YOU CAN DRAW

YOU CAN DRAW - ALL YOU NEED IS A PENCIL AND SOME PAPER.

Once you're comfortable with the basics, try other materials and work on your techniques. Even if your first drawing isn't a masterpiece, don't worry! The more you draw, the better you'll become. Look long and hard at whatever it is you want to draw, too. The more you look, the more you'll see!

Follow the steps to try the projects in this book, and then vary them how you like. Maybe try ink instead of paint, orange instead of blue, swirls instead of lines. It's up to you!

PICK UP A PENCIL, OPEN TO ANY PAGE, AND GET DRAWING!

This edition published by Parragon Books Ltd in 2013

Parragon Books Ltd
Chartist House
15–17 Trim Street
Bath BA1 1HA, UK
www.parragon.com

ISBN 978-1-4723-3673-6

Printed in China

YOU CAN Draw

Parragon

Bath • New York • Singapore • Hong Kong • Cologne • Delhi
Melbourne • Amsterdam • Johannesburg • Shenzhen

CONTENTS

Materials 6
Techniques 8
Portraits 10
Hedgehog 12
Hot-air Balloons 14
Fashion Girls 16
Grizzly Bear 18
Racing Car 20
Profile 22
Penguins 24
Electric Guitar 26
Rose 28
Fashion Boys 30
Meerkats 32
T-Shirts 34
Pirate Ship 36
High Street 38
Statue of Liberty 40
Quad Bike 42
Mega Dessert 44
Ninja 46
Moustaches 48
Alien Invasion 50
Giraffe Face 52
Pop Star 54
Line Designs 56
Rock Star Drum Kit 58
Alien UFO 60
Cartoon Monsters 62
Monkeys 64
Speech Bubbles 66
Skateboards 68
Diver 70
Bullet Train 72
Peacock 74
Eiffel Tower 76
Hairstyles 78
Aerial Display 80
Dancing Dog 82
Snowboarder 84
Fantasy Map 86
Trainers 88
Spy Car 90
Rock Star 92
Belts 94
Superhero 96
Cartoon Explosions 98
Space Rocket 100
Elephant 102
Street Art 104
Skateboarder 106
Pizza 108

Geometric Patterns ... 110
T. rex ... 112
Motorcycle Stunt Rider ... 114
Wild Hats ... 116
Haunted House ... 118
Manga Girl ... 120
Urban Bridge ... 122
Cartoon Wild Animals ... 124
Jetpack ... 126
Monster Plant ... 128
World's Tallest Hamburger ... 130
Circular Patterns ... 132
Zombie ... 134
Candy Machine ... 136
Shark! ... 138
Skyscrapers ... 140
Basketball Player ... 142
Volcano ... 144
Weird Beards ... 146
Speedboat ... 148
Frames ... 150
Caricatures ... 152
Crocodile ... 154
Tornado ... 156
Monster Mash-up ... 158
Ferris Wheel ... 160
Scaredy-Cat ... 162
Cyborg ... 164
Funky Cake ... 166
Robot ... 168
Pictures in Lights ... 170
Cartoon Cute Animals ... 172
Surfer ... 174
Cool Shades ... 176
Frankenstein's Monster ... 178
Woodland Animals ... 180
Mountain Bike ... 182
Straight Patterns ... 184
Twisty Tree ... 186
Manga Boy ... 188
Submarine ... 190
Troll ... 192
Hockey Player ... 194
Gyrocopter ... 196
Dragon ... 198
Cartoon Expressions ... 200
Spaceship Controls ... 202
Superheroine ... 204
Animal Patterns ... 206
Fishbowl ... 208
Towering Buildings ... 210
French Café ... 212
Optical Illusions ... 214
Streetdancer ... 216
Creepy Mansion ... 218
Index ... 220
About the Artists ... 222
Acknowledgements ... 224

MATERIALS

THERE ARE LOTS OF SPECIAL MATERIALS THAT ARE FUN TO TRY OUT. BUT, REALLY, ANYTHING THAT MAKES A MARK ON PAPER IS GREAT FOR DRAWING! YOU CAN GET THESE MATERIALS AT CRAFT SHOPS.

GRAPHITE PENCILS range from hard to soft. H pencil leads are hard and good for light sketching and fine lines. B pencil leads are softer and great for shading and thick lines. HB is in the middle.

PAPER textures can make a big difference to how your drawing looks. Smooth copy paper will give you a sharp, crisp line. Cartridge paper is heavier and more textured, so your line will look softer. Watercolour paper absorbs ink or watercolour paints. Coloured paper gives an unusual effect and ready-made background.

WATERCOLOUR PENCILS usually come in sets. There is a huge variety of colours available. They work like ordinary coloured pencils, but can be blended together with a wet brush. Regular coloured pencils are a great material too, especially for animal fur.

ERASERS come in handy when you are happy with your final drawing lines and want to get rid of guidelines. Don't rub hard or the surface of the paper will suffer. Instead, gently roll a corner of the eraser on the paper to lift the pencil off.

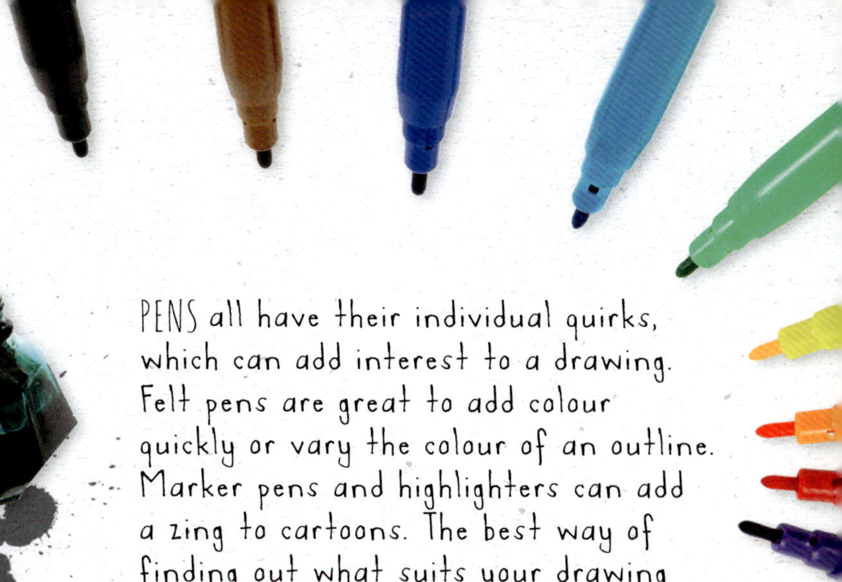

PEN-AND-INK is a popular way to lift a drawing with heavy lines and give the picture character with varied line widths. Use a dip pen or a fine-tipped brush to apply various colours of ink. Practise first as once it's on, it won't come off! You can also use a cartridge pen for a similar effect.

PENS all have their individual quirks, which can add interest to a drawing. Felt pens are great to add colour quickly or vary the colour of an outline. Marker pens and highlighters can add a zing to cartoons. The best way of finding out what suits your drawing style is to experiment!

CRAYONS are great for colour lines and colour texture. Try wax, chalk or oil crayons in your drawings.

BRUSHES come in a variety of shapes and sizes. Round brushes are used for applying washes and are a good, all-round paintbrush. Pointed brushes are good for line and detail. Flat brushes are ideal for painting stripes or applying larger areas of colour evenly. Always wash your brushes between colours and when you have finished painting.

PAINTS – whether you choose poster, watercolour or acrylic will depend on what effect you want to achieve. Poster paints tend to be flat but easy to use. Watercolours blend well together to produce an interesting surface and soft look. Acrylics are very vibrant.

TECHNIQUES

HERE ARE A FEW SIMPLE TECHNIQUES THAT WILL HELP YOU GET THE MOST OUT OF YOUR DRAWING.

BASIC SHAPES AND GUIDELINES help you plan your drawing before you add any detail. They're a good way of checking proportions, direction of movement and position on the page. Simple lines and rectangles can make up bodies and limbs, while circles and oval ellipses are useful stand-ins for heads and hands. A centre line is useful if you are drawing anything symmetrical, where the drawing on one side of the line mirrors the details on the other side.

simple lines and shapes

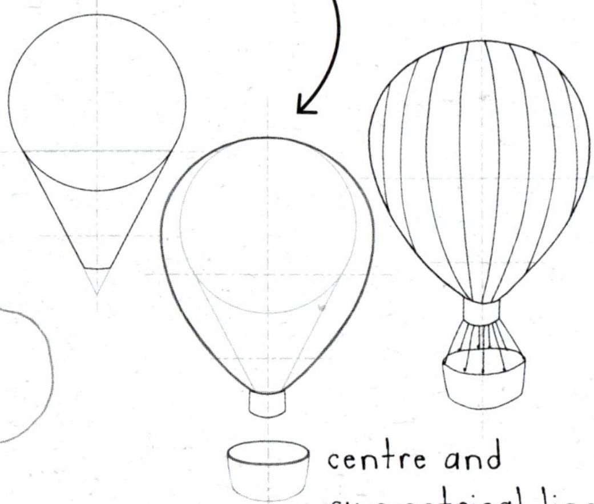

centre and symmetrical lines

LIGHT AND SHADE add dimension and realism to your drawing. Think about your light source – where the light is coming from in your drawing – for where shadows will fall. Leave white highlights in the parts nearest to the viewer and add shade where the shape is furthest from the viewer for depth.

PENCIL STROKES can add character to a drawing. There are a number of shading techniques you could use. Try holding the pencil side-on to the paper for a rubbed effect. Or, use the point of the pencil to crosshatch lines in opposing directions, almost like a grid, to build up shading. Experiment with changing the pressure on the pencil as you make your marks, using short flicks or longer, sweeping strokes.

crosshatching

rubbed edge effect

changing pressure of pencil to flick and sweep

PROPORTION needs to be fixed at the earliest stage of your drawing. Check the sizes of your basic shapes in relation to each other, making adjustments as needed. This is especially useful when breaking down where to position face and body features.

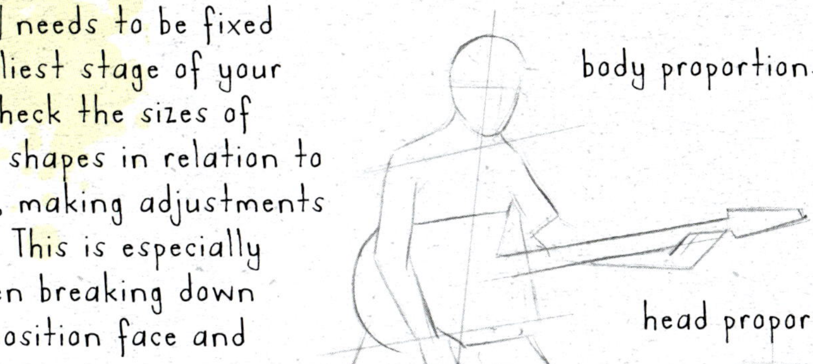

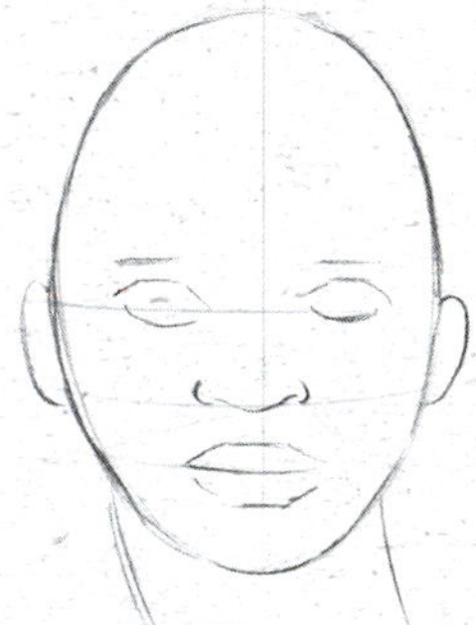

COLOUR completes your picture and can add mood. Experiment with complementary colours, which go well together, such as red and green, or contrasting colours, such as red and yellow. Complementary colours are opposite each other on a colour wheel. Two colours mixed together produce a new colour tone. Adding white to a colour produces a soft tint that is useful for highlights. Shades produced by mixing black to a colour are good for shadows. Try tones of the same colour for depth.

WORKING DIGITALLY is very popular nowadays. You can scan your sketch into a computer and then open it using image-editing software. Use special tools in the software, such as paintbrushes or spray cans, to add colour, do touch-ups or even draw the whole thing on screen!

colour wheel

PERSPECTIVE gives your drawing depth. Planning a horizon line (the place where the ground meets the sky) and vanishing points (where lines in the distance come together) will provide a clear foreground and background to your picture. Objects in the foreground will appear larger than objects in the background.

PORTRAITS

1 DRAW AN OVAL SHAPE FOR THE HEAD AND ROUGH GUIDELINES FOR THE POSITIONS OF THE EYES, NOSE AND MOUTH, POSITIONED AS SHOWN. ADD A VERTICAL GUIDE TOO.

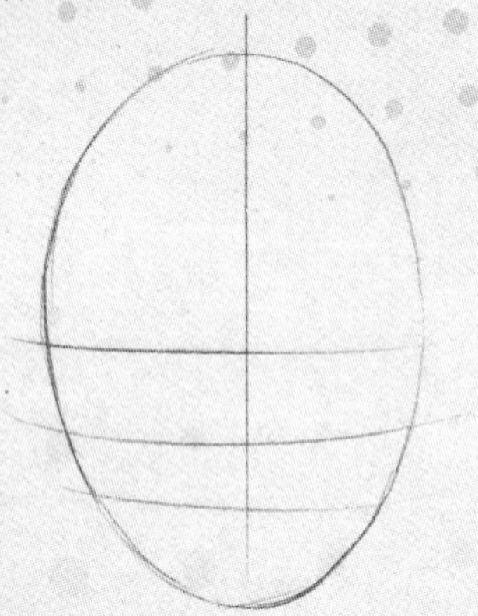

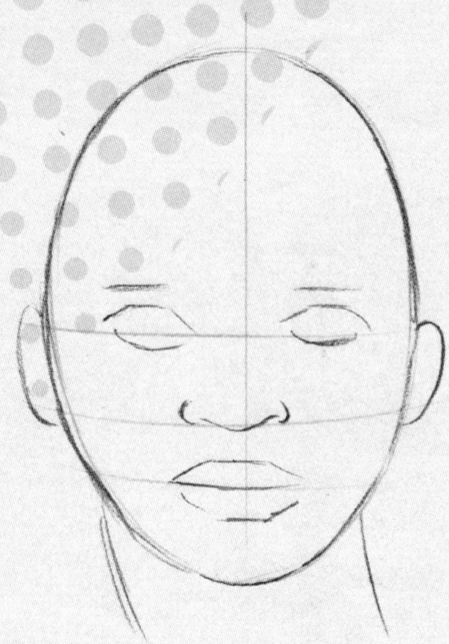

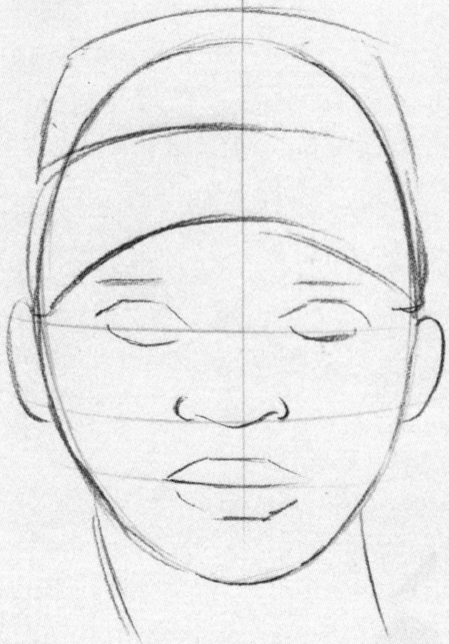

2 USING THE VERTICAL GUIDE TO HELP YOU WITH SYMMETRY, SKETCH SOME ROUGH SHAPES FOR THE EYES, EYEBROWS AND EARS. USE CURVED LINES FOR THE NOSE, WITH LARGER CURVES FOR THE LIPS. ADD A NECK SHAPE.

3 SKETCH TWO CURVED RECTANGLES TO FORM A CAP SHAPE. MAKE THE TOP LINE A LITTLE HIGHER THAN THE TOP OF THE PERSON'S HEAD.

Add sketchy cheekbone lines for a chiselled cheek look.

4 SKETCH THE SHAPE OF THE BRIM AND WORK UP THE FACIAL FEATURES. REFINE THE SHAPES OF THE EYES, ADDING CIRCLES FOR THE IRISES AND PUPILS. ADD NOSTRILS AND DETAILS TO THE EARS. DRAW A SLIGHTLY ANGULAR JAWLINE FOR AN OLDER BOY.

5 USING A HEAVY PENCIL SUCH AS A 4B, FIRM UP THE FEATURES A BIT MORE. IMAGINE THE LIGHT IS COMING IN FROM THE LEFT AND DRAW A LINE UNDER THE EYES TO MARK THE SHADOW CAST BY THE BRIM. ADD MORE SHADOW LINES TO THE NECK AND THE SIDE OF THE NOSE.

6 USING SLANTED PENCIL STROKES, SHADE IN THE FOREHEAD AND NECK AREAS YOU'VE JUST MARKED OFF. SHADE AROUND THE NOSE AND ADD SHADING TO THE CAP TO SHOW THE CREASES IN THE MATERIAL.

7 ADD COLOUR! NOW THE SHADING DETAIL CAN BE MORE SUBTLE. USE SLIGHTLY DARKER TONES FOR THE AREAS OF SKIN THAT ARE IN SHADOW, MAKING SOME AREAS COMPLETELY BLACK FOR DRAMATIC CONTRAST. ADD A FEW PALE HIGHLIGHTS TO THE CAP.

Once you've tried drawing someone face-on, follow these steps to try drawing a face at an angle. This can be more dynamic, visually interesting and cheeky!

HEDGEHOG

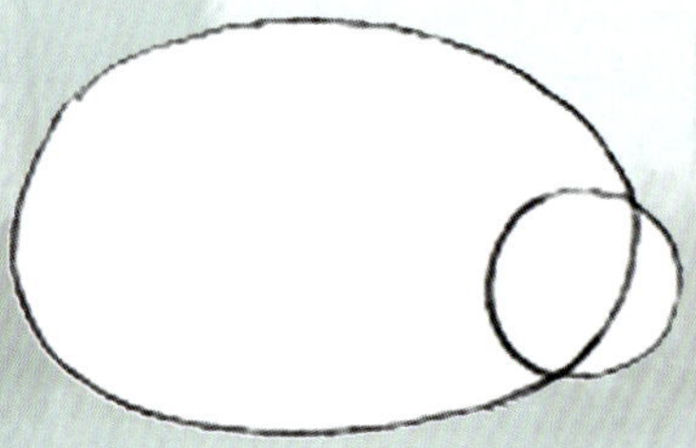

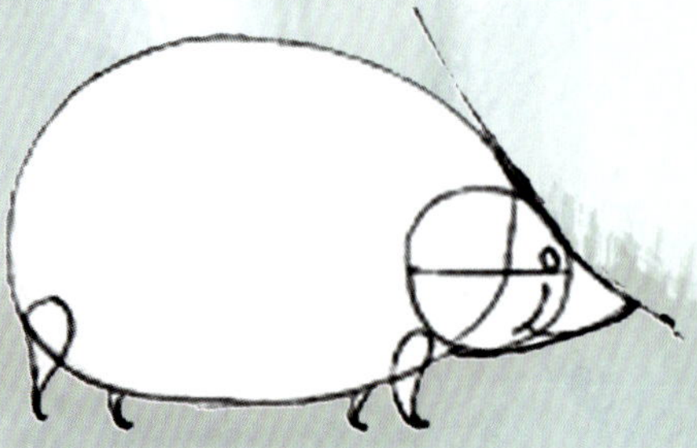

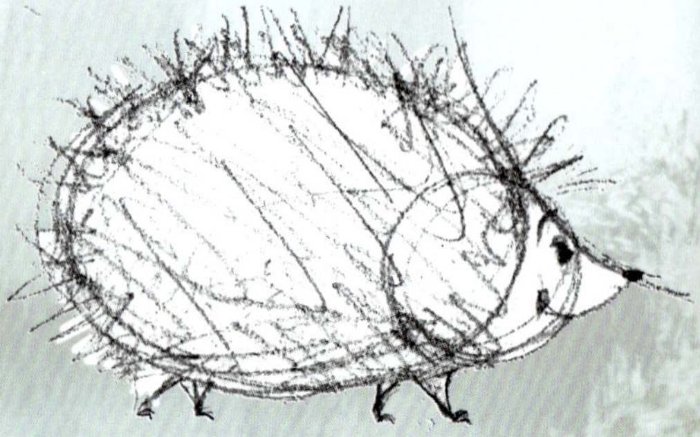

1

DRAW AN OVAL SHAPE FOR THE HEDGEHOG BODY. ADD AN OVERLAPPING SMALL CIRCLE FOR THE HEAD.

2

SHAPE THE HEAD ON A CURVE TO CREATE A SNOUT, AS SHOWN. ADD LEGS, AN EYE AND A MOUTH.

3

ROUGHLY SKETCH OUT THE REST OF THE HEDGEHOG DETAILS, INCLUDING PRICKLY LINES AND A LITTLE ROUND NOSE.

4

COLOUR THE HEDGEHOG WITH THE BASE COLOURS, THEN ADD LIGHT AND DARK AREAS FOR A REALISTIC EFFECT. ADD AN EYEBROW AND WHISKERS FOR PERSONALITY.

Build up the scene with little footprints, matching them to the placement of your hedgehog's legs.

1

FOR A HEDGEHOG IN A BALL, DRAW A ROUND SHAPE FOR THE BODY AND A SMALLER ROUND SHAPE INSIDE FOR THE HEAD.

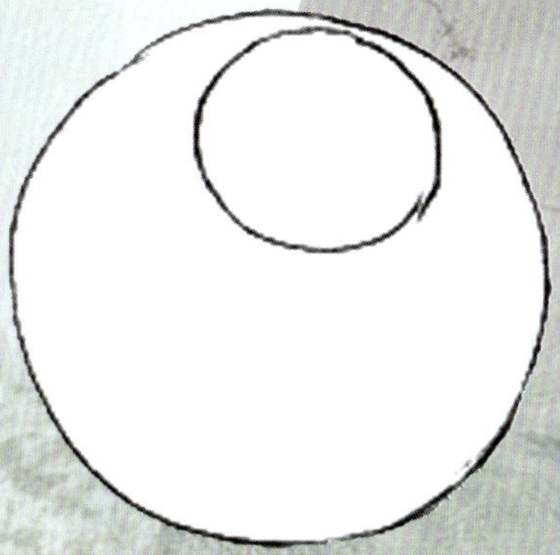

2

ADD EARS, EYES, A SNOUT, A NOSE AND LEGS FOLLOWING THE GUIDE FOR PLACEMENT BELOW.

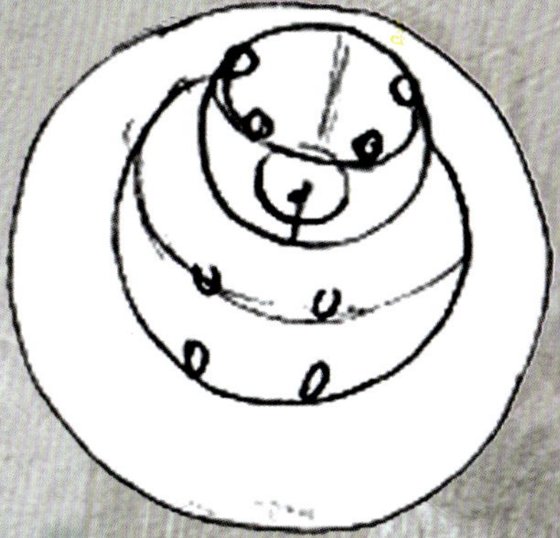

3

ROUGHLY SKETCH OUT THE REST OF THE HEDGEHOG, KEEPING IT LOOSE. SKETCH YOUR PRICKLES OUTWARDS TO BUILD THE BALL EFFECT.

Use your imagination to vary the pose. Simply changing the eyes morphs an alert hedgehog into a sleeping one.

Tell a story and build character with your drawing, adding little touches such as a stuck-on leaf to this baby.

4

ADD COLOUR AS BEFORE. THINK ABOUT WHERE THE LIGHT WOULD BE COMING FROM IN THE PICTURE TO ADD HIGHLIGHTS AND SHADOWS.

Hot-air balloons

Drawing faint guidelines helps you with the symmetry and proportions of your balloons. Use a compass if you want a perfect circle guide.

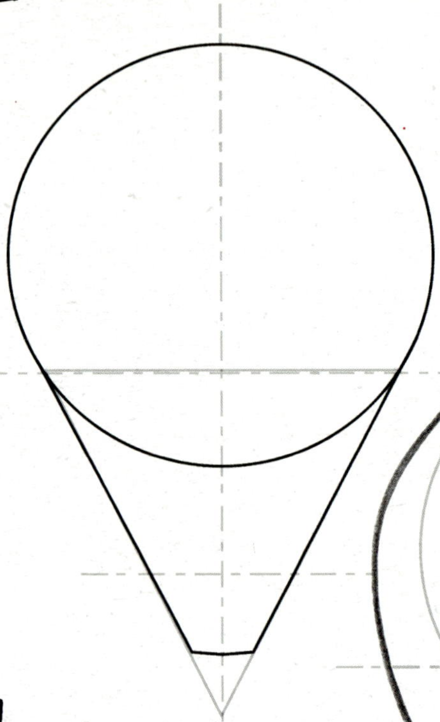

1

USING A PENCIL, DRAW A CIRCLE FOR THE BALLOON, THEN DIVIDE IT IN HALF WITH A FAINT VERTICAL LINE. ATTACH A BIG V SHAPE, STARTING ABOUT THREE-QUARTERS OF THE WAY DOWN THE CIRCLE. ADD A HORIZONTAL GUIDE WHERE THE TWO SHAPES MEET, PLUS A PARALLEL GUIDELINE BELOW THAT.

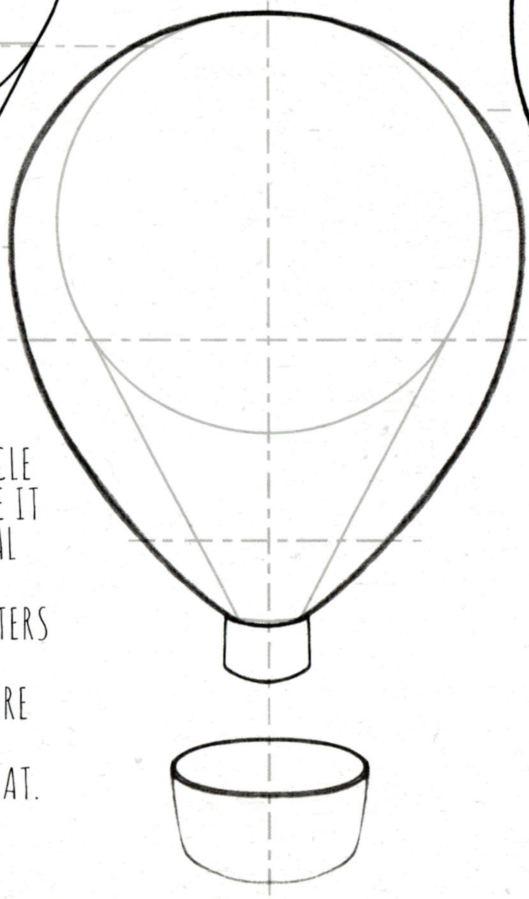

2

USING THE BASIC SHAPES AS A GUIDE, DRAW A LARGER BALLOON OUTLINE. ADD A CYLINDER SHAPE AT THE BOTTOM AND A BASKET BELOW. WHEN YOU'RE HAPPY WITH YOUR SHAPES, TRACE OVER THE OUTLINES WITH WATERPROOF INK.

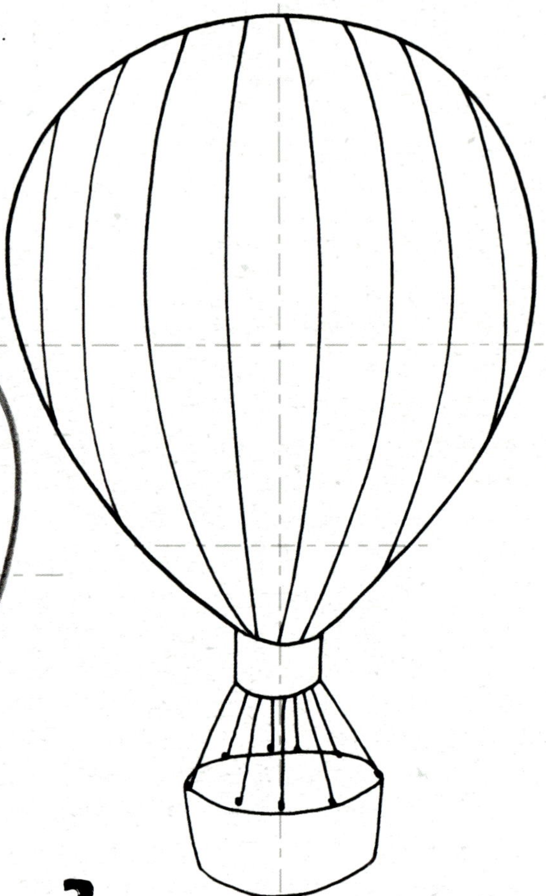

3

USING YOUR INK PEN, ADD CURVED, VERTICAL LINES TO YOUR BALLOON. THESE WILL HELP YOU DESIGN THE BALLOON'S PATTERN. DRAW MORE LINES CONNECTING THE CYLINDER SHAPE TO THE TOP EDGE OF THE BASKET.

Use other shapes to decorate your balloon. This chequered design uses squares and curved lines.

4

USE THE VERTICAL LINES TO HELP YOU DRAW A ZIG-ZAG PATTERN. ADD TWO ROWS OF LEAF SHAPES. THEN USE CIRCLES AND ELLIPSES TO DRAW IN SOME SAND BAGS.

5

USE WATERCOLOUR INKS OR WATERCOLOUR PAINTS TO COLOUR YOUR BALLOON. VARY THE TONES FROM LIGHT TO DARK TO HELP MAKE IT LOOK MORE 3D. BRING OUT SOME OF THE SHAPES IN A CONTRASTING COLOUR.

If you use a waterproof pen for your linework, it won't bleed or smudge when you add watery paint on top.

Fashion girls

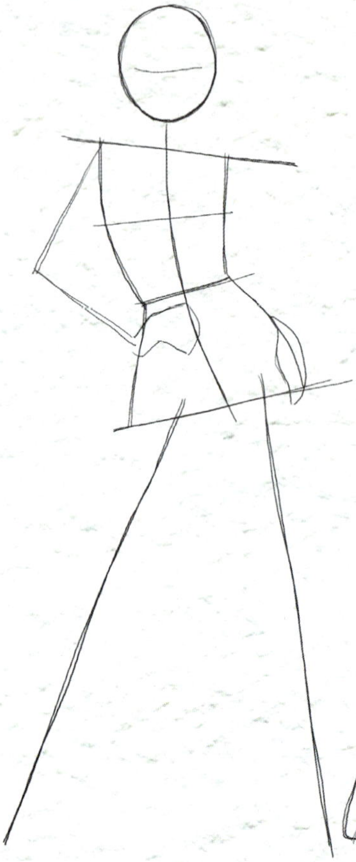

1

SKETCH A ROUND SHAPE FOR THE HEAD AND THEN GUIDELINES FOR THE TORSO, ARMS AND LEGS.

2

DRAW ROUGH ARM AND LEG SHAPES AROUND YOUR GUIDELINES.

3

SKETCH OUT A TOP, BELT, TROUSERS AND SHOES TO ADD CLOTHES.

4

FINISH THE HANDS AND SKETCH OUT LONG HAIR AND A FACE. ERASE ANY ROUGH GUIDELINES. NOW ADD COLOUR! USE ONLY ACCENTS TO KEEP THE DRAWING SOPHISTICATED.

Find inspiration for patterns and colours from magazines. You could even cut out some samples and glue them onto your model to make a collage effect.

OUT AND ABOUT

Use the technique on the opposite page to create a basic body, then change the outfits for different occasions.

Try drawing the girl standing side-on, and add accessories, such as an umbrella!

Add beachwear for a sunny-day pose!

Experiment with colour combinations before you colour in the outfits.

GRIZZLY BEAR

TIPS

Keep your pencil sharp for the detailed features, such as the eyes and nose.

Once you've mastered the techniques, try some different grizzly poses.

Experiment with pen and ink, coloured pencils and different line weights for various fur textures.

1

USING A SHARP, LIGHT PENCIL SUCH AS GRADE H, DRAW THE BASIC SHAPE OF A YOUNG BEAR.

2

USING A SHARP, HEAVIER GRADE PENCIL, DARKEN THE EYES AND EYEBROWS. FILL IN THE NOSE, USING A HEAVY PRESSURE ON THE LEFT-HAND SIDE AND GRADUALLY TAKING OFF PRESSURE TOWARDS THE RIGHT. DARKEN THE INNER EARS.

3

ADD DETAIL TO THE OUTLINE OF THE BEAR, USING EACH PENCIL LINE AS A PIECE OF FUR. DRAW THE KNOTS OF THE TREE THEN ADD ROUGH VERTICAL LINES FOR BARK.

4

FLICK YOUR PENCIL TO CREATE EACH LINE OF FUR, FOLLOWING THE DIRECTION OF THE BEAR'S BODY. WORK FROM THE FACE DOWNWARDS SO YOU DON'T SMUDGE THE DRAWING.

To keep the fur looking soft, use your pencil without sharpening it. The smoother the better!

5

COLOUR THE BEAR WITH COLOURED PENCILS. ADD TONE BY SHADING CERTAIN AREAS WHERE THE TREE CASTS A SHADOW ON THE BEAR'S TUMMY.

RACING CAR

Draw light guidelines to help with the shape.

1 START WITH A SIMPLE OUTLINE. DON'T WORRY IF THERE ARE A FEW WOBBLES HERE AND THERE. IT ALL ADDS TO THE CHARACTER!

2 ADD A BUMPER AND SOME WHEELS. TRY SLOPING THEM TO GIVE THE IMPRESSION OF MOVEMENT.

3 ADD THE DETAILS! HAVE FUN WITH THIS – IT'S HOW YOU CAN REALLY PERSONALIZE YOUR DRAWING.

4 DRAW YOUR DRIVER – AND MAYBE EVEN A BEMUSED PASSENGER.

5 NOW ADD SOME HEAVIER LINES WITH INK AND A FINE BRUSH. THIS INDICATES WEIGHT AND SHADOWS. AGAIN, A FEW WOBBLES JUST ADD TO THE ENERGY OF THE LINE.

Don't be afraid to be really heavy with your ink.

BADGE DESIGN IDEAS

Try designing your own badges and emblems for your racing car.

6 ADD COLOUR! COMPLETE THE PICTURE WITH SPEED LINES AND SHADOWS BEHIND THE WHEELS SO YOUR CAR ISN'T FLOATING.

Add a finish flag to make your car look like a winner.

PROFILE

If you think of the shape of a skull, it will help you draw the shape of the head.

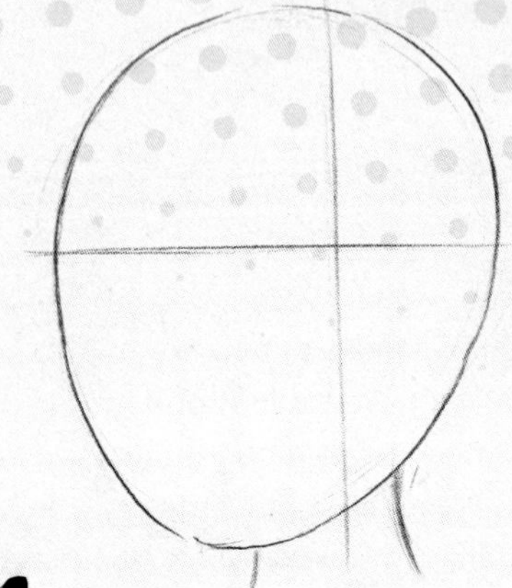

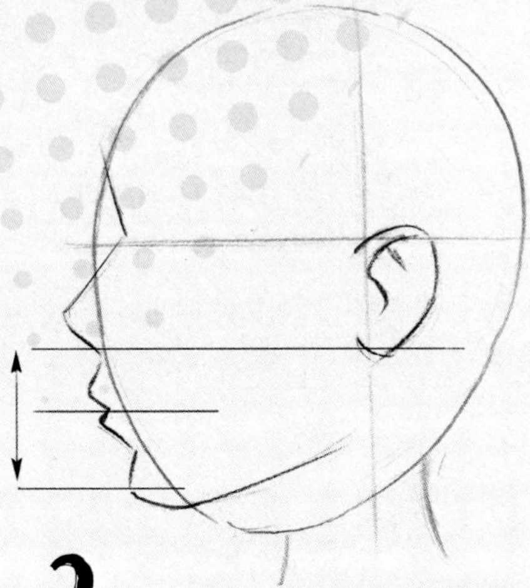

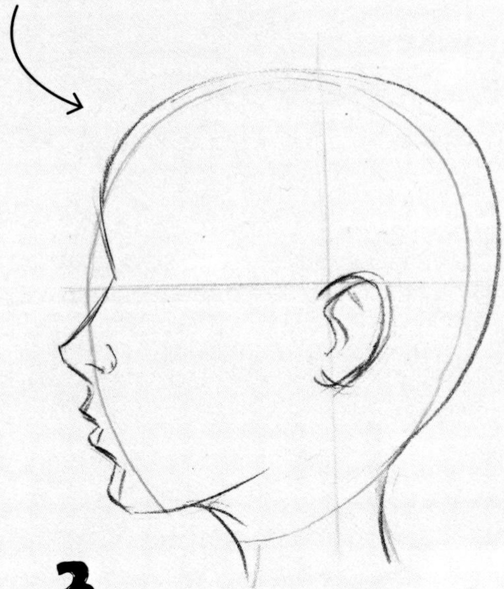

1

SKETCH AN OVAL FOR THE HEAD. MARK A HORIZONTAL LINE WHERE THE EYES SHOULD FALL AND A VERTICAL LINE WHERE THE EAR WOULD LIE. DRAW IN THE NECK.

2

DRAW THE TOP OF THE EAR IN LINE WITH THE EYE. DRAW A GUIDELINE FROM THE BOTTOM OF THE EAR TO LINE UP THE BOTTOM OF THE NOSE. SKETCH THE PROFILE AND JAW.

3

START TO DRAW THE PROFILE IN MORE DETAIL. LOOK CLOSELY AT THE OUTLINE AND DISTANCE BETWEEN THE FEATURES. KEEP USING A LIGHT PENCIL.

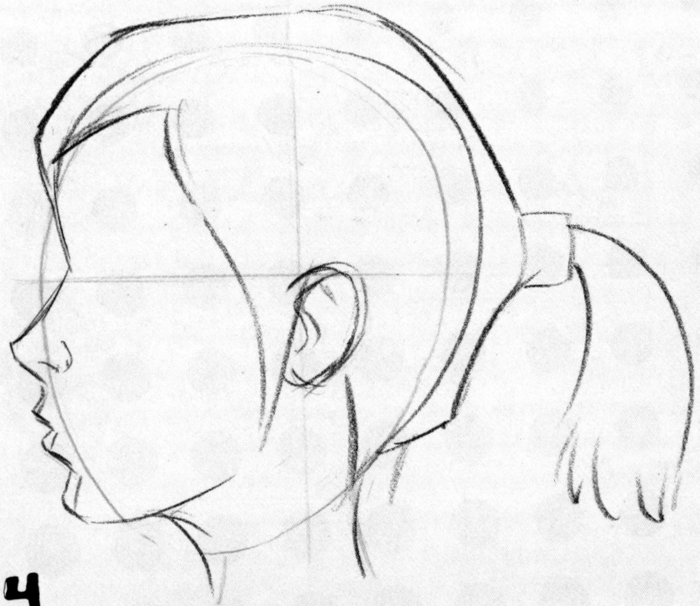

4

ONCE YOU'RE HAPPY WITH THE PROFILE, ADD THE SHAPE OF THE HAIR. HAIR NEARLY ALWAYS HAS VOLUME, SO DON'T MAKE IT TIGHT TO THE HEAD (UNLESS IT'S A CREW CUT!).

5

ADD THE EYE – IT SITS INSIDE A SOCKET AND THE LIDS FOLD OVER TO PROTECT IT. BEGIN TO ADD DETAIL TO THE HAIR, LIPS AND EARS. THINK ABOUT SHADING BELOW THE EYE, NOSE AND CHIN.

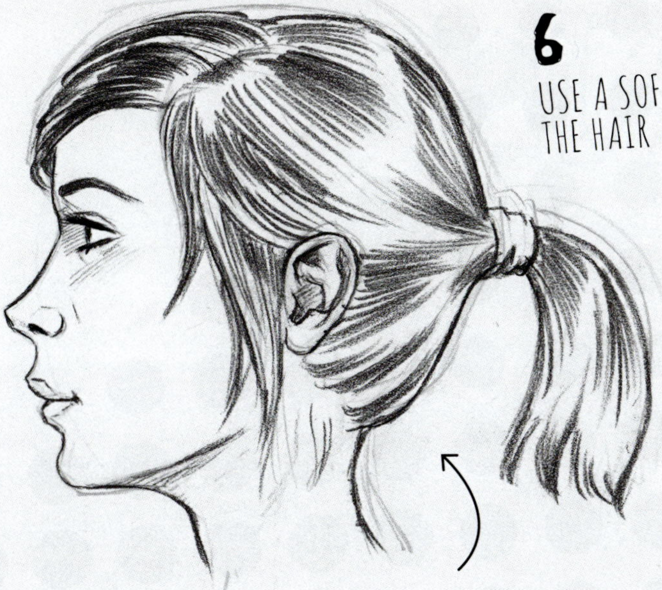

6

USE A SOFT PENCIL TO WORK UP THE HAIR AND FEATURES.

Remember to keep your wrist relaxed so that the drawing is flowing and alive.

7

WHEN YOU ARE READY TO COLOUR YOUR PROFILE, VARY THE TONES TO REFLECT THE LIGHT AND SHADE IN THE DRAWING.

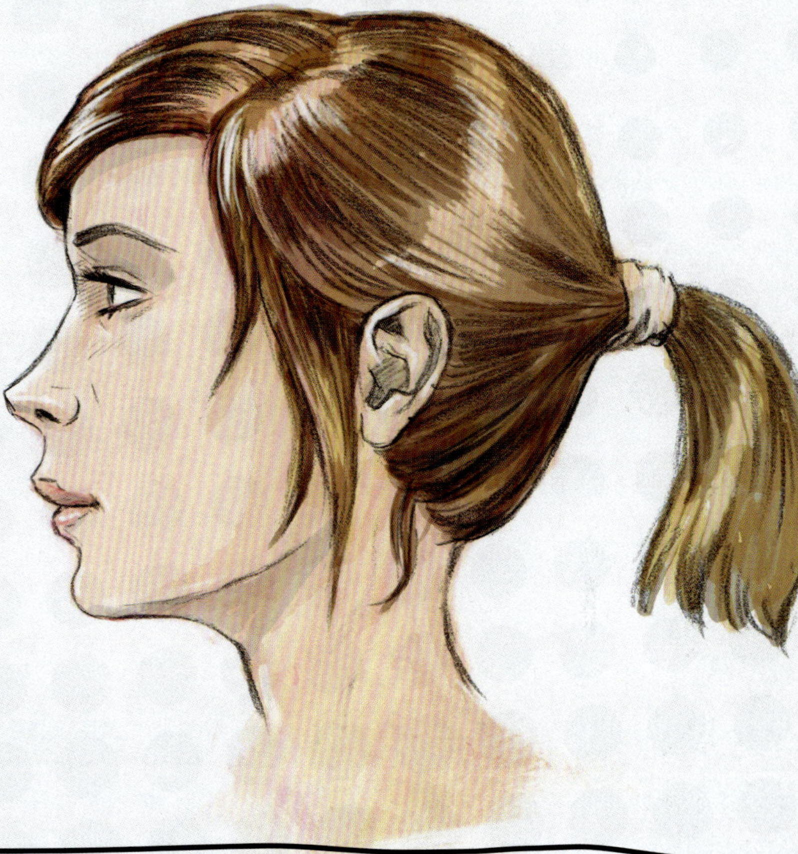

PROFILE FEATURES

EYES

The eyeball is exactly that - a ball that sits in the socket and is protected by folds of skin, or lids. It's easier to draw them when you understand what's going on under the surface.

NOSE AND MOUTH

Look how various areas of the face stick out in profile. Nudging these in or out changes the character of the face. The length and angle of the nose changes the profile. Look at whether the nose turns up or juts out. Look where the forehead and chin lie in relation to the nose too.

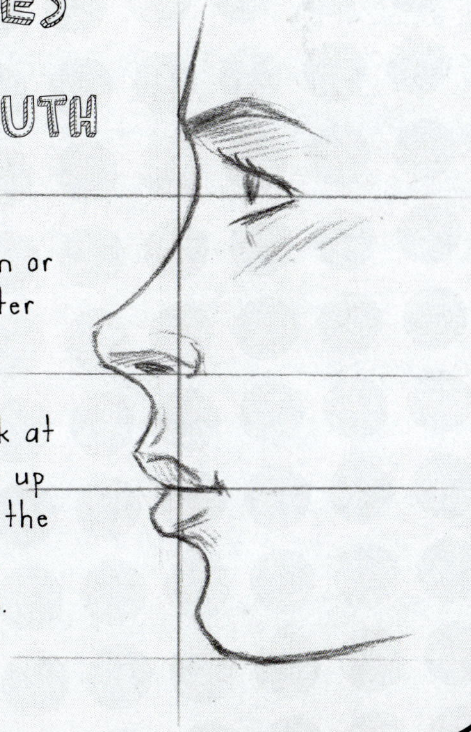

PENGUINS

1 USING A LIGHT PENCIL SUCH AS A GRADE H, SKETCH A BASIC PENGUIN SHAPE: DRAW A SMALL ROUNDED SHAPE FOR THE HEAD AND A LARGE OVAL FOR THE BODY. ADD THE TAIL.

2 ADD SOME MORE BASIC SHAPES FOR YOUR PENGUIN'S LIMBS. DRAW A POINTED BEAK, SIMPLE FLIPPER SHAPES, A LEG AND A CLAWED FOOT. DON'T FORGET THE BEADY EYE!

3 DEFINE THE OUTLINE. USE LOOSE LINES FOR THE BIRD'S BELLY. DRAW DETAIL ON THE BEAK AND HEAD. ADD SHADING AROUND THE EYE. RUB OUT ANY UNNEEDED GUIDELINES.

1 FOR A BABY PENGUIN, SKETCH ONE SMALL CIRCLE FOR THE HEAD AND AN OVERLAPPING EGG SHAPE FOR THE BODY. DRAW A LINE OF ICE TO GROUND HIM.

2 CONTINUE ADDING BASIC BODY SHAPES. SKETCH SOME SIMPLE SAUSAGE SHAPES FOR THE FLIPPERS AND SMALL OVALS FOR THE FEET. VARY THE FLIPPERS FOR PERSONALITY.

3 SKETCH THE FACE, WHICH IS SIMILAR TO A HEART SHAPE. DEFINE THE PENGUIN'S OUTLINE, ADDING FEET, EYES AND A BEAK. RUB OUT UNNEEDED GUIDES.

Try holding your pencil at a 45-degree angle when shading the feathers. This will make your pencil marks appear smoother.

Use white painted marks to highlight the feathers on the belly and give a great 3D effect.

4 SHADE THE BEAK AND HEAD WITH THE EDGE OF A PENCIL, THEN MOVE DOWN THE PENGUIN'S BODY, BACK AND FLIPPERS. ADD PRESSURE TO YOUR PENCIL FOR THE DARKER AREAS.

5 ADD COLOUR! USE A BLUE-GREY PENCIL FOR THE PENGUIN'S BODY, WITH A LIGHT YELLOW FOR THE PATCH ON THE SIDE OF ITS HEAD. USE A CREAMY COLOUR FOR THE BELLY, WITH BRIGHT ORANGE FOR THE BEAK AND FEET.

4 BEGIN THE TONAL WORK BY SHADING THE HEAD AND BEAK. GRADUATE THE SHADING FOR ADDED VISUAL INTEREST. THEN SHADE THE FEET AND EYE AREAS.

5 BABY PENGUINS ARE FLUFFY, SO USE SENSITIVE PENCIL STROKES TO ACHIEVE A SOFT, FURRY EFFECT. IT'S FINE TO DRAW OVER THE OUTLINE! USE DOWNWARDS STROKES.

6 COLOUR WITH A LIGHT-GREY WASH FOR THE BODY AND GREY FOR THE BEAK. TRY A DARK BLUE PENCIL FOR THE OUTLINE TO CONTRAST WITH THE GREY. TRY VARYING THE FLIPPERS TOO.

ELECTRIC GUITAR

1

DRAW TWO SIMPLE GUIDE SHAPES – AN OVAL FOR THE BODY AND A LONG, OVERLAPPING RECTANGLE FOR THE GUITAR NECK.

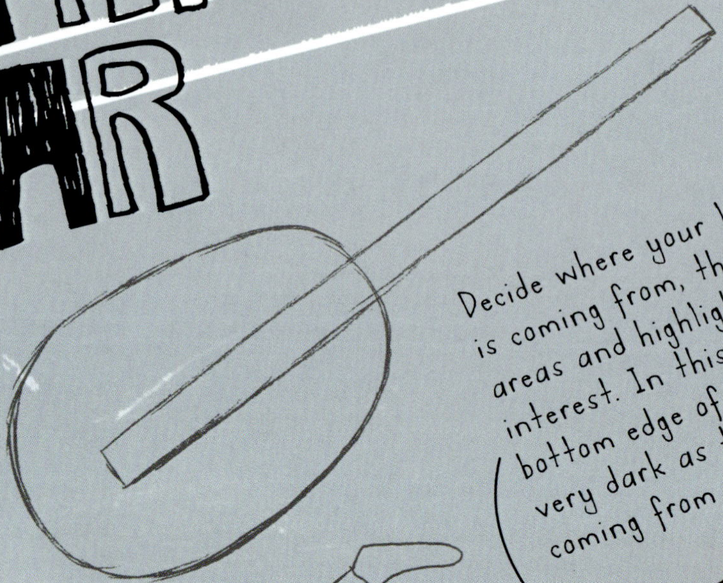

2

DRAW WAVY LINES AROUND THE OUTSIDE OF THE OVAL SHAPE TO GIVE THE EFFECT OF FLAMES FANNING DOWN TO THE LEFT. THEN RUB OUT THE OVAL GUIDE SHAPE.

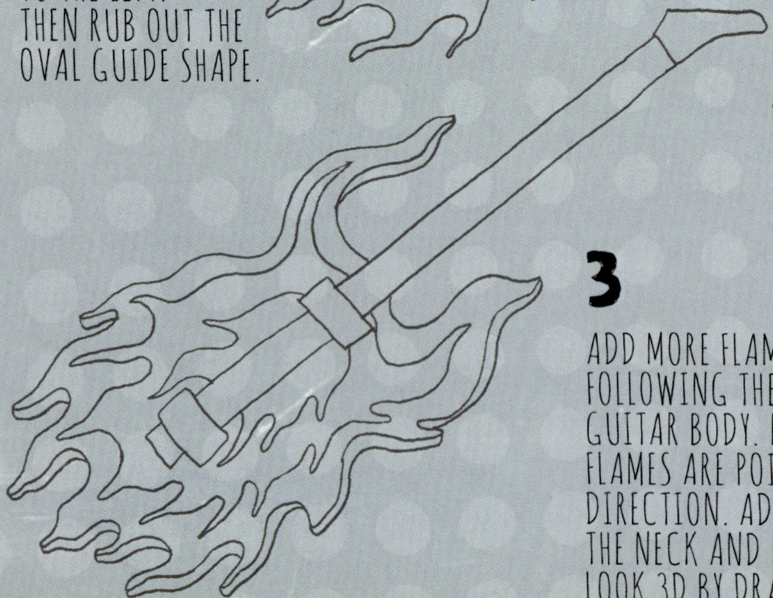

3

ADD MORE FLAME DESIGNS, FOLLOWING THE OUTLINE OF THE GUITAR BODY. MAKE SURE THE FLAMES ARE POINTING IN THE SAME DIRECTION. ADD MORE DETAILS TO THE NECK AND MAKE THE GUITAR LOOK 3D BY DRAWING EXTRA WAVY LINES IN THE PLACES SHOWN.

Decide where your light source is coming from, then use shaded areas and highlights for visual interest. In this picture, the bottom edge of the guitar is very dark as the light is coming from the top right.

4

USE BRIGHT COLOURS FOR THE BODY OF THE GUITAR AND A DARKER COLOUR FOR THE NECK AND HEAD. DRAW FIVE DASHED LINES IN A LIGHT COLOUR FOR THE STRINGS, THEN ADD TUNING PEGS AT THE TOP.

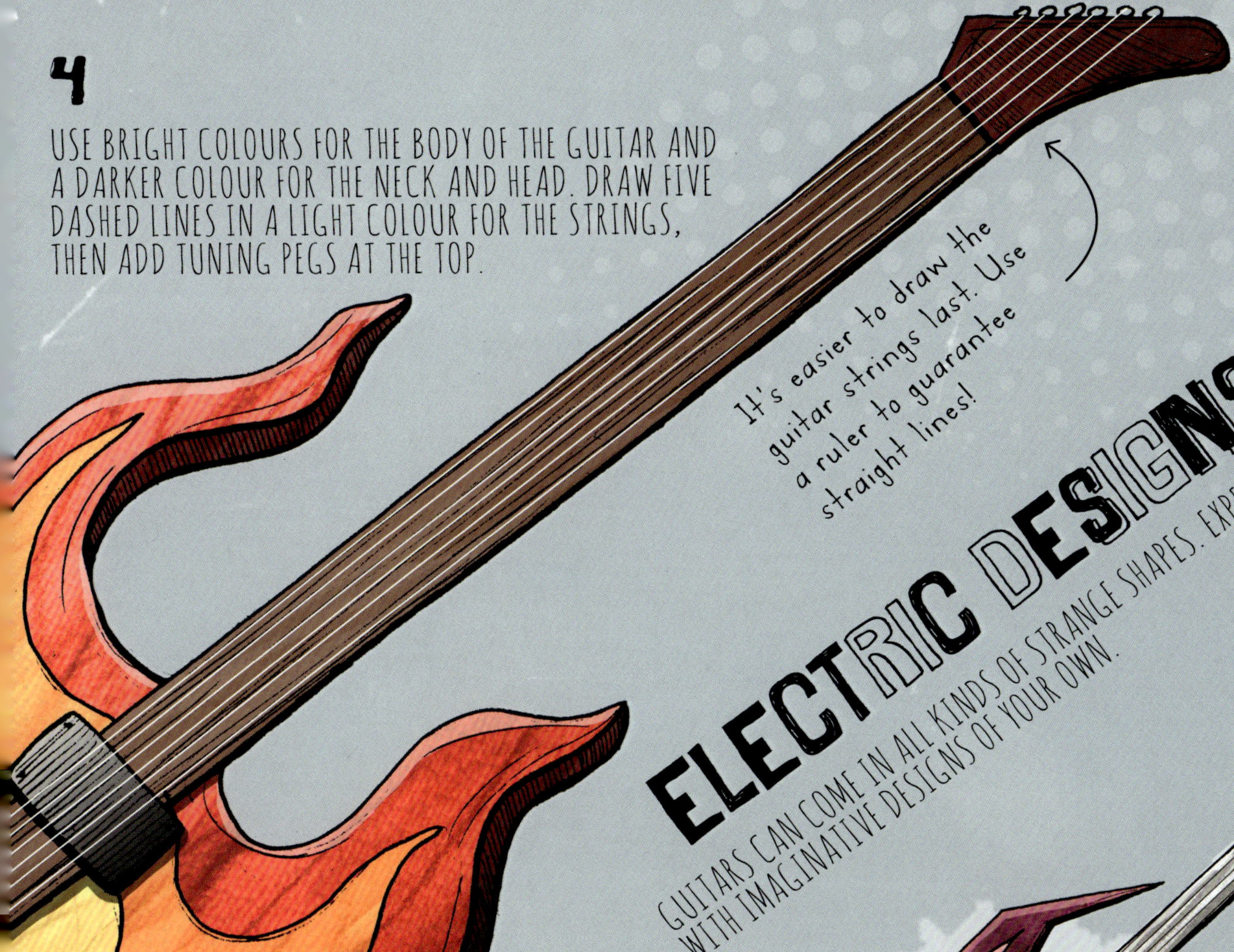

It's easier to draw the guitar strings last. Use a ruler to guarantee straight lines!

ELECTRIC DESIGNS

GUITARS CAN COME IN ALL KINDS OF STRANGE SHAPES. EXPERIMENT WITH IMAGINATIVE DESIGNS OF YOUR OWN.

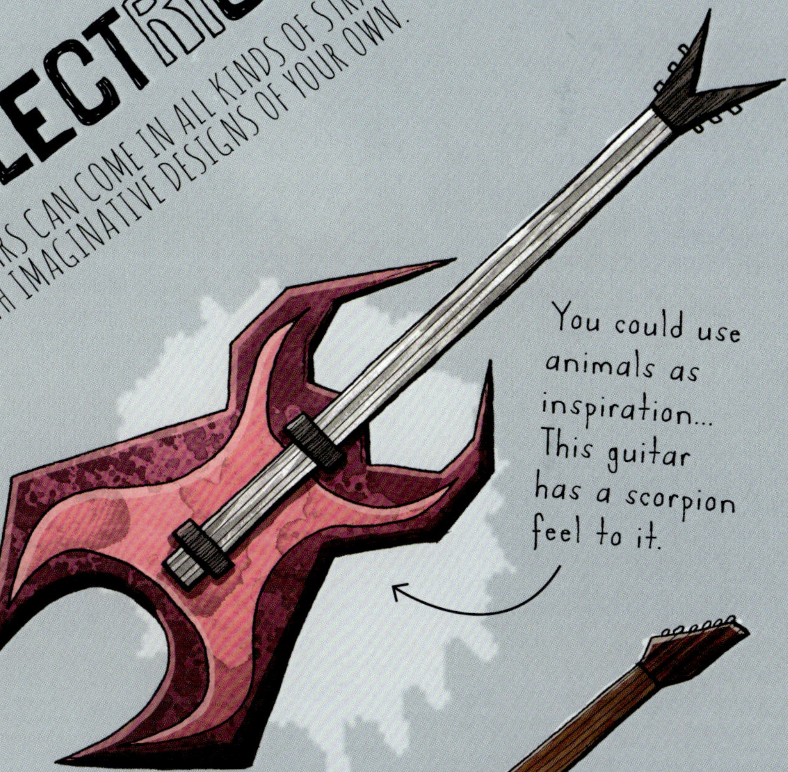

You could use animals as inspiration... This guitar has a scorpion feel to it.

Streamlined designs look good, such as this triangular-shaped guitar.

A rounded edge makes for a more classic-looking electric guitar.

ROSE

1 START BY CREATING THE BASIC STRUCTURE. DRAW A SIMPLE SPIRAL, KEEPING THE TOP TIGHTER THAN THE BOTTOM TO TILT THE ANGLE OF THE ROSE THEN DRAW A HALF CIRCLE BELOW.

2 USING THE SPIRAL AS YOUR BASE, ADD SMALL PETALS, STARTING FROM THE CENTRE. THESE CENTRAL PETALS SHOULD BE SMALL AND UPRIGHT.

3 DRAW THE REST OF THE PETALS, FOLLOWING THE SPIRAL SHAPE. BUILD UP THE FLOWER FURTHER FROM THE CENTRE, MAKING THE PETALS LARGER AND FLATTER TOWARDS THE OUTER EDGE.

4 ADD SOME DETAILS TO THE PETALS. DEFINE THE LINES WITH A DARK PENCIL LINE AND ADD VOLUME BY SHADING TOWARDS THE BOTTOM OF EACH PETAL.

Adding lines at the edge of your shading will suggest the petal is folding outwards, creating a rose in full bloom!

5 ADD SOME COLOUR! THINK ABOUT YOUR LIGHT SOURCE AND WHERE IT WOULD FALL ON THE ROSE PETALS. TRY DIFFERENT SHADES OF RED TO DEFINE LIGHT ZONES AND SHADOWS.

Add a stem and leaves to finish your rose, and maybe even a few thorns if you're feeling brave.

Rose leaves have a spiky edge. Sketch a leaf shape first, then go over the outline, keeping the points of the zig-zag facing towards the tip of the leaf.

CLOSED ROSE

Fashion boys

1

SKETCH AN OVAL SHAPE FOR THE HEAD AND GUIDELINES FOR THE SHOULDERS, BODY, HIPS, ARMS AND LEGS.

2

DRAW ARM AND LEG SHAPES AROUND YOUR GUIDELINES. ADD HANDS AND FEET.

3

ADD A HOODY AND JEANS TO THE SHAPE. USE WAVY LINES TO SHOW CREASES AT THE ELBOWS AND KNEES.

Use light and dark shades of the same colour to vary the texture. Try rubbing chalk or wash a damp paintbrush over a colour.

You can add some texture to the clothes to make it more realistic.

4

ADD HAIR AND A FACE AND FINISH OFF THE DETAILS SUCH AS LACES, POCKETS AND ZIPS. ERASE ANY GUIDELINES THAT ARE STILL SHOWING BEFORE COLOURING THE FINISHED FIGURE.

Make up swatches of colours you think will look good together.

OUT AND ABOUT

Try drawing a figure holding a skateboard. Look at the way this boy's shoulders and hips are tilted and one foot is turned up.

Add skater graphics to make your drawing more realistic. Make up your own or take inspiration from your favourite brands and logos.

MEERKATS

1 SKETCH A STICK FIGURE TO GIVE YOU THE BASIC POSE AND BODY PROPORTIONS OF YOUR MEERKAT. USE VERTICAL LINES FOR THE NECK AND BODY, WITH HORIZONTAL LINES TO MARK THE POSITIONS OF THE LEG JOINTS AND SHOULDERS.

2 ADD SOME GUIDE SHAPES TO FLESH OUT THE DIFFERENT PARTS OF THE MEERKAT'S BODY.

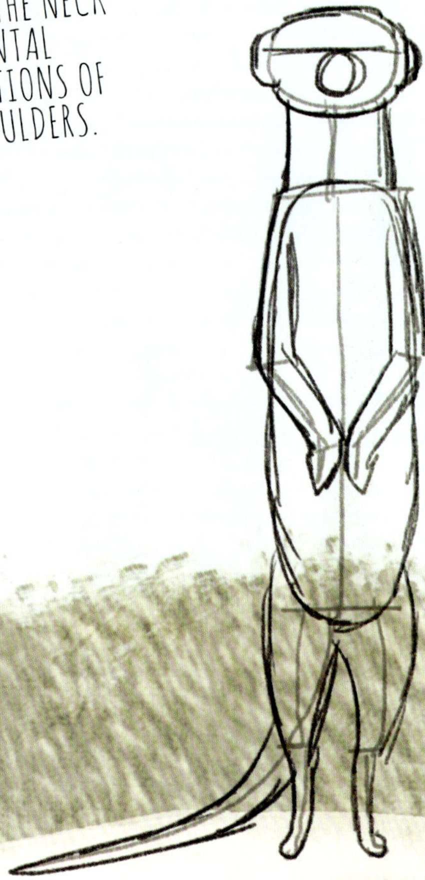

3 SKETCH THE MEERKAT'S OUTLINE THEN RUB OUT THE CONSTRUCTION LINES. ADD THE FACIAL FEATURES. USE SHADING TO CREATE A FURRY TEXTURE AND TO SHOW WHERE THE SHADOWS FALL.

Set the scene for your characters by painting a background first. Try a light wash for the sand with darker shapes to suggest rocks and stones.

4 PAINT YOUR MEERKAT, STARTING WITH A FLAT, DARK BROWN FOR THE BODY THEN BUILDING UP THE FUR TEXTURE IN A LIGHTER COLOUR USING SMALL BRUSH STROKES.

Varying the orientation of each meerkat can create a quirky and comical effect.

5 ADD MORE MEERKATS TO THE SCENE. TRY SOME SIDE-ON VIEWS AND HAVE OTHERS PEEPING OUT FROM BEHIND DIFFERENT OBJECTS OR GRASS.

To achieve the effect of sand-covered rocks, add specks of a contrasting colour. Rub your finger across the end of a brush to flick tiny specks of paint onto the darker areas.

T-SHIRTS

A T-SHIRT IS THE PERFECT FASHION ITEM – A BLANK CANVAS FOR ANY KIND OF DESIGN YOU CAN IMAGINE. PRACTISE DRAWING THE BASIC SHAPES FIRST, THEN GET CREATIVE!

DRAW A BASIC CREW-NECK T-SHIRT SHAPE USING A PENCIL OR PEN AND INKS. ADD CREASES TO THE ARMPIT AREAS. DRAW EXTRA STITCHING LINES IF YOU LIKE, SUCH AS AROUND THE NECK AND SLEEVES.

FOR A VEST, LEAVE OFF THE ARMS AND DRAW LINES CURVING INWARDS ON EACH SIDE. AND AN EXTRA LINE FOR INTEREST.

FOR A MORE FEMININE-LOOKING DESIGN, DRAW A SHALLOW V-NECK WITH THIN, VERTICAL STRAPS ATTACHED TO THE TOP.

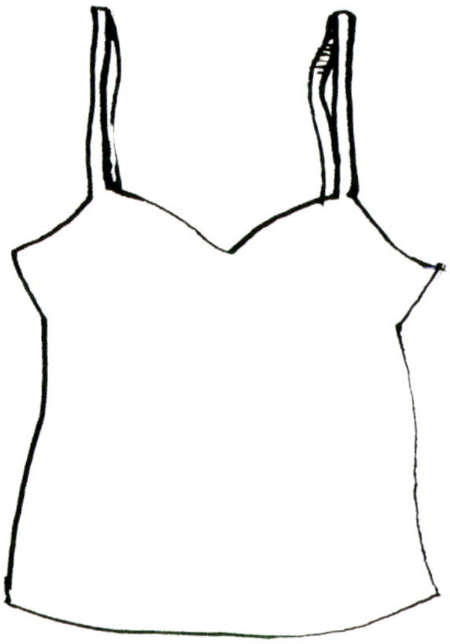

ANOTHER POPULAR T-SHIRT SHAPE IS THE V-NECK SHIRT.

DRAW A POCKET BY SKETCHING A SQUARE WITH A POINTED BASE. ADD EXTRA LINES OF DETAIL.

Draw simple dashed lines like these for the stitching detail. Add these lines around the base, neck and sleeves.

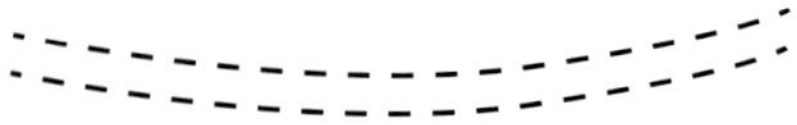

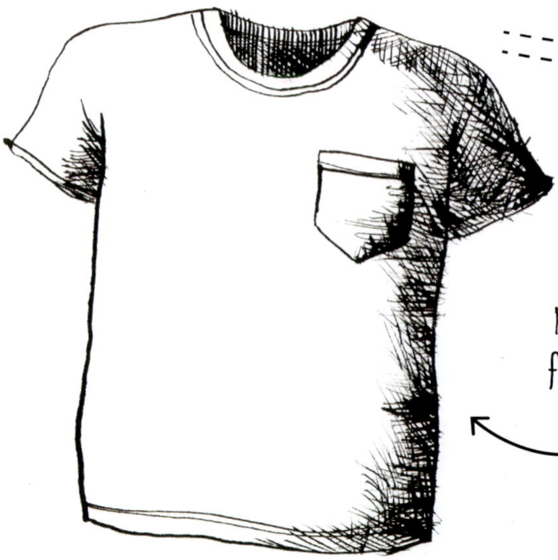

To add depth, use simple crosshatching for the areas that would be in the shadows. Here, the light source is coming in from the left.

HERE ARE SOME T-SHIRT DESIGNS TO GIVE YOU INSPIRATION.

MUSIC

Draw objects hanging on either side of the neck, such as these cool headphones.

BEAR

A large image bleeding off the bottom of the T-shirt looks very striking. Big faces have a lot of impact as well!

PATTERNED NECK

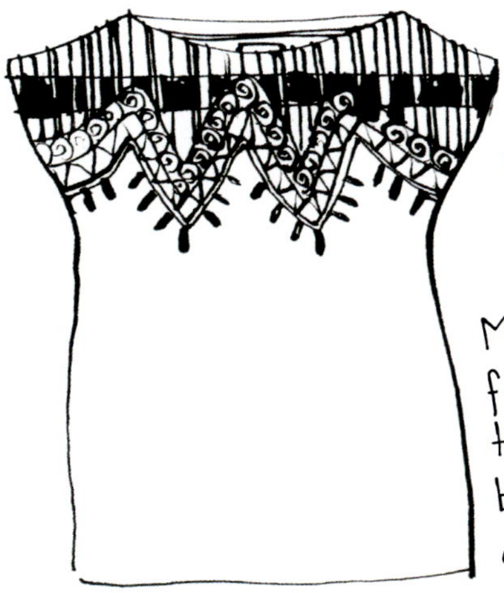

Make a feature of the neckline by drawing an intricate pattern.

STRIPY

Pull out the pocket using different patterns and colours.

BLOCK STRIPE

Irregular-shaped bands of colour are simple but highly effective.

ZIG-ZAG

Bold patterns in contrasting colours look cool and on-trend.

POLKA DOT

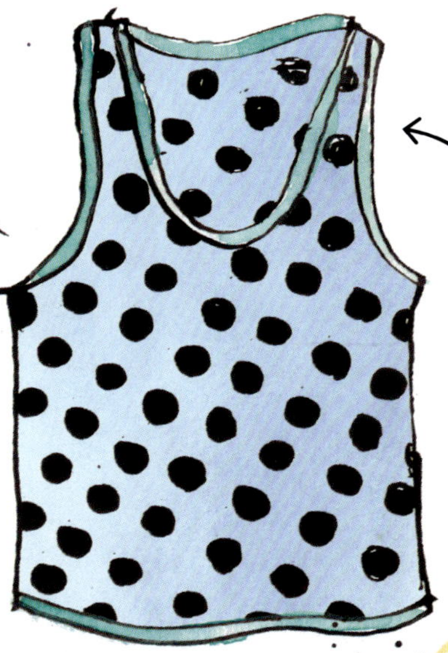

To soften the impact of a strong pattern, try using a contrasting colour for the edges.

PIRATE SHIP

1 DRAW THE OUTLINE OF THE SHIP'S HULL. IMAGINE IT AS A LONG BOX, WITH ANOTHER BOX BALANCED ON TOP OF IT AT THE FAR END. DRAW A BEAM AT THE FRONT AND THREE SETS OF PARALLEL LINES FOR THE MASTS.

To help you get the shape right, try looking at a boot or shoe with the toe end tilted slightly towards you. The ship is similar in shape.

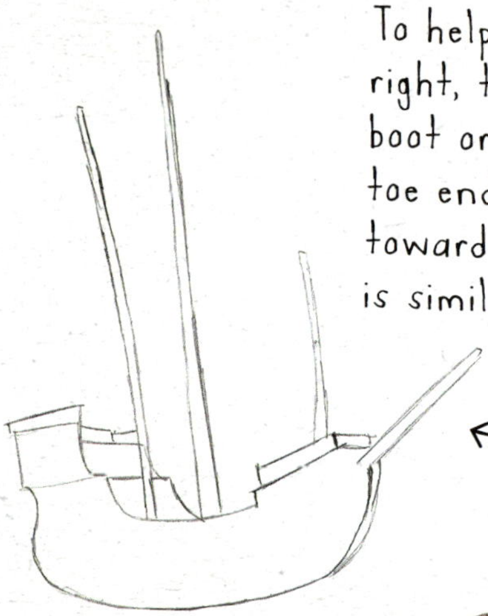

2 DRAW SOME BEAMS AT RIGHT ANGLES TO THE MASTS, THEN ADD THE VARIOUS SAILS. THE MAIN SAILS ARE LIKE RECTANGLES WITH CURVED EDGES. ADD A POINTED FLAG, A CROW'S NEST NEAR THE TOP AND EXTRA DETAIL AT THE FRONT OF THE SHIP.

To get the shape of the sails right, bend a piece of paper and observe it at an angle that matches that of your ship.

3 ADD CANNON PORTS TO THE HULL OF YOUR SHIP BY DRAWING SOME SMALL RECTANGLES. SKETCH AN ANCHOR ON ITS SIDE NEAR THE FRONT. RUB OUT THE BITS OF THE SHIP THAT ARE VISIBLE THROUGH THE SAILS, SUCH AS THE MASTS.

4 USING LONG, WIGGLY LINES, ADD FLAGS TO THE TOP OF THE MIDDLE AND REAR MASTS. DRAW CANNONS PEEPING OUT OF THE HULL AND ADD HORIZONTAL LINES TO CREATE THE PORT COVERS. SKETCH A LANTERN, ROPES AND A SKULL AND CROSSBONES.

Start shading darker areas, such as inside the cannon ports.

5 WORK ON THE FINE DETAILS. SKETCH A CROSSHATCH DESIGN ON THE REAR WINDOWS AND ADD HORIZONTAL LINES TO THE RIGGING. DRAW THE SHIP'S WHEEL, AS WELL AS PATCHES AND TEARS ON THE SAILS.

Fine detail will add extra visual interest. Add extra lines to the hull, beams and balconies.

6 USE DARK AND MUTED COLOURS TO GIVE YOUR PIRATE SHIP AN OMINOUS AND MYSTERIOUS FEEL. THINK ABOUT WHERE THE SHADOWS WILL FALL, SUCH AS ON THE DECK AREA AND AT THE REAR OF THE SHIP.

Add slightly lighter areas of grey to the black sails to achieve the effect of creased material billowing in the wind.

HIGH STREET

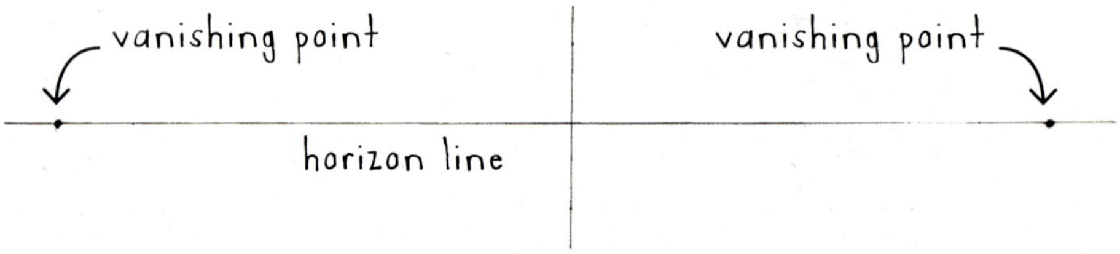

1

USE A RULER TO DRAW A HORIZONTAL LINE. DRAW A DOT AT EACH END OF THE LINE. THESE ARE THE VANISHING POINTS, WHERE ALL LINES WILL COME TOGETHER. NEXT, DRAW A VERTICAL LINE – THIS WILL BE THE HEIGHT OF THE BUILDINGS AT THE FRONT OF THE PICTURE.

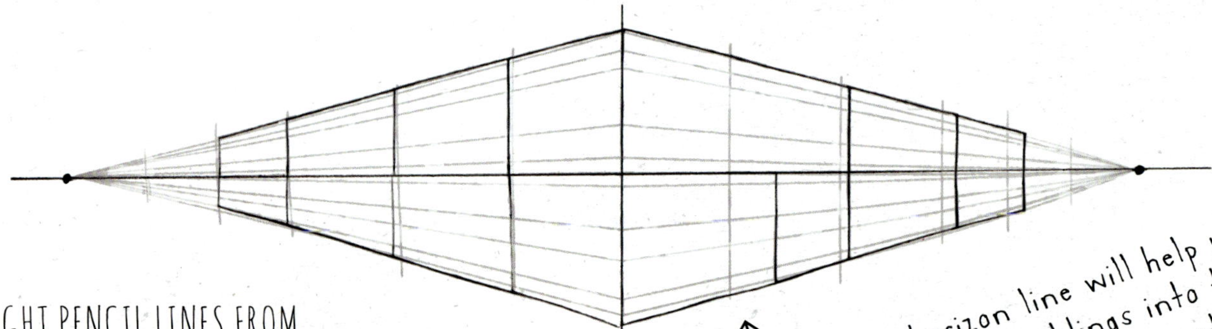

2

DRAW LIGHT PENCIL LINES FROM THE VANISHING POINTS TO THE TOP AND BOTTOM OF THE VERTICAL LINE. ADD MORE VERTICAL LINES TO DIVIDE THE HIGH STREET INTO INDIVIDUAL SHOPS.

The horizon line will help you divide the buildings into the upstairs and the downstairs.

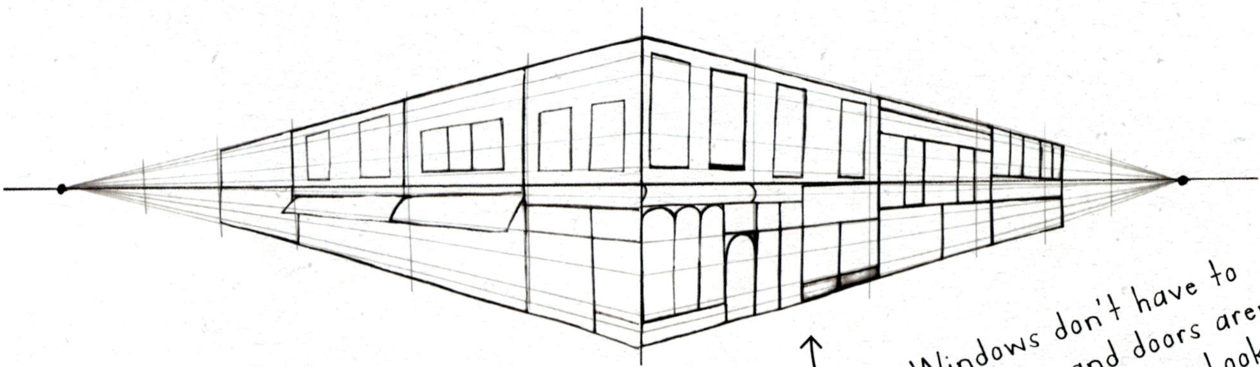

3

ADD EXTRA GUIDELINES TO HELP YOU POSITION SHOP DETAILS. START FROM THE VERTICAL LINE AND END AT THE VANISHING POINT, DRAWING THE SAME LINES ON BOTH SIDES. USING THE VERTICAL AND HORIZONTAL LINES AS GUIDES, DRAW THE WINDOWS, DOORS AND AWNINGS.

Windows don't have to be square and doors aren't always rectangles. Look at the high street near you to get some ideas.

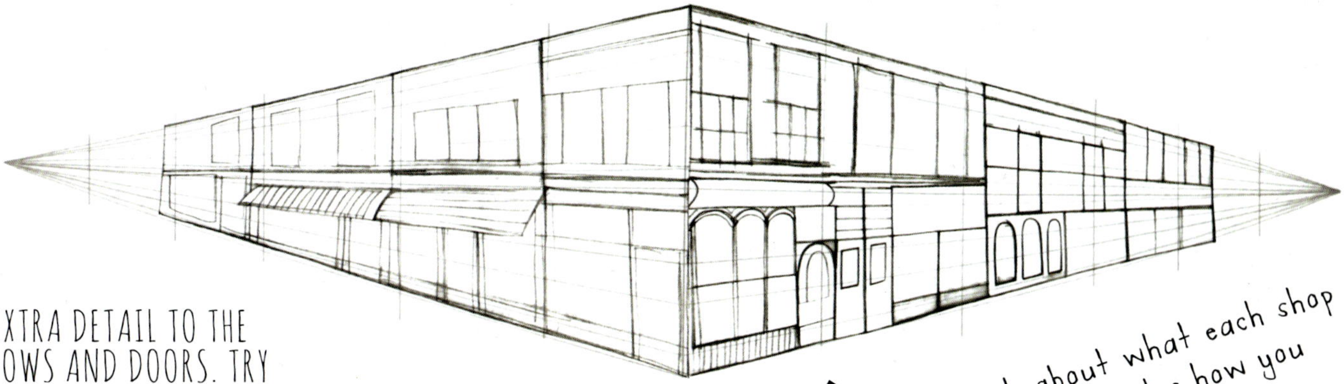

4

ADD EXTRA DETAIL TO THE WINDOWS AND DOORS. TRY TO MAKE THEM ALL DIFFERENT TO KEEP EACH BUILDING INDIVIDUAL. THIS WILL ADD CHARACTER TO YOUR DRAWING. WHEN YOU ARE HAPPY WITH THE DRAWING, ERASE THE GUIDELINES.

Think about what each shop sells to consider how you draw and decorate them.

5

USE AN INK PEN TO OUTLINE YOUR BUILDINGS AND ADD ANY DECORATIVE DETAIL TO THEM. USE WATERCOLOUR WASHES TO PAINT THE BUILDINGS AND SHOW REFLECTIONS ON THE WINDOWS. PAINT WITH THE PALEST COLOURS FIRST AND WORK UP TO THE DARKER SHADES.

Let the paint dry in between working on each building so the colours don't bleed together.

STATUE OF LIBERTY

1

USING A LIGHT PENCIL, SKETCH BASIC SHAPES. DRAW CIRCLES FOR THE HEAD AND FLAME, AND LOOSE RECTANGLES FOR THE BODY, FOLLOWING THE LINE OF MOVEMENT OF THE STATUE.

2

ADD GUIDELINES TO PLAN THE FACE OF THE STATUE IN YOUR DRAWING. ADD THE CROWN OF RAYS FROM THE HEAD AND OUTLINE THE GOWN.

Find a photo of the Statue of Liberty for inspiration. This will help you decide which details are important to capture in your drawing.

Using darker colours on one side and lighter colours on the other on the statue some gives the statue some dimension. White highlights in the centre add form too.

3

START ADDING SOME DETAIL. DRAW THE HANDS HOLDING THE TORCH AND TABLET. USE SWEEPING LINES TO SHOW THE PLEATS AND FOLDS OF THE GOWN TO CREATE THE IDEA OF MOVEMENT AROUND THE BODY OF THE STATUE.

4

CHECK YOUR DRAWING AGAINST YOUR REFERENCE PICTURE TO MAKE SURE YOU HAVEN'T MISSED ANY IMPORTANT DETAIL BEFORE YOU START TO ADD SOME COLOUR. ADD A PLATFORM TO GROUND YOUR STATUE.

5

NOW ADD SOME COLOUR USING WATERCOLOUR PENCILS. BRUSH WATER IN SOME PLACES TO BLEND THE COLOURS. LEAVE SOME AREAS WITHOUT COLOUR TO CREATE HIGHLIGHTS. FINALLY, DRAW THE OUTLINE IN BLACK AND DON'T BE AFRAID TO USE HEAVY LINES FOR SHADOWS AND PLEATS.

QUAD BIKE

1 DRAW A ROUND SHAPE FOR THE BIKE RIDER'S HEAD AND THEN USE OVAL SHAPES FOR HIS TORSO, ARMS, HANDS, LEGS AND FEET, LIKE THIS.

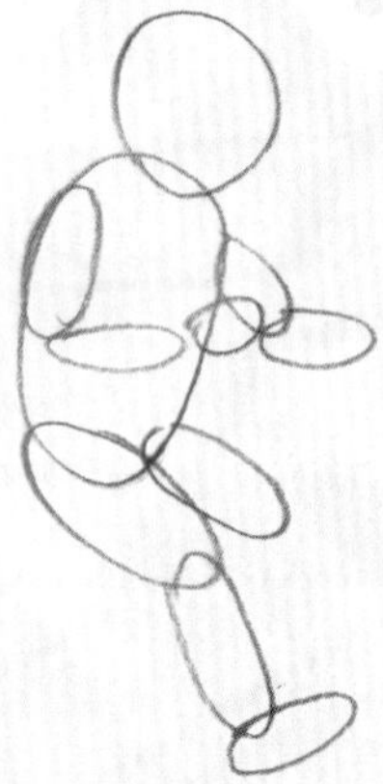

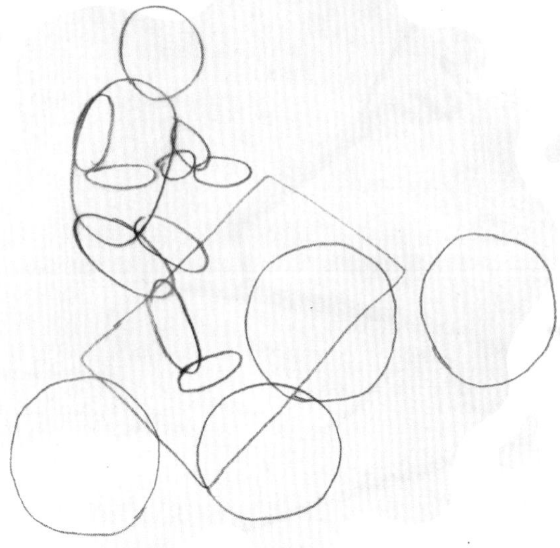

2 SKETCH A LARGE, ANGLED RECTANGLE SHAPE IN FRONT OF THE RIDER FOR THE MAIN BODY OF THE BIKE. THEN DRAW FOUR BIG CIRCLES FOR THE WHEELS.

3 ADD DETAIL TO THE SKETCH BY DRAWING THE TOP OF THE RIDER'S HELMET AND A PAIR OF GOGGLES. THEN ADD MORE DETAIL TO THE QUAD BIKE, AS SHOWN.

4 SHADE THE DARKER SECTIONS UNDERNEATH THE BIKE. CONTINUE TO ADD DETAIL TO THE DRAWING. ADD THE STAR DESIGN ONTO THE SUIT AND HELMET.

5 TRACE OVER THE PENCIL WITH INK. ONCE THE INK IS DRY, CAREFULLY RUB OUT ANY REMAINING PENCIL. ADD PLENTY OF EXTRA DETAIL IN INK, SUCH AS HANDLEBARS AND SHADOWS.

Add shading under the rider's arms and knees to give him more depth.

Putting the bike in the air creates an exciting picture full of action.

6 USE PAINT TO ADD COLOUR TO THE BIKE AND RIDER. TO MAKE IT LOOK AS IF THE BIKE IS MOVING, SPLATTER FLECKS OF BROWN PAINT ON A MUDDY TRACK.

MEGA DESSERT

1

DRAW THE OUTLINE OF A DESSERT BOWL, ADDING LOTS OF OVERLAPPING CIRCLES FOR THE ICE-CREAM AND FRUIT. USE WAVY LINES TO BUILD UP THE LAYERS OF TOPPING. ADD A WIDE CONE SHAPE FOR THE UMBRELLA.

2

DRAW KIWI SLICES, A CHERRY, BOWL DETAIL AND SQUARES FOR PINEAPPLE CHUNKS. CREATE AN ORANGE SLICE BY ADDING MORE CIRCLES AND LINES TO ONE OF THE ROUND SHAPES.

Vary the thickness of the black linework and create extra visual interest by adding thick coloured outlines.

3

ADD DETAIL AND TEXTURE. DRAW STRAIGHT LINES ON THE UMBRELLA, RADIATING OUTWARDS FROM THE CENTRE. DRAW CURVED LINES ON THE TOP LAYER TO MAKE LAYERS OF WHIPPED CREAM. SKETCH WAVY LINES ON THE BLOBS OF ICE-CREAM.

Use contrasting tones to bring out the texture and shape of the ice-cream.

4

NOW FOCUS ON THE FINE DETAIL. DRAW LOTS OF TINY DOTS, STARS AND NUGGET SHAPES FOR THE SPRINKLES. RUB OUT ANY UNWANTED OVERLAPPING LINES.

5

USE A RANGE OF BRIGHT COLOURS TO MAKE YOUR DESSERT LOOK AS APPETIZING AS POSSIBLE! CREATE A FLOWERY PATTERN FOR THE UMBRELLA USING LOTS OF OVERLAPPING ELLIPSES.

NINJA

1 DRAW A SIMPLE SKELETON SHAPE, SHOWING YOUR NINJA IN AN ACTION POSE. DRAW STRAIGHT LINES FOR HIS OUTSTRETCHED ARM AND LEG, WITH ANGLED LINES FOR HIS OTHER LIMBS.

2 DRAW ROUNDED SHAPES FOR THE CHEST, PELVIS AND JOINTS. FLESH OUT THE NINJA'S BODY, USING YOUR GUIDES TO GET THE PROPORTIONS RIGHT. MAKE HIS LEFT ARM AND LEG LOOK BULKIER, AS THEY ARE IN A BENT POSITION – THE MUSCLES WILL BE BULGING!

3 DRAW LOOSE CLOTHING ON THE NINJA'S BODY. ADD A SLIT TO HIS MASK AND REFINE THE SHAPES OF HIS HANDS AND FEET. DRAW HIS HEADBAND TRAILING BEHIND HIM, AS IF HE'S FLYING THROUGH THE AIR.

Add more ninjas to your scene. Try and think of poses that contrast with the typical high-kicking main action pose. For example, this ninja is crouching down, ready to pounce!

5 PAINT YOUR NINJA MAINLY BLACK. ADD PATCHES OF LIGHT GREY ON TOP TO BRING OUT THE HIGHLIGHTED AREAS AND THE CREASES ON HIS CLOTHES.

4 GO OVER THE OUTLINE OF THE NINJA AND RUB OUT ANY UNWANTED GUIDELINES. WORK ON THE FINE DETAIL BY DRAWING THE FINGERS AND FACIAL FEATURES. ADD LINES AND SHADING TO SHOW THE CREASES IN THE CLOTHING.

Paint the background a flat colour, adding darker brick shapes and windows. Give it a gritty, urban texture by scratching away the painted surface with a coin or wire brush.

MOUSTACHES

LEARN HOW TO DRAW SOME SIMPLE TWIRLY MOUSTACHES, THEN TRY CREATING YOUR OWN STYLES - THE MORE OUTLANDISH, THE BETTER!

SHORT STROKES

1 DRAW THE BASIC OUTLINE OF A MOUSTACHE. THINK OF IT AS A WIDE, SOFT 'M' SHAPE WITH CURLS ON EACH SIDE.

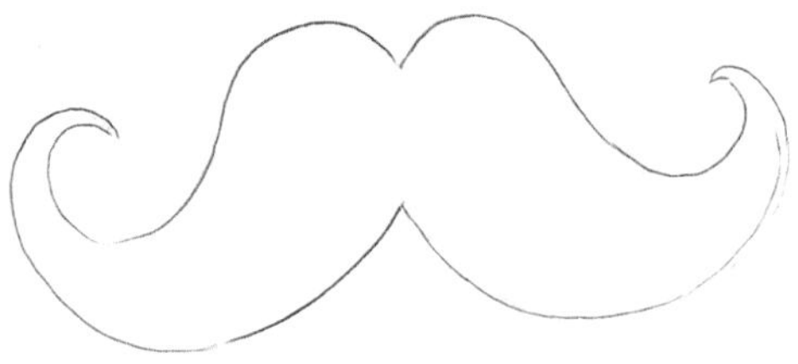

2 USING A SOFT-GRADE PENCIL, ADD LOTS OF SHORT MARKS FOLLOWING THE CURVED SHAPE OF THE MOUSTACHE. START WITH THE OUTLINE, THEN FILL IN THE MIDDLE. THE MARKS WILL LOOK LIKE INDIVIDUAL HAIRS.

CONTOUR LINES

1 DRAW A CURLIER MOUSTACHE – THE KIND AN OLD-FASHIONED CIRCUS RINGMASTER MIGHT HAVE HAD! USE LONG, CURVED LINES TO DRAW THE LEFT SIDE FIRST, THEN SKETCH THE OTHER HALF TO MATCH. DON'T WORRY IF IT'S NOT EXACTLY SYMMETRICAL. IT WILL LOOK EVEN QUIRKIER IF IT'S NOT COMPLETELY PERFECT.

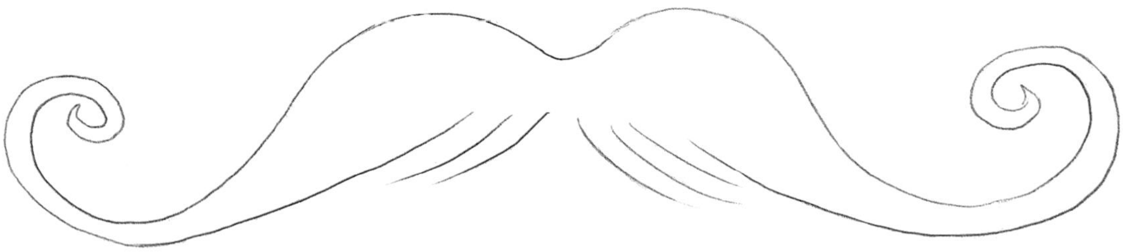

2 ADD SOFTER CURVED LINES, FLOWING FROM THE MIDDLE OF THE MOUSTACHE ALMOST TO THE END OF EACH CURL. VARY THE PRESSURE ON YOUR PENCIL TO CREATE THE IMPRESSION OF DEPTH IN YOUR DRAWING.

Think about how your moustache designs can be used on faces. This eccentric professor is wearing a suitably mad-looking moustache!

AFTER YOU'VE MASTERED THE BASIC MOUSTACHE, TRY VARYING THE SHAPES AND EXPERIMENT WITH DIFFERENT TECHNIQUES FOR ADDING TEXTURE.

PENCIL STROKES

USE DIFFERENT PENCIL STROKES FOR THESE MOUSTACHES, AND USE PENCIL CRAYONS TO COLOUR THEM IN.

Mimic the moustache contours with a number of heavier lines. Then add softer shading between them.

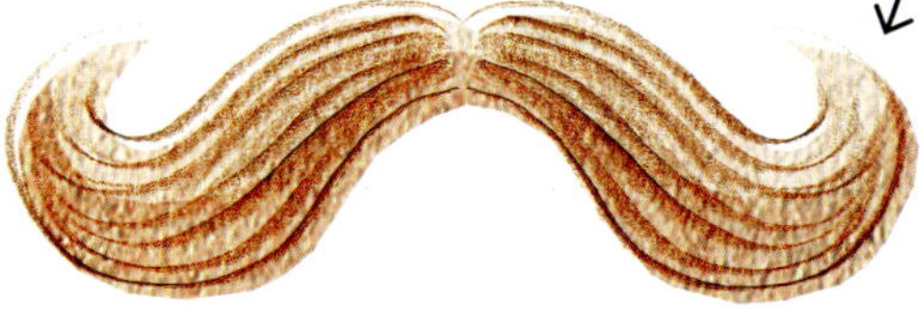

THE HANDLEBAR

Draw each of these short lines with a quick flick of the pencil to make the moustache look bristly.

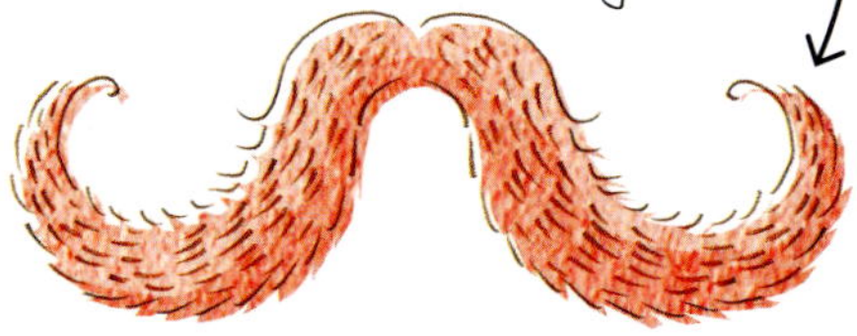

THE SERGEANT MAJOR

This simple crescent-shaped moustache looks quite neat. Fill the shape with dashed marks to create a uniform pattern.

THE VILLAIN

PATTERNED

FILL YOUR MOUSTACHE DESIGNS WITH DOODLES AND PATTERNS. THESE DESIGNS WERE CREATED USING FINE-LINE MARKER PENS.

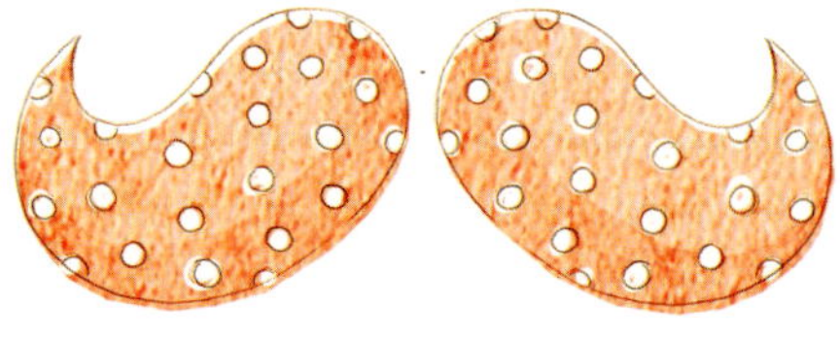

THE POLKA DOT

THE SWIRLY

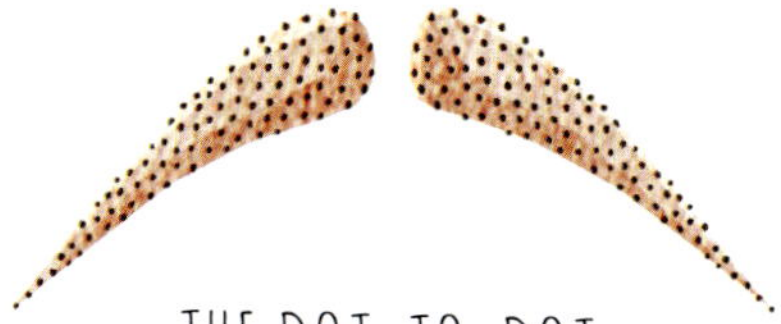

THE DOT-TO-DOT

WACKY STYLES

MOUSTACHE DESIGNS CAN BE AS STRANGE AND OVER-THE-TOP AS YOU WANT. LET YOUR IMAGINATION RUN WILD!

Draw multiple swirls, then fill them with long, sweeping curves.

THE HEXOPUS

This curved design has a handy gap in the middle for the person's mouth.

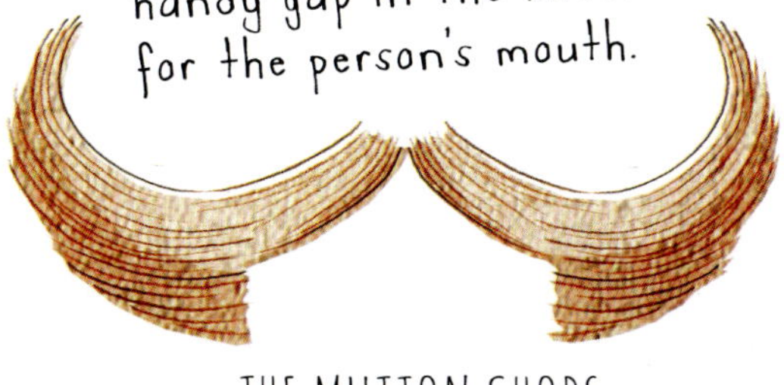

THE MUTTON CHOPS

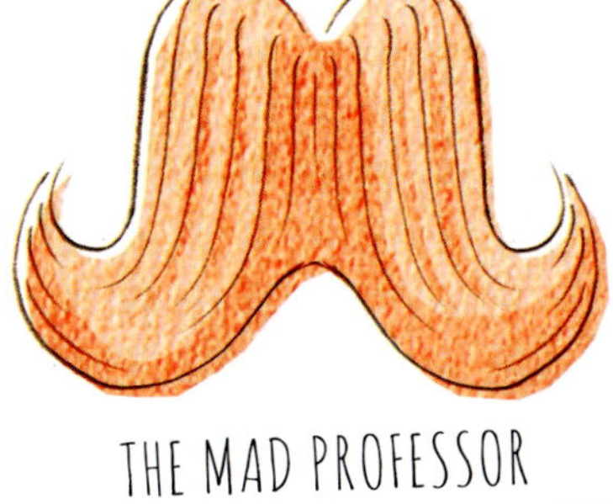

THE MAD PROFESSOR

ALIEN INVASION

1 TO START YOUR BASIC ALIEN, DRAW THREE OVERLAPPING SHAPES, INCLUDING A CIRCLE FOR THE HEAD.

2 DRAW SOME LONG, CURVED LIMBS, PLUS WAVY TENTACLES AND CIRCULAR EYES. ADD LIPS TO THE ALIEN'S BIG MOUTH.

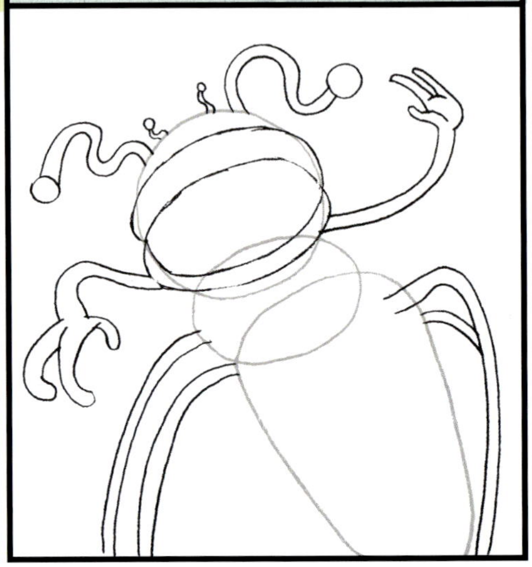

3 DRAW A BIG TONGUE AND LOTS OF SHARP, JAGGED TEETH. ADD SUCKER SHAPES TO THE FINGERS AND TENTACLES.

4 TO DRAW THE BUILDINGS, FIRST SKETCH SOME ANGLED RECTANGLES, AS IF YOU'RE LOOKING DOWN ON SKYSCRAPER ROOFS. THEN DRAW VERTICAL GUIDELINES DOWN FROM EACH CORNER.

5 ADD WINDOWS USING A VARIETY OF SQUARE AND RECTANGULAR SHAPES. DRAW JAGGED LINES AT THE ENDS OF SOME OF THE BUILDINGS TO SHOW WHERE THE ALIEN HAS RIPPED THEM APART!

6 GO OVER YOUR LINEWORK IN INK. DRAW TINY CIRCLES TO GIVE THE SKIN SOME TEXTURE AND ADD CURVED LINES TO THE ALIEN'S HEAD AND BODY. ADD NOSTRILS. ADD SHADING TO THE AREAS THAT SHOULD BE DARKER.

7 USE STRONG COLOURS TO HELP YOUR ALIEN STAND OUT FROM THE SKY-BLUE BACKGROUND. ADD A STARBURST TO BUILD UP THE ACTION AND COMMOTION TOO!

GIRAFFE FACE

2

ADD MORE SIMPLE SHAPES: A ROUGH SEMI-CIRCLE FOR THE MOUTH AND SAUSAGE SHAPES FOR THE HORNS AND EARS.

1

START BY SKETCHING THREE BASIC SHAPES: A SKEWED RECTANGULAR SHAPE FOR THE NECK, A LARGE CIRCLE FOR THE HEAD AND A SMALLER ONE FOR THE EYE.

3

USING THE BASIC SHAPES AS A GUIDE, SKETCH THE OUTLINE OF THE GIRAFFE. GIVE HER SOME LOVELY UPTURNED EYELASHES – THE EYES ON A GIRAFFE ARE A BIG FEATURE! RUB OUT YOUR GUIDELINES.

4

USE SUBTLE SHADING TO BRING OUT THE FACIAL FEATURES. FOR THE PATTERN, DRAW SOME ROUGH CIRCULAR SHAPES, THEN SHADE EACH AREA, ADDING DARKER TONES TO THE CENTRE OF EACH ONE.

5

PAINT AN ORANGEY WATERCOLOUR WASH ALL OVER YOUR SKETCH. USE A BROWN COLOURED PENCIL TO TRACE OVER THE OUTLINE AND ADD SHADING, INCLUDING IN THE EARS AND ON THE HORNS AND NOSTRILS.

To create expressive, life-like eyes, colour the pupils dark then add two spots of white paint on top - one larger than the other for glints.

Try drawing on textured cartridge paper to give your illustration added visual interest.

POP STAR

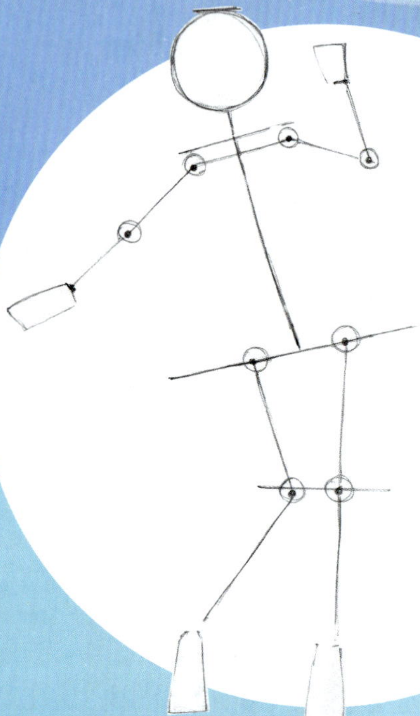

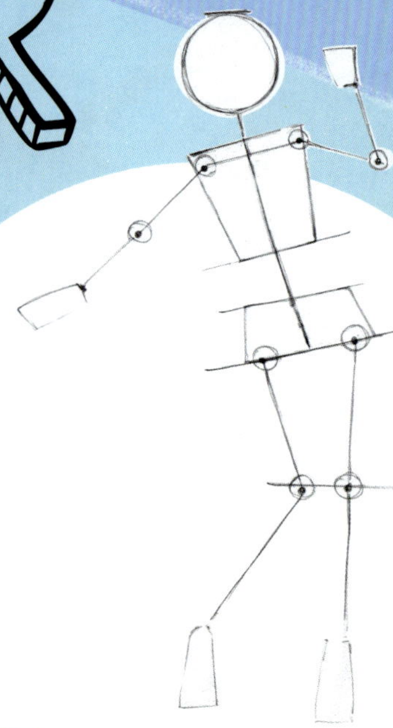

1

SKETCH A CIRCLE FOR THE HEAD AND A STRAIGHT, VERTICAL LINE FOR THE NECK AND SPINE. ADD A PERPENDICULAR LINE FOR THE HIPS AND MORE LINES FOR THE ARMS AND LEGS. DRAW CIRCLES FOR THE JOINTS AND RECTANGLES FOR THE HANDS AND FEET, AS SHOWN.

2

DRAW A TAPERED RECTANGULAR SHAPE FOR THE TORSO. ADD A SMALLER RECTANGULAR SHAPE BELOW IT TO FORM THE LOWER PART OF THE BODY.

3

START FLESHING OUT THE BODY PARTS. DRAW A CIRCLE BETWEEN THE HIPS AND THE CHEST, THEN ADD ROUGH SAUSAGE SHAPES FOR THE ARMS AND LEGS.

4

JOIN THE LIMB SHAPES TOGETHER WITH MORE DISTINCT OUTLINES AND DRAW STRONG LINES TO BRING OUT THE CURVES AND CONTOURS OF THE BODY.

Add facial features and some shading for your pop star's stage make-up.

Try adding a two- tone background, choosing colours that contrast with your pop star.

6

ADD SOME COLOUR TO YOUR POP STAR. USE SUBTLE SHADING ON THE JEWELLERY WITH ADDED HIGHLIGHTS TO BRING OUT THE BLING!

5

FOCUS ON THE FINER DETAILS OF YOUR FIGURE, ADDING HAIR, CLOTHES AND ACCESSORIES. IT'S OFTEN THE SMALLER DETAILS THAT HELP TO ADD REAL CHARACTER.

Draw a podium to ground your singer so she doesn't look like she's floating in space.

LINE DESIGNS

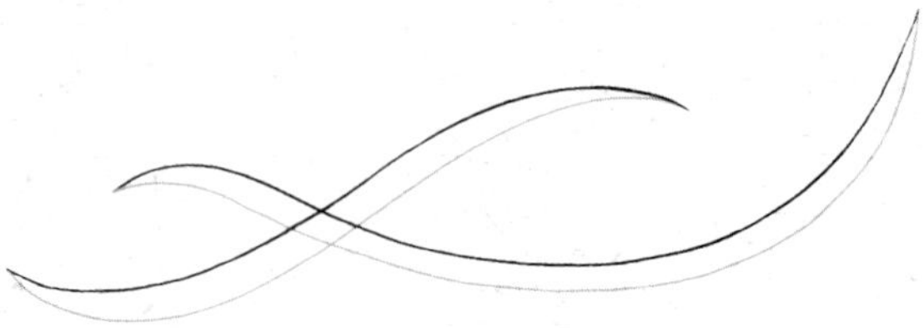

1

USE A PENCIL TO DRAW TWO WAVY LINES OF SIMILAR LENGTHS. THE LINES WILL LOOK LESS WOBBLY IF YOU DRAW THEM QUICKLY. A LINE DESIGN SHOULD BE POWERFUL, DRAMATIC AND MEMORABLE!

2

GIVE YOUR TWO LINES A BIT MORE DEPTH BY ADDING ANOTHER TWO PENCIL LINES BENEATH THEM, LIKE THIS, MAKING THE LINES LOOK AS IF THEY HAVE BEEN CREATED WITH TWO CLEAN, SWEEPING BRUSH STROKES.

3

ADD SOME SPIRALS AND MORE SWEEPING LINES INTO YOUR DESIGN. MAKE IT LOOK NATURAL. AGAIN, DO THIS QUICKLY AND CONFIDENTLY.

4

USE AN INK PEN TO FILL IN THE DESIGN. A SOLID BLACK COLOUR CREATES A VERY STRIKING IMAGE.

MORE!

Be as creative and imaginative as you like with line designs and come up with your own to draw on your things. These ones are spiky, dramatic and memorable!

SYMMETRICAL

1 2 3 4

Draw a vertical pencil line. Whatever you sketch on one side of the line, repeat the mirror image on the other side. For this butterfly design, build up the image gradually until you have a striking set of symmetrical swirls and patterns.

SPIRAL

1

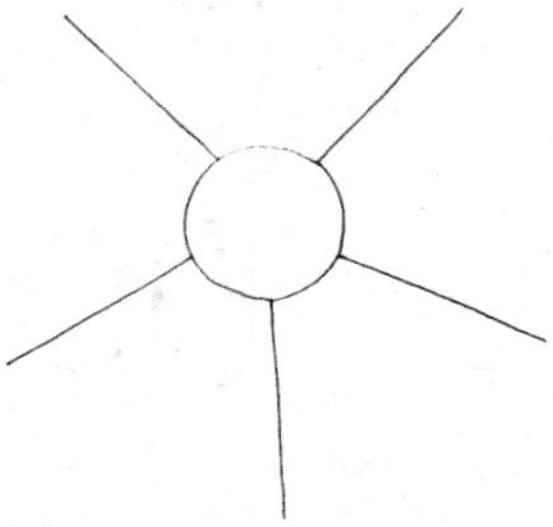

Use a pencil to sketch a small circle then draw five lines, like this.

2

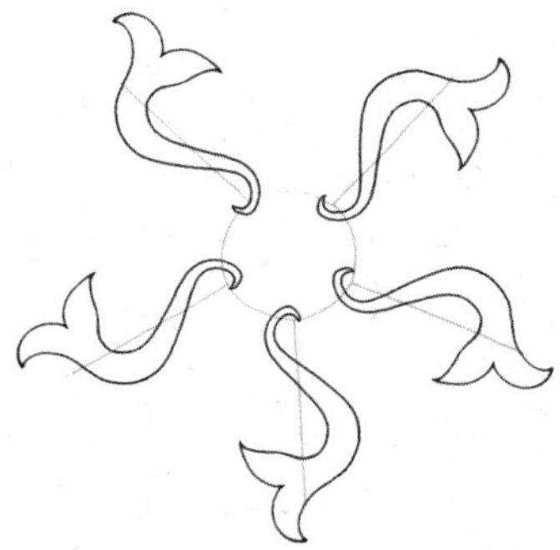

On each line, roughly draw in the outline of the same little leg shapes.

3

In the five spaces between the legs, draw in a slightly different pattern.

4

Add a spiky design to the circle in the middle of your pattern.

5

Using ink, colour in your design. Doing this quickly creates a bolder image.

6

Finally, add some little dots to the image to complete your cool spiral design.

ROCKSTAR DRUM KIT

1 DRAW A LARGE CIRCLE FOR THE BASS DRUM AND THEN SKETCH IN SOME SMALLER OVAL SHAPES FOR THE OTHER BITS OF THE DRUM KIT AROUND THE BIGGER CIRCLE.

2 SKETCH IN THE SAME SHAPES REFLECTING THE ORIGINAL ONES. THIS IS GOING TO HELP MAKE THE DRUMS LOOK 3D.

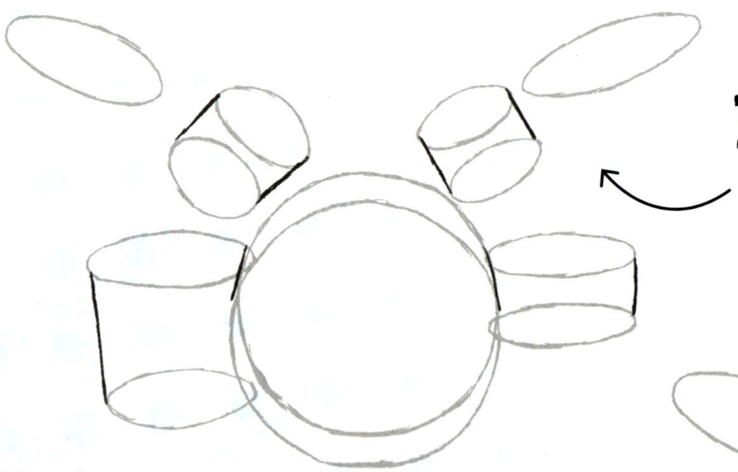

3 CONNECT EACH SET OF SHAPES BY DRAWING A SERIES OF STRAIGHT LINES, LIKE THIS.

4 ADD MORE DETAIL TO YOUR DRAWING. DRAW LINES AROUND EACH OF THE DRUMS, SKETCH IN THE STANDS FOR THE CYMBALS AND SMALLER DRUM AND ADD LEGS AND FEET FOR ALL THE KIT.

5 TO MAKE THE DRUM KIT STAND OUT, DESIGN YOUR OWN BLACK LINE DRAWING ON THE FRONT OF THE BASS DRUM. OR, GIVE YOUR BAND A NAME AND ADD A SPECIAL LOGO WITH THE NAME IN THE SAME SPACE.

For inspiration for the line design, see pages 56 and 57.

6 COLOUR YOUR FINISHED PICTURE WITH GOLDEN COLOURS FOR THE CYMBALS AND WOODEN COLOURS FOR THE DRUMS. ADD DARK STANDS AND A COOL ROCK-STAR BACKGROUND.

ALIEN UFO

1 DRAW THREE PAIRS OF ELLIPSES, MAKING EACH NEW PAIR NOTICEABLY BIGGER AS YOU MOVE DOWNWARDS. DRAW THE SHAPES AT A SLIGHT ANGLE.

2 TO MAKE THREE SHALLOW CYLINDRICAL SHAPES, USE VERTICAL LINES TO JOIN EACH PAIR OF ELLIPSES AT THE FAR EDGES. FOR WINDOWS, ADD A ROW OF SMALL CIRCLES TO THE SIDE OF EACH CYLINDER. DRAW MORE CYLINDERS UNDERNEATH THE UFO'S BODY TO FORM THE BOOSTERS. ADD MORE DOMES AND CYLINDERS AS SHOWN.

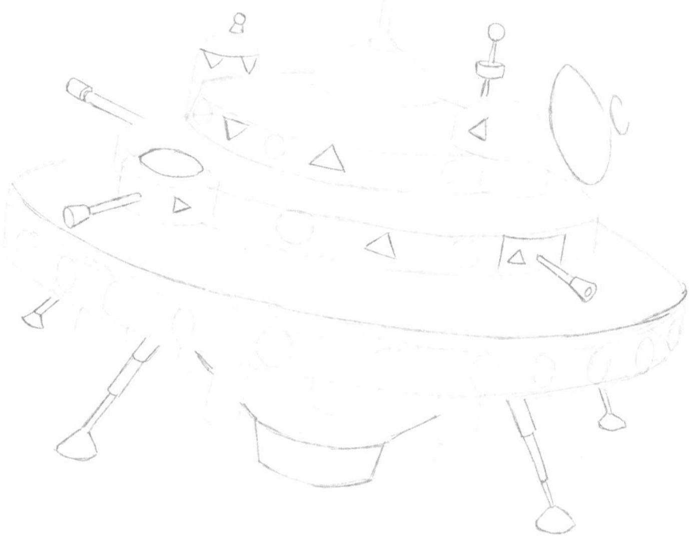

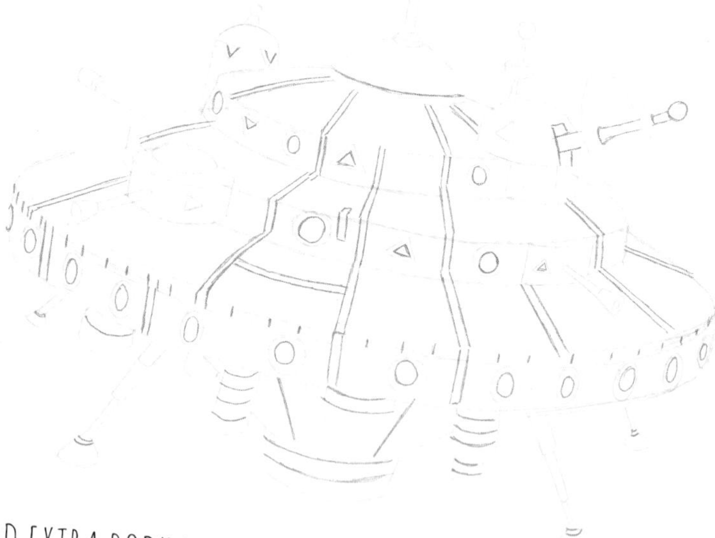

3 ADD MORE WINDOWS BY SKETCHING SOME TRIANGULAR SHAPES. ADD LEGS AND ARMS USING LONG RECTANGLES WITH TRIANGULAR OR 3D CONE SHAPES AT THE ENDS. ADD AN ELLIPSE TO FORM THE BASIC SHAPE OF A SATELLITE DISH. DRAW A LARGE CYLINDER UNDERNEATH THE UFO.

4 ADD EXTRA BODY DETAIL. DRAW MORE CIRCLES AND TRIANGLES AROUND THE WINDOWS. EMPHASIZE THE SENSE OF PERSPECTIVE BY DRAWING PAIRS OF PARALLEL LINES THAT FOLLOW THE STEPPED SHAPE OF THE UFO, SEPARATING SLIGHTLY AS THEY APPROACH THE VIEWER. ADD EXTRA CURVES TO THE BOOSTERS, LEGS AND TURRETS.

5 PAINT YOUR UFO! THEN USE CHALKS OR PASTELS TO ADD A SOFT GLARE EFFECT AROUND THE OUTER EDGES OF THE WINDOWS. MAKE THE BODYWORK LOOK SMOOTH AND METALLIC BY ADDING PLENTY OF REFLECTIONS AND LARGE HIGHLIGHTED AREAS.

Use watercolour washes to create a beam of light. Start with a pale blue and fade it out as you approach the centre, leaving only the white paper showing. Leave to dry then repeat with the purple colour, starting further away and fading out where the two colours overlap.

CARTOON MONSTERS

EXPRESSIVE EYES

SAD

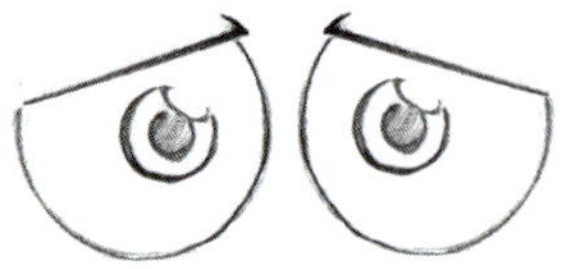

ANGRY

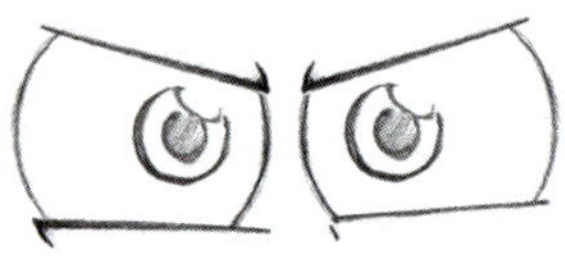

HAPPY

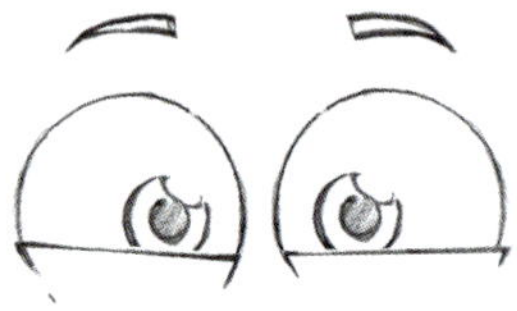

Eye shapes can completely change a monster's mood! Use eyebrows to create even more expression.

PUZZLED

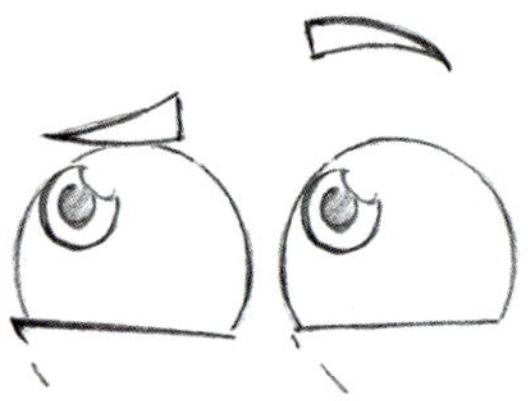

SURPRISED

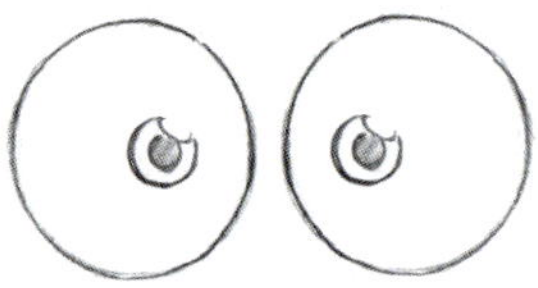

CRAZY

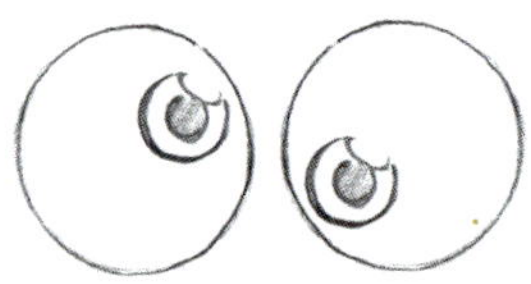

FUR TEXTURE

FUR FALLS IN ONE DIRECTION. SKETCH A RAGGED OUTLINE AND ADD CLUMPS INSIDE.

CREATE TEXTURE WITH LIGHT AND SHADOWS BETWEEN THE CLUMPS OF FUR. USE LINES IN ONE DIRECTION.

MONSTER MOUTHS

SQUAT AND SQUARE

I'M MELTING!

SMALL SPIKES

LOTS OF SPOTS

Draw eyes pointing in different directions for a goofy monster.

Experiment with different monster bodies - tall, short, four arms or none!

STRIPE FRIGHT

FOUR ARMED

TINY TONGUE

HAIRY HORROR

Add stripes, spots, blobs and more to give each monster its own personality.

ANGRY LEGS

BEASTIE BLOB

MONKEYS

1

DRAW A BASIC STICK FIGURE SHOWING YOUR MONKEY IN AN ACTION POSE. USE SHORT LINES TO SHOW THE POSITIONS OF THE SHOULDER AND ARM JOINTS.

2

SKETCH THE OUTLINE OF YOUR MONKEY'S BODY USING THE STICK FIGURE AS A GUIDE.

Note how the monkey's body and his right leg follow one continuous line of action. Since the line is curved rather than straight, it makes the overall pose feel dynamic and interesting.

3

DRAW MORE GUIDES TO DEFINE THE MONKEY'S BODY, LIMBS AND TAIL. ADD ROUGH SHAPES FOR HIS FACIAL FEATURES.

4

RUB OUT ALL THE CONSTRUCTION LINES, LEAVING THE OUTLINE OF YOUR MONKEY. REFINE THE FACIAL DETAILS AND DRAW IN THE FINGERS AND TOES.

5

PAINT THE FACE, EARS AND FEET PALE PINK. USE PENCIL CRAYONS FOR THE FUR. MAKE THE BASE TONE DARKER THAN YOU WANT THE FINAL FUR COLOUR TO APPEAR AND ADD A LIGHTER TONE ON TOP, USING VERY FINE PENCIL STROKES DOWNWARDS. FINALLY, ADD AN EVEN LIGHTER TONE FOR HIGHLIGHTS.

If you want to paint the fur texture instead of using pencils, first paint your monkey in a solid colour. Add fine brush strokes on top in a lighter colour. Follow the form of the animal so the fur all lies in the same direction.

SPEECH BUBBLES

TRY DRAWING SPEECH BUBBLES IN ALL SORTS OF SHAPES AND SIZES. ADD THEM TO PICTURES OF PEOPLE AND ANIMALS, OR USE THEM TO CREATE YOUR OWN COMIC STRIPS.

START BY PRACTISING SOME COMMON SPEECH BUBBLE SHAPES SUCH AS OVALS AND RECTANGLES.

ROUND BUBBLES

1 Draw a simple oval shape. It doesn't matter if it's a little wobbly.

2 Add a curved triangular shape to the outer edge, pointing towards the person who is speaking.

3 To create a 3D effect, draw an extra outline that mimics part of the bubble. Shade in the gap created.

RECTANGULAR BUBBLES

1 Sketch a simple rectangular shape with rounded corners.

2 Add the curved triangular shape. It can be quite long if you want, like a dog's tail.

3 The 3D effect is better if you make some areas a bit darker, as if in shadow.

NOW TRY THESE

Practise drawing 3D versions of oval and rectangular bubbles in different positions.

Depending on the space you have, speech bubbles can be fat or thin.

Vertical shading strokes help sell the 3D effect. The lines are similar to the edges of a coin.

Longer tails are useful when the bubble is far away from the speaker.

Use curved lines joined together to create a cloud-shaped thought bubble. Add small circles underneath.
Drawing lots more curves helps to create an even fluffier cloud shape.
HELLO
Try using a wiry or loopy line!
Experiment with colour, perhaps using a contrasting tone for the sides.
A zig-zag tail and red stripes can make a bubble feel like a warning.
BYE
Give your bubble a frame and add a coloured pattern to it.
Using long zig-zag lines is a great way to add interest to your words.
Instead of shading the sides, try a chequered pattern, curving the squares to follow the bubble shape.
NO
Experiment with different kinds of tails. Try loops or even knots for a fun effect!
Add a pattern to the outside edge for extra impact. These dots look like light bulbs from a dressing-room mirror.
Use varied line widths to add depth to your speech bubbles.
Thicker, contrasting black lines help grab attention!

Skateboards

THE BASIC SHAPE OF A SKATEBOARD IS VERY EASY TO DRAW. THE FUN PART IS COMING UP WITH AN EXCITING AND ORIGINAL PATTERN!

1

DRAW A LARGE RECTANGULAR SHAPE WITH TWO ROUNDED ENDS. SKETCH IN TWO GUIDELINES. THIS WILL HELP YOU ADD THE WHEELS TO THE BOTTOM OF THE SKATEBOARD.

2

SKETCH IN THE SIMPLE SHAPES OF THE SKATEBOARD'S WHEELS AND AXLES, USING THE LINES TO HELP. MAKE SURE THEY ARE THE SAME DISTANCE APART AT EACH END.

3

DRAW THE PATTERN FOR YOUR SKATEBOARD. DIVIDING THE DESIGN INTO THREE PARTS WILL HELP. WHEN YOU ARE HAPPY WITH IT, GO OVER THE PENCIL LINES IN INK.

BOARD DESIGNS

Use your imagination to come up with original designs for the bottom of your board. Colour in the skateboards brightly to make the patterns look striking!

Make the board appear 3D using perspective, like this angle.

4

USE PAINTS TO COLOUR IN YOUR SKATEBOARD. GIVE DEPTH TO THE DESIGN WITH A SLIGHTLY HEAVIER LINE USING A FINE BRUSH AND INK AROUND BITS OF THE PATTERN.

DIVER

1

SKETCH A DIVING STICK FIGURE. THIS IS VERY BASIC AND HELPS YOU FIND A POSE QUICKLY. EXPERIMENT WITH DIFFERENT POSES UNTIL YOU FIND ONE YOU ARE HAPPY WITH.

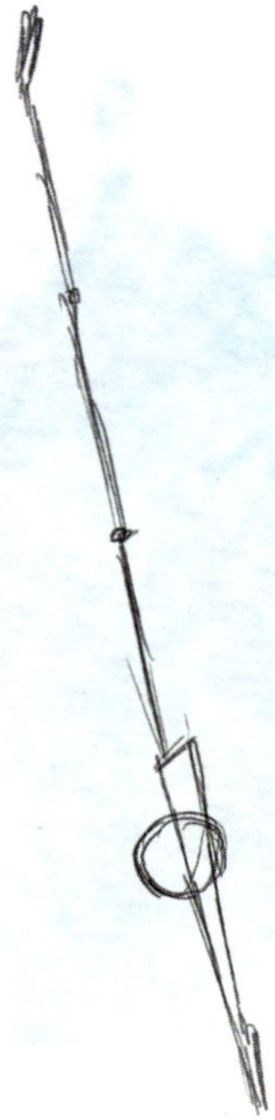

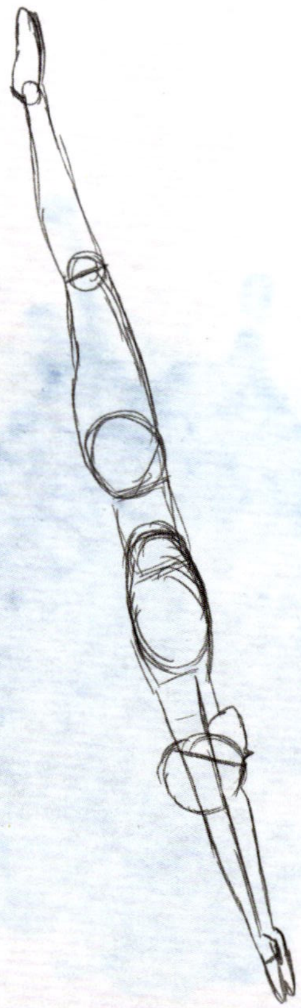

2

DRAW IN THE SHAPES THAT MAKE UP THE DIVER'S BODY. TO MAKE IT EASIER TO DRAW AN UPSIDE-DOWN FIGURE, JUST TURN THE PAPER THE OTHER WAY AROUND WHILE YOU SKETCH IN THE DETAILS.

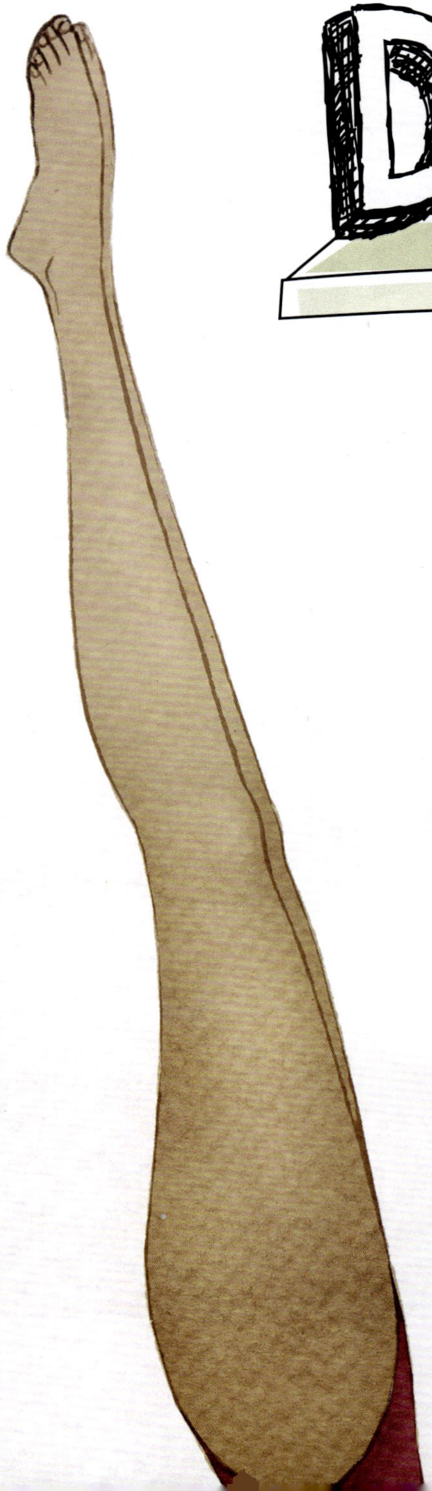

OTHER DIVING POSITIONS

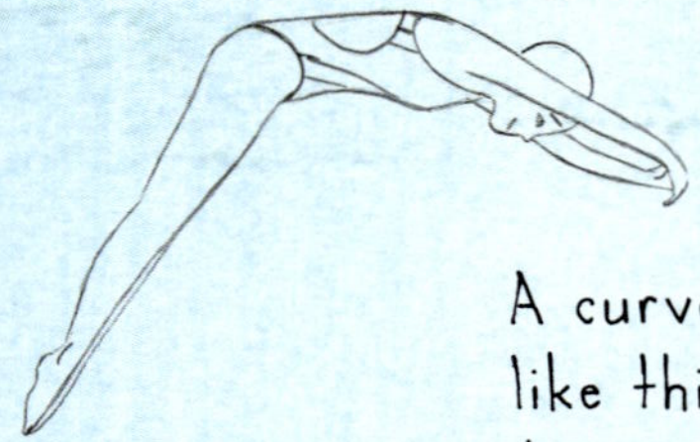

A curved position like this shows a diver jumping off the board.

For a forward spin, the head will curve right round and the legs will remain completely straight.

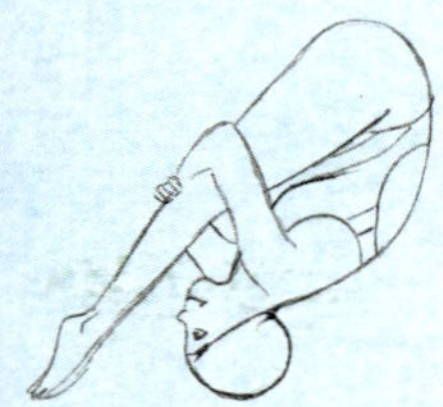

For an extra-special trick, the diver might grab her legs like this... before a big splash!

3

SKETCH THE SWIMSUIT AND FACE AND GO AROUND THE OUTLINE CAREFULLY. RUB OUT ANY PENCIL GUIDELINES.

4

FILL IN THE FINAL BITS OF THE LINE DRAWING. ADD SHADING TO THE SWIMSUIT AND SWIMMING CAP.

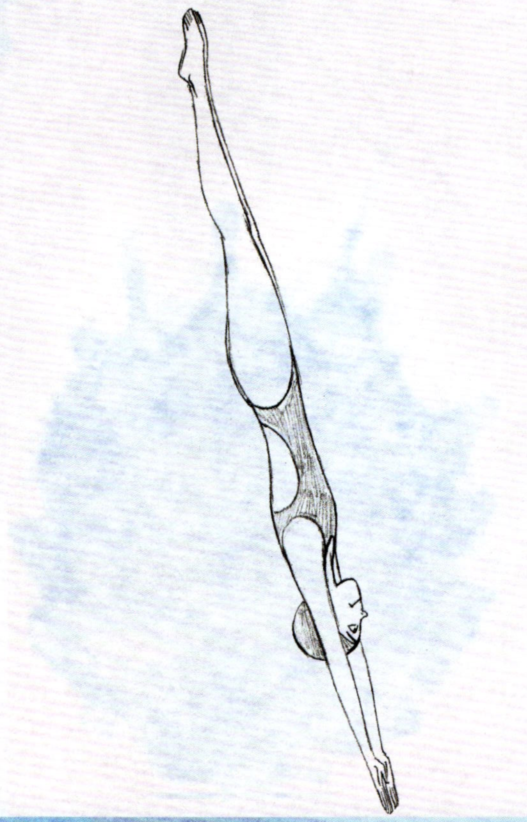

5

CHOOSE STRIKING COLOURS FOR YOUR DIVER'S SWIMSUIT. START WITH A FLAT DARK COLOUR AND THEN BUILD UP THE PICTURE WITH LIGHTER COLOURS. USE A SOFT BRUSH TO PAINT THE SKIN.

Paint splashes around the diver hitting the water. Move your hand quickly and freely with a wet, watered-down brush.

Use a big wet brush for the water. Mask off the water line for a nice crisp edge for the diver to jump into.

BULLET TRAIN

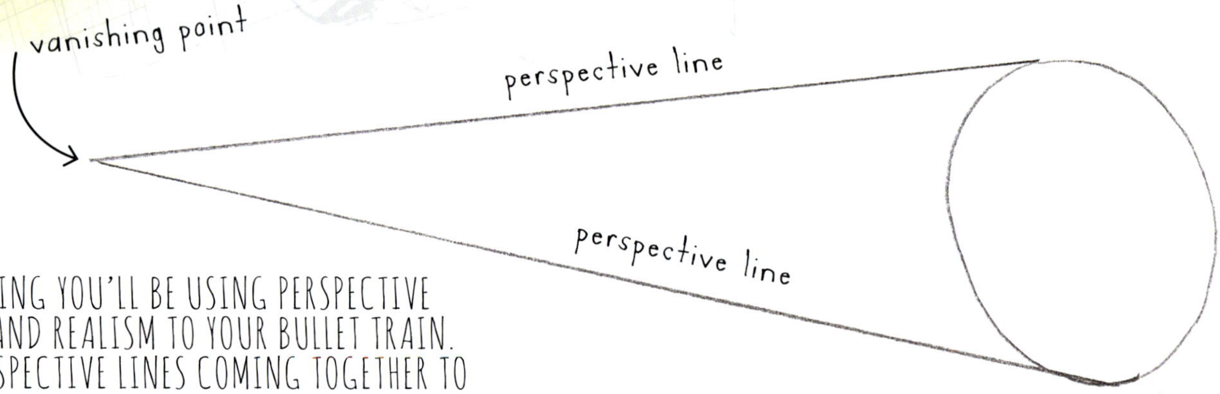

1

FOR THIS DRAWING YOU'LL BE USING PERSPECTIVE TO ADD DEPTH AND REALISM TO YOUR BULLET TRAIN. DRAW TWO PERSPECTIVE LINES COMING TOGETHER TO ESTABLISH THE VANISHING POINT OF THE PICTURE. DRAW A LARGE OVAL AT THE OTHER END.

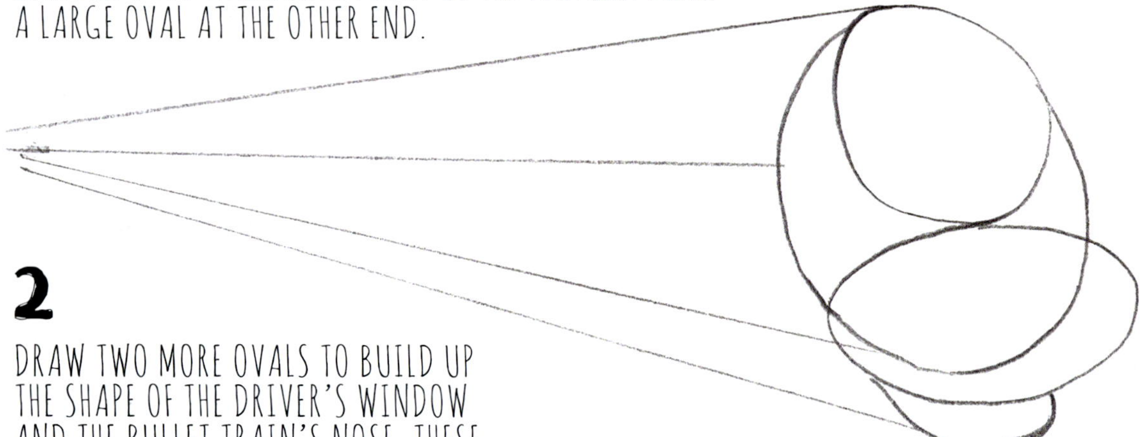

Add a couple more perspective lines to help build your drawing.

2

DRAW TWO MORE OVALS TO BUILD UP THE SHAPE OF THE DRIVER'S WINDOW AND THE BULLET TRAIN'S NOSE. THESE SHAPES NEED TO BE BIG, AS THIS PART OF THE TRAIN IS IN THE FOREGROUND.

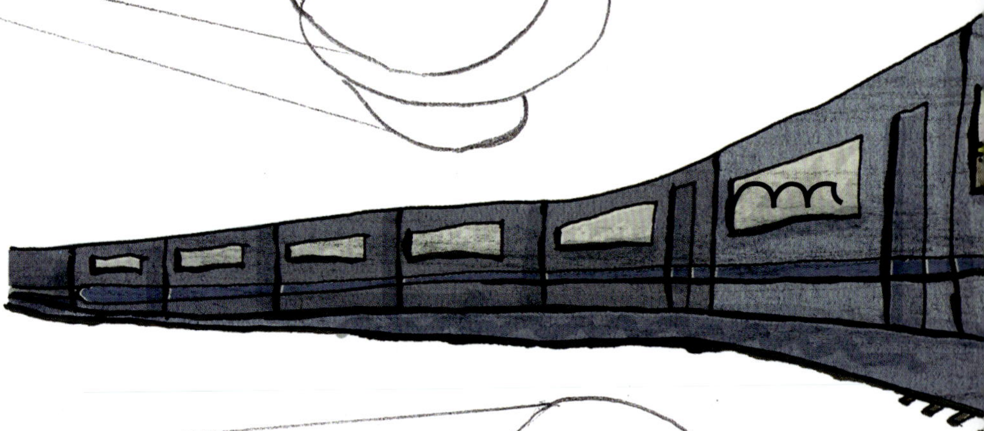

Adding a simple curved guideline to the train's nose will help it to look more 3D.

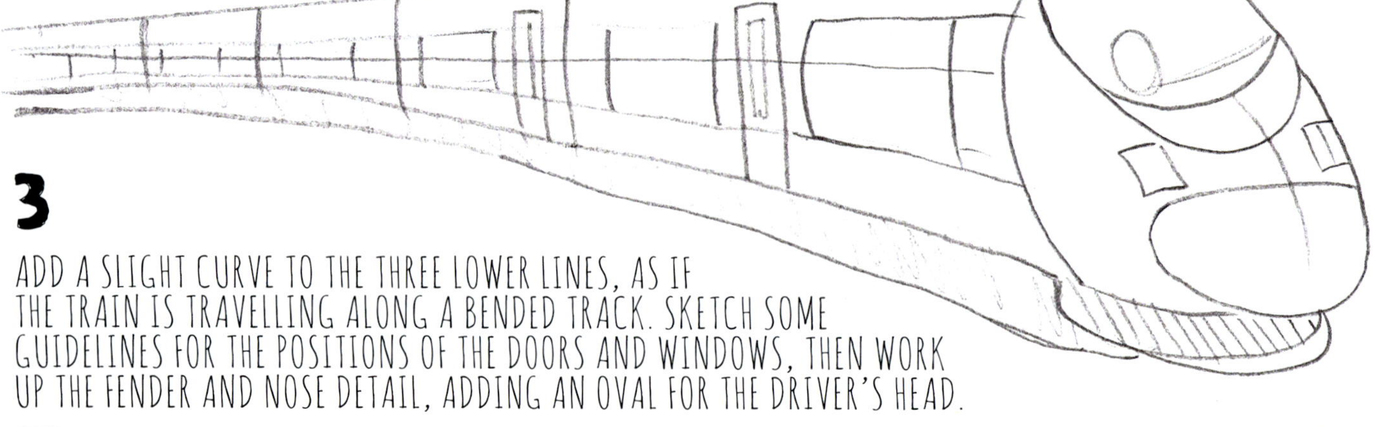

3

ADD A SLIGHT CURVE TO THE THREE LOWER LINES, AS IF THE TRAIN IS TRAVELLING ALONG A BENDED TRACK. SKETCH SOME GUIDELINES FOR THE POSITIONS OF THE DOORS AND WINDOWS, THEN WORK UP THE FENDER AND NOSE DETAIL, ADDING AN OVAL FOR THE DRIVER'S HEAD.

To make your train appear sleeker and more aerodynamic, alter the top perspective line to give it more of a curved shape.

4

DRAW MORE OVALS FOR THE PASSENGERS' HEADS. ADD MORE DECORATIVE DETAIL TO THE TRAIN'S EXTERIOR AND SKETCH MORE LINES ON THE LIGHTS AND FENDER. CONTINUE THE LOWER GUIDELINES TO HELP YOU DRAW IN A SIMPLE TRACK.

Don't worry if your final linework is a bit wobbly. It's a feeling of movement you want to get across, rather than an impression of technical perfection!

5

COLOUR YOUR TRAIN, PAYING SPECIAL ATTENTION TO LIGHT AND SHADE. HERE, A LIGHTER FRONT SECTION REINFORCES THE SENSE OF PERSPECTIVE, MAKING THE TRAIN APPEAR TO COME OUT OF THE PAGE TOWARDS US.

PEACOCK

1

DRAW THE BASIC OUTLINE OF THE PEACOCK. USE CIRCLES FOR ITS HEAD AND BODY WITH CURVED LINES FOR ITS NECK. DRAW A FAN SHAPE FOR THE TAIL AND ADD IN GUIDELINES FOR THE FEATHERS. THESE NEED TO CURVE OUTWARDS FROM THE CENTRE.

2

USE THE GUIDE SHAPES TO HELP YOU REFINE THE OUTLINE OF THE PEACOCK'S BODY. DRAW FEATHERS ON ITS HEAD AND ADD SHADING AROUND ITS EYE. DRAW ROWS OF HALF CIRCLES FOR THE FEATHERS BEHIND ITS NECK. ADD SOME CLAW-LIKE FEET.

To create a feathered effect, use quick flicks of your pencil, easing off the pressure as you make each stroke.

3

SKETCH EYE SHAPES ALONG EACH OF THE CURVED GUIDELINES. FOR EACH ONE, DRAW A 'U' SHAPE WIH A DOT IN THE CENTRE. DRAW VERTICAL STROKES AT THE TOP OF EACH 'U' SHAPE. ADD SHADING AND FEATHER MARKS TO THE PEACOCK'S BODY AND FEET.

4

ADD THE FEATHERS IN BETWEEN THE EYE SHAPES BY DRAWING LOTS OF SHORT, SLANTED MARKS ON EACH SIDE OF THE CURVED GUIDELINES.

5

USE A BLUE WASH FOR THE PEACOCK'S BODY, TRACING THE OUTLINE WITH A DARK BLUE PENCIL. USE A GREEN WASH FOR THE FEATHERED FAN AND PICK OUT THE FEATHERED DETAIL WITH A DARK GREEN PENCIL. LEAVE SOME AREAS WHITE TO GIVE THE PEACOCK MORE OF A 3D LOOK.

For the 'eyes', use bright felt-tip pens. Try blue for the centre, with a caramel-coloured ring. Add yellow and green curves around the 'U' shapes.

The Eiffel Tower was completed in 1889 and is the tallest building in Paris, France. It is also pretty easy to draw!

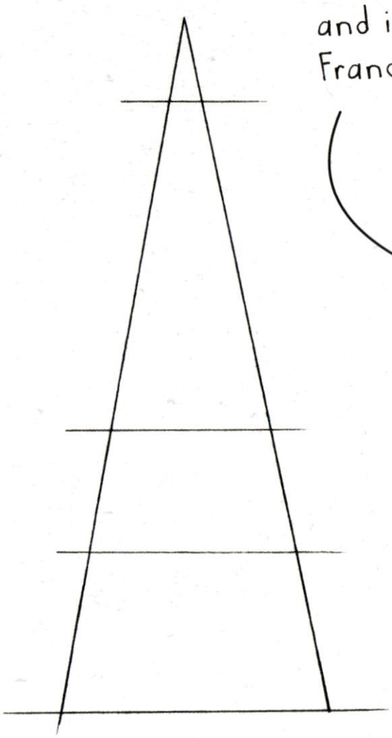

1

USE A PENCIL AND RULER TO DRAW A TALL, TRIANGULAR GUIDELINE SHAPE. BREAK THE SHAPE UP WITH FOUR HORIZONTAL LINES, POSITIONED AS SHOWN.

2

USE YOUR GUIDELINES TO SKETCH OUT THE SHAPE OF THE TOWER. THE STRUCTURE IS WIDE AT THE BASE AND RISES TO A SINGLE POINT.

3

ADD MORE DETAIL TO YOUR TOWER BY DIVIDING THE DRAWING INTO SHAPES AND SECTIONS WITH A PENCIL. WHEN THE SHAPE IS COMPLETE, YOU CAN RUB OUT THE GUIDELINES.

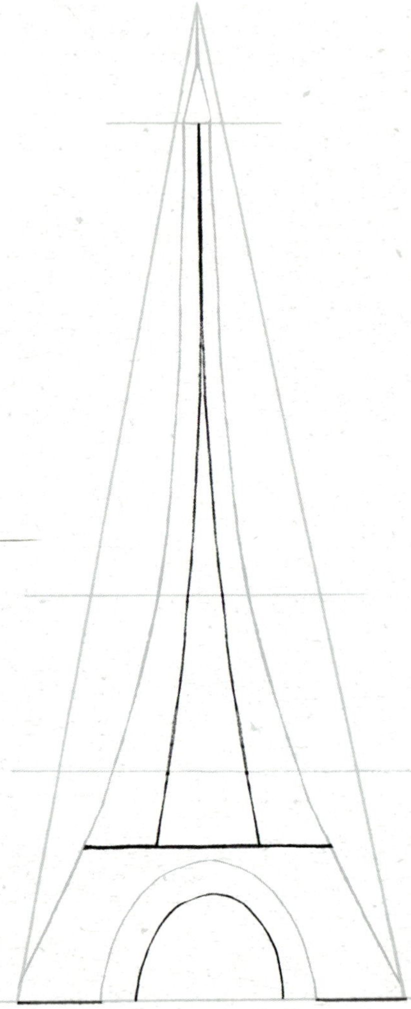

The design of the Eiffel Tower can look complicated close up! Break it down into small sections to create the intricate detail. The design is full of triangle and square shapes, as well as decorative swirls. Have fun practising your linework drawing!

EIFFEL TOWER

4

USE A FINE INK PEN AND A RULER TO BREAK THE DRAWING INTO EVEN SMALLER SHAPES, LIKE THIS. A RULER WILL HELP MAKE SURE THE LINES ARE NEAT AND AT THE SAME LEVEL.

When your Eiffel Tower is finished, give your picture a wow-factor background. Watercolour paints or inks are good for this. Using a large brush loaded with water, wet the paper. Add on the inks or paint and watch the colours bleed together.

5

USING A FINE WATERPROOF PEN, ADD LOTS OF DECORATIVE DETAIL TO FINISH THE DESIGN OF THE TOWER. DRAW IN SOME SILHOUETTED PEOPLE AT THE BOTTOM TO GIVE AN IDEA OF HOW IMPRESSIVELY TALL THE TOWER IS.

HAIRSTYLES

LEARN HOW TO DRAW A VARIETY OF HAIRSTYLES TO USE ON YOUR PORTRAITS. EXPERIMENT WITH COLOUR AND TEXTURE!

1

FOR A BASIC BOY'S HAIRSTYLE, START BY THINKING HOW THE HAIR WILL FALL ON THE FACE. DRAW THE BASIC OUTLINE ON THE TOP OF THE HEAD, LIKE THIS.

Think about the direction of the hair. Use long, confident strokes for someone who has longer hair, like this.

2

SKETCH IN THE HAIR DETAIL. MAKE SURE LINES ARE CLOSE TOGETHER AND VARY THE LIGHTNESS AND DARKNESS TO SHOW SHADING, USING DIFFERENT PENCILS TO ACHIEVE THIS VARIATION.

1

FOR A BASIC GIRL'S HAIRSTYLE, AGAIN START WITH A ROUGH OUTLINE FOR THE SHAPE OF THE GIRL'S HAIR ON A SIMPLE FACE, LIKE THIS.

For longer hair, make sure that the strokes of hair are of similar length. Add a bit of shape to them to show movement.

2

SKETCH IN THE HAIR WITH DOWNWARD PENCIL STROKES. THINK ABOUT THE SHADOWS AND HIGHLIGHTS.

NOW TRY THESE COOL HAIRSTYLES!

AERIAL DISPLAY

1 DRAW AN ELONGATED OVAL SHAPE FOR THE MAIN BODY OF THE PLANE WITH A PENCIL. ADD TWO SMALL WING SHAPES AT ONE END.

It is always easier to draw a light outline to start with.

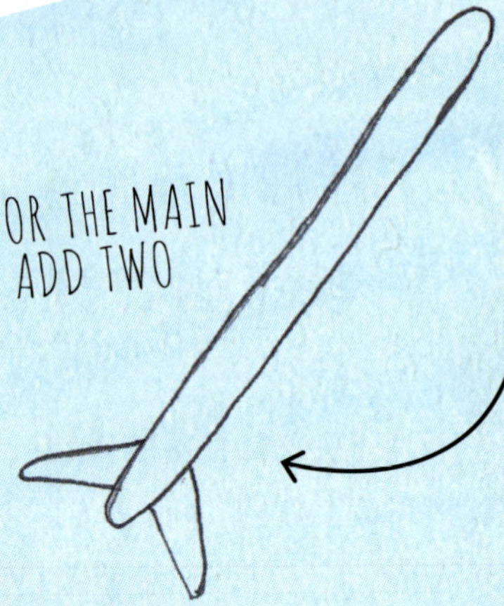

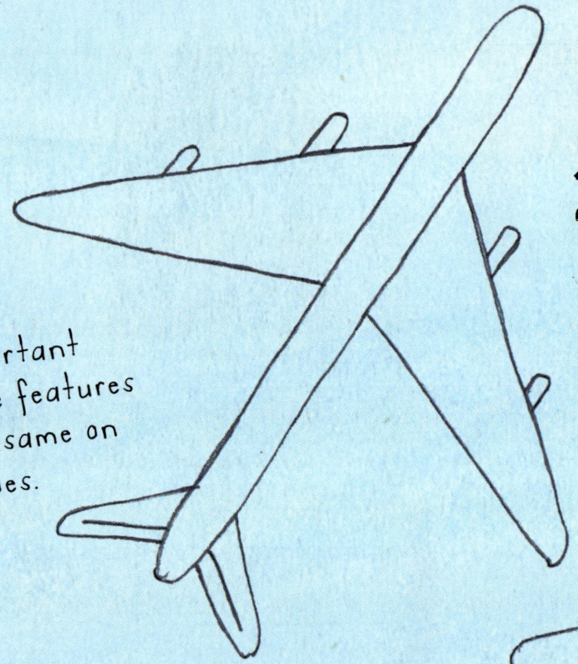

2 DRAW IN TWO LARGE WINGS. THEY SHOULD BE COMPLETELY SYMMETRICAL. SKETCH IN FOUR ENGINES ONTO THE WINGS AND ADD A BIT OF DETAIL TO THE SMALL BOTTOM WINGS.

It's important that the features are the same on both sides.

3 ADD A TARGET DESIGN TO THE WINGS. THIS GIVES A BIT OF INTEREST TO THE PLANE. AGAIN, THESE SHOULD BE SYMMETRICAL. ADD WIGGLY LINES AT THE BOTTOM FOR THE PLANE'S VAPOUR TRAIL.

The trail should look soft and fluffy, so use soft, light strokes.

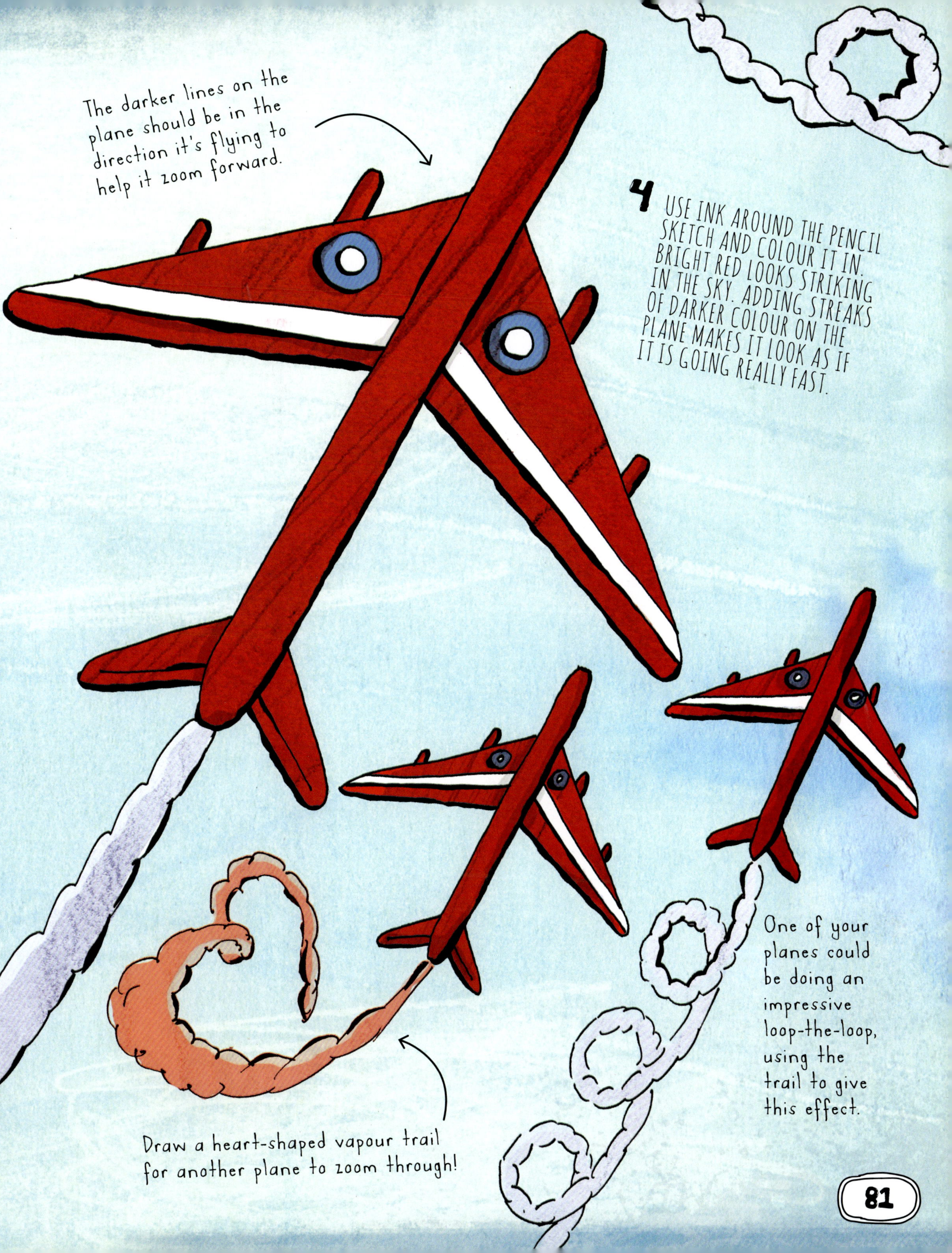

The darker lines on the plane should be in the direction it's flying to help it zoom forward.

4 USE INK AROUND THE PENCIL SKETCH AND COLOUR IT IN. BRIGHT RED LOOKS STRIKING IN THE SKY. ADDING STREAKS OF DARKER COLOUR ON THE PLANE MAKES IT LOOK AS IF IT IS GOING REALLY FAST.

One of your planes could be doing an impressive loop-the-loop, using the trail to give this effect.

Draw a heart-shaped vapour trail for another plane to zoom through!

DANCING DOG

1

DRAW SIMPLE SHAPES TO USE AS GUIDELINES. USE A CIRCLE SHAPE FOR THE HEAD, A BEAN SHAPE FOR THE BODY AND RECTANGLES FOR THE LEGS AND SNOUT.

2

ADD PERKY EARS, EYES AND A TAIL. DRAW LIGHTLY OVER YOUR GUIDELINES TO BEGIN TO SMOOTH OUT THE SHAPES.

3

FOLLOW THE OUTLINE OF THE CHIN AND DRAW A VERY BIG SMILE. ADD THE EYEBALLS, LEAVING WHITE DOTS TO MAKE THE EYES LOOK LIVELY. WORK UP THE EARS AND FEET.

Try this goofy expression for your dancing dog.

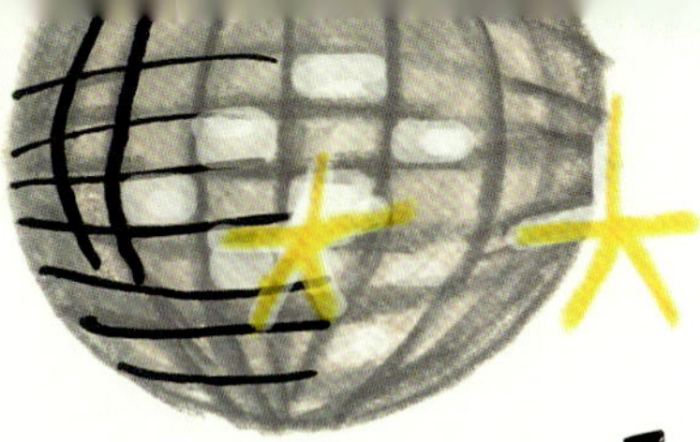

4

ADD WHISKER SPOTS TO THE SNOUT AND SHADE IN THE NOSE AND EARS.

To draw the fur of the dog, make short, irregular lines.

5

USE SOME WATERCOLOUR PENCILS TO BLEND DIFFERENT BROWNS AND YELLOWS. ONCE THE WATERCOLOUR IS DRY, DRAW THE OUTLINE IN A MIXTURE OF BROWN AND BLACK.

SNOWBOARDER

Draw trees partway down the mountain - not right on the top.

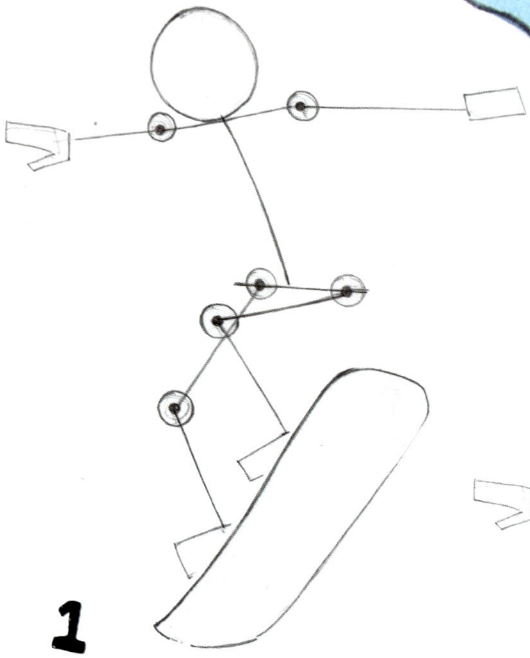

1

START WITH SIMPLE GUIDELINES. SKETCH A CIRCLE FOR THE HEAD AND LINES FOR THE BODY, ARMS AND LEGS. USE CIRCLES FOR JOINTS AND RECTANGLES FOR THE HANDS, FEET AND SNOWBOARD.

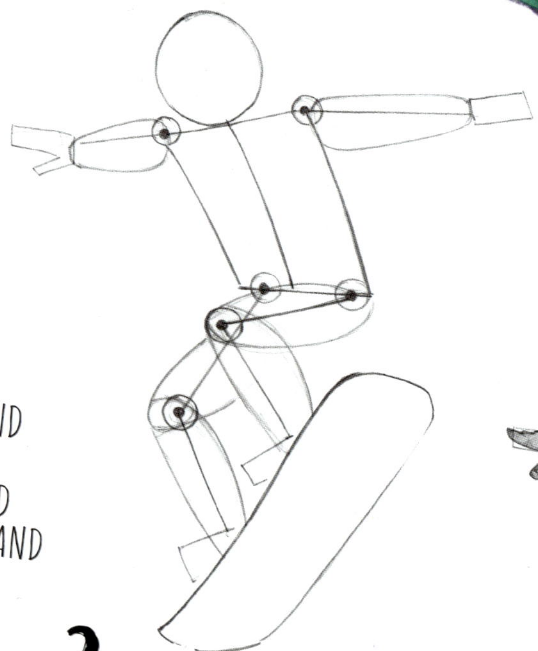

2

START OUTLINING THE BODY SHAPES. DRAW A VERTICAL RECTANGLE FOR THE TORSO AND CYLINDERS FOR THE ARMS AND LEGS.

3

JOIN THE SHAPES TOGETHER WITH A STRONGER OUTLINE, ADDING CLOTHING AND SNOW KIT SHAPES AS WELL.

Add steep snowy mountains for a dazzling background. Add grey patches to indicate steep rock faces, giving the impression of the snowboarder being way up high on the mountain!

4

NOW FOCUS ON THE DETAILS OF THE DRAWING. DRAW THE FACIAL FEATURES AND WORK UP THE HELMET, MASK AND CLOTHING.

5

ADD SOME COLOUR, USING MARKER PENS OR WATERCOLOUR. THINK ABOUT THE LIGHT SOURCE TOP LEFT AND ADD DARKER SHADOWS ON THE OPPOSITE SIDE.

FANTASY MAP

LEARN HOW TO DRAW THE DIFFERENT PARTS OF A FANTASY MAP, THEN PUT THEM ALL TOGETHER TO CREATE YOUR OWN DESIGN!

1

DRAW A SIMPLE COASTLINE FOR YOUR MAP. EXPERIMENT WITH DIFFERENT SHAPES – PERHAPS IT COULD RESEMBLE THE HEAD OF A DRAGON OR SOME OTHER MYTHICAL BEAST. SKETCH WAVY LINES AROUND THE OUTLINE TO REPRESENT THE SEA.

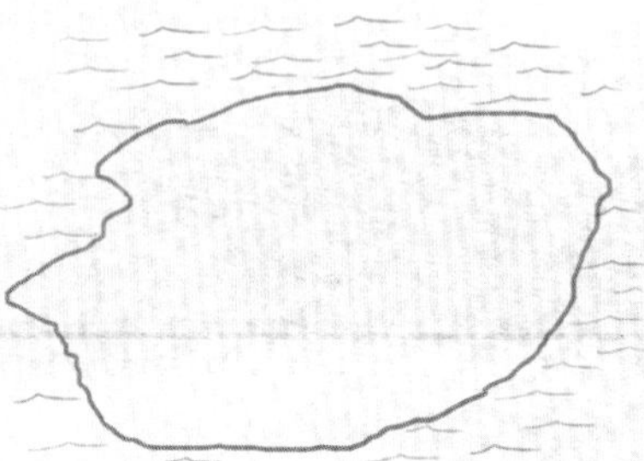

2

DRAW THE SHAPE OF A MOUNTAIN RANGE. FOR ROUNDED HILLS, ADD SHADING USING STROKES THAT FLOW IN ONE DIRECTION. FOR JAGGED PEAKS, DRAW A SHARP OUTLINE, ADDING STROKES THAT CUT INTO EACH OTHER AT DIFFERENT ANGLES.

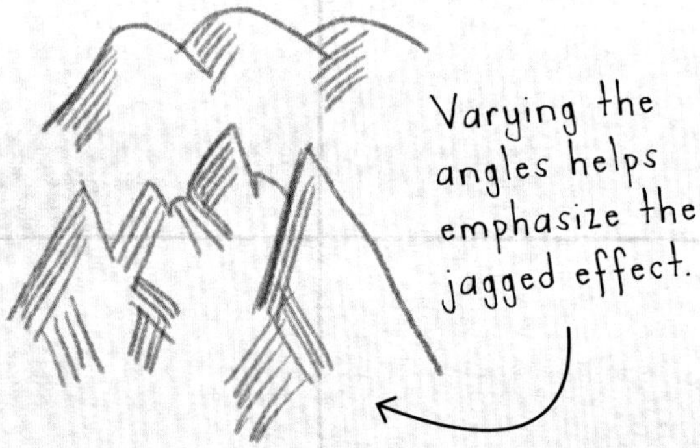

3

SKETCH A CASTLE, BUILDING IT UP FROM DIFFERENT SHAPES SUCH AS TRIANGLES AND RECTANGLES. ADD FLAG POLES AND SKETCH WAVY LINES FOR FLAGS FLAPPING IN THE BREEZE.

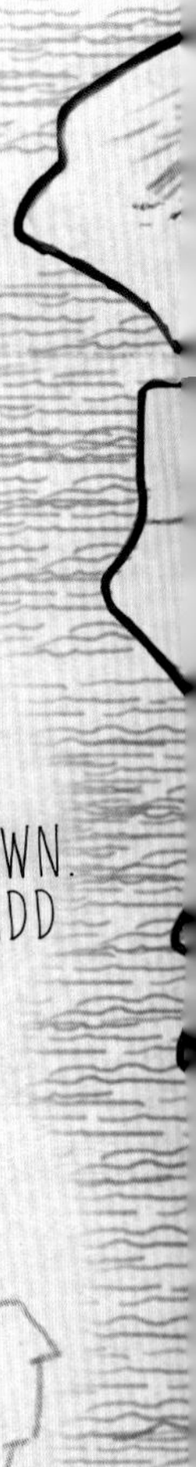

4

TO DRAW A TREE, SKETCH A ROUGH CLOUD SHAPE WITH A TRUNK ATTACHED, ADDING SOME DIAGONAL LINES BELOW FOR SHADE. TO SKETCH A CLUSTER OF TREES, DRAW THE CLOUD SHAPES BUNCHED TOGETHER, ADDING TRUNKS TO THE NEAREST ONES.

5

BRIDGES, RIVERS AND STREAMS CAN BE DRAWN VERY SIMPLY. DRAW TWO CURVED LINES FOR A BRIDGE, WITH MORE CURVES UNDERNEATH FOR THE RIVER. ADD MORE LINES TO SUGGEST RUNNING WATER.

6

USE LITTLE GROUPS OF HOUSES TO INDICATE THE LOCATION OF A TOWN. DRAW AN OUTLINE FIRST, THEN ADD SIMPLE, OVERLAPPING ROOF AND BUILDING SHAPES, WITH DOORS AND WINDOWS.

To create the effect of old paper, paint a flat wash over the entire area, then add splotches of darker tones and blend them in. You can also draw false crease lines to show where the map might have been folded.

Trainers

1 USE CURVED LINES TO DRAW THE SIMPLE SHAPE OF A TRAINER VIEWED SIDE ON. ADD A LIGHTLY CURVED HORIZONTAL LINE TO CREATE THE SHAPE OF THE SHOE'S SOLE.

2 DRAW THE SHAPE OF THE SHOE'S TONGUE. SKETCH A PARALLEL LINE SLOPING DOWN TOWARDS THE FRONT, WITH ANOTHER CURVE SEPARATING OFF THE TOE AREA. ADD A DOTTED HORIZONTAL LINE AT THE BOTTOM.

Patterns

Use contrasting colours to create punchy patterns for your trainers. Try drawing groups of circles, and paint some of them in light colours against a dark background. Or, try a simple overlapping rectangular design.

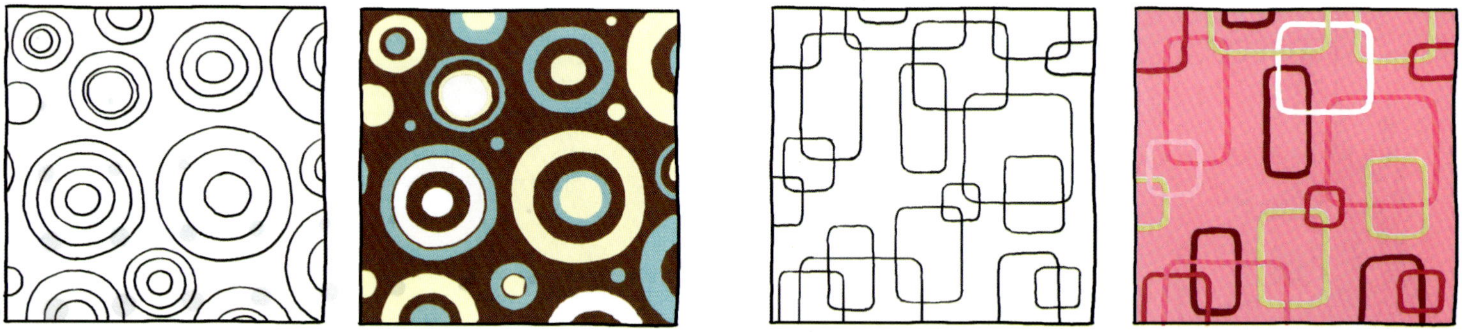

Angles

Try sketching a shoe at different angles. It's an effective way to understand perspective and will help improve your drawing skills.

Choose a colour for the laces that contrasts with the main colour scheme. Yellow works well here against the various shades of blue.

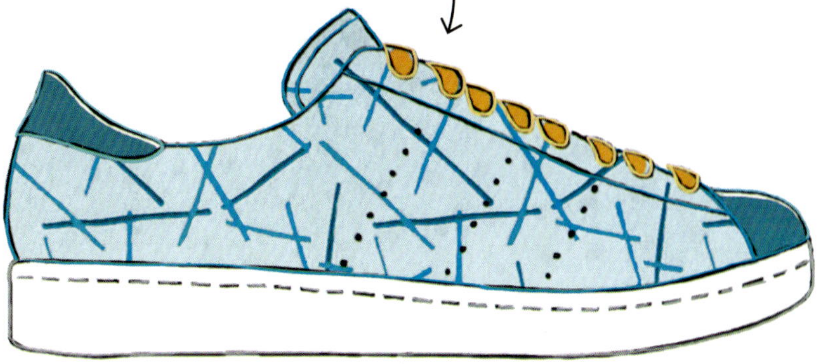

3 ADD LACES BY DRAWING EIGHT SMALL SQUARES ALONG THE TOP OF THE SHOE, STOPPING SHORT OF THE TOE AREA. ADD STITCHING DETAIL BY DRAWING THREE SLANTED, DOTTED LINES.

4 ADD COLOURS AND FUN PATTERNS. TO CREATE THIS PATTERN, PAINT THE SHOE WITH A LIGHT BLUE WASH. ADD LOTS OF ANGLED LINES IN CONTRASTING TONES. PICK OUT THE TOE AND HEEL AREAS IN A DARKER COLOUR.

Try a simple gingham print by drawing lots of criss-crossing lines to make squares. Use alternating tones of blue, interspersed with white squares, as shown. Or, try a smaller circular pattern. This one uses rows of little circles on top of a light green wash.

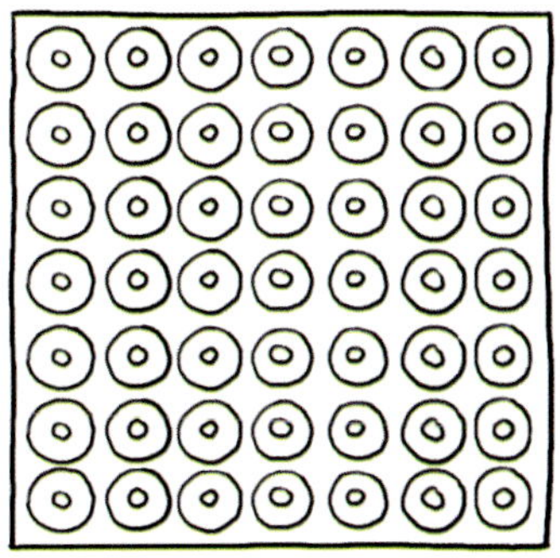

Shapes

Use your imagination to come up with fun designs that build on the basic trainer shape. As a starting point, think about how you can radically alter one part of the shoe at a time. These designs should inspire you!

EAGLE WINGS

HIGH HEELS

CROCODILE TEETH

SPY CAR

1 CARS ARE SYMMETRICAL, SO DRAW A VERTICAL GUILDELINE AND SKETCH THE BASIC SHAPE OF A CAR ON ONE HALF. KEEP IT SIMPLE SO THAT YOU CAN COPY IT AS A MIRROR IMAGE ONTO THE OTHER HALF.

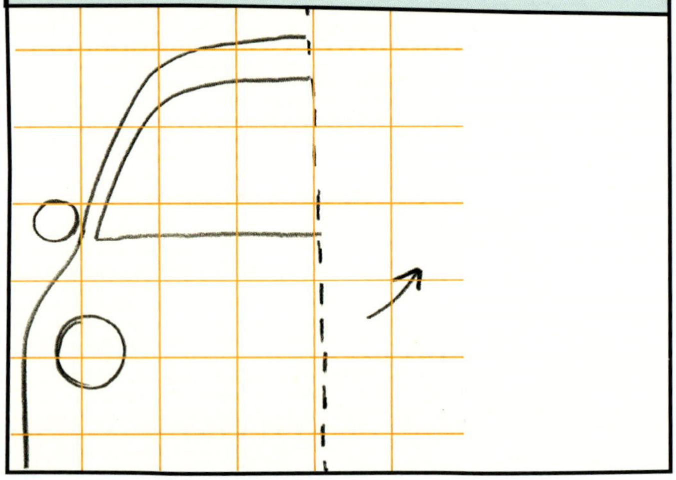

2 ADD SOME DETAILS SUCH AS SEATS AND A BONNET, FOLLOWING THE SHAPE OF THE CAR. ADD CIRCLES FOR HEADLIGHTS AND WING MIRRORS.

3 TO ADD A SECRET CAMERA, DRAW A GRID, LIKE THE ONE BELOW, WHERE ALL THE LINES LEAD TOWARDS A VANISHING POINT. USE THE GRID TO SKETCH IN THE CAMERA. THE PERSPECTIVE WILL HELP THE CAMERA LOOK AS IF IT'S CLOSE UP FRONT.

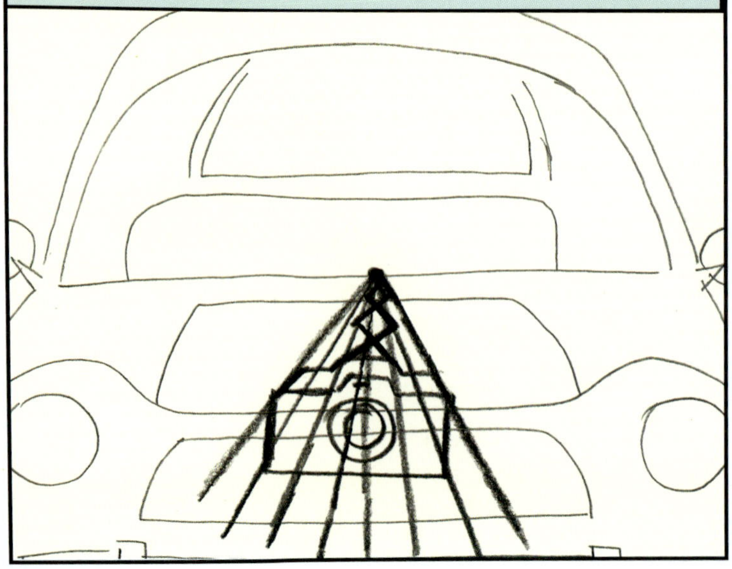

4 ADD A USEFUL MICROPHONE ON A TRIPOD TO THE ROOF OF THE CAR. THEN START DRAWING THE SHAPE OF THE SECRET AGENT AND STEERING WHEEL USING BASIC SHAPES.

5 TO CREATE A CITY SCENE BEHIND THE CAR, DRAW SIMPLE RECTANGLES IN THE BACKGROUND. VARY THE HEIGHT AND WIDTH OF THE BUILDINGS AND USE GRIDS TO CREATE SLEEK CITY WINDOWS. DRAW VERTICAL LINES TO BUILD UP THE GRILL ON THE FRONT OF THE CAR.

6 FINALLY, ADD COLOUR AND EXTRA DETAIL, SUCH AS CROSSHATCH SHADING ON THE SEATS. USE WATERCOLOUR PENCILS IN COOL COLOURS, THEN FINISH THE DRAWING WITH BLACK INK, ESPECIALLY FOR THE BUILDINGS IN THE BACKGROUND. TRY INVENTING MORE GADGETS FOR THE SPY CAR!

Block in some of the windows with yellow to look as though the lights are turned on.

Make your spy look mysterious with a hat, shades and turned-up collar.

1 SKETCH SOME STRAIGHT LINES TO PLAN THE ANGLE OF YOUR ROCK STAR'S POSE: USE SLIGHTLY SKEWED HORIZONTAL LINES TO MAKE THE ANGLES OF THE SHOULDERS AND HIPS. ADD A NEAR-VERTICAL LINE RUNNING THROUGH THEM FOR THE POSITION OF THE HEAD AND TORSO.

Keep the initial outline of your figure simple. If it helps, imagine you're drawing around a body at a crime scene!

2 USING A 2H PENCIL, SKETCH THE OUTLINE OF YOUR ROCK STAR, CONCENTRATING ON GETTING HIS BODY SHAPES AND PROPORTIONS RIGHT. USE THE ANGLED GUIDELINES TO HELP YOU DRAW A DYNAMIC POSE – IN THIS CASE, THE FIGURE'S FEET ARE APART AND HE'S LEANING FORWARDS A LITTLE.

3 DRAW THE SHAPE OF THE ROCK STAR'S CAP AND HAIR. ADD BASIC FACIAL FEATURES. SKETCH THE SHAPE OF THE CLOTHES, SHOES AND STRAP, AND FIRM UP THE OUTLINE OF THE GUITAR. DRAW THE ROCK STAR'S FINGERS RESTING ON THE GUITAR'S NECK. ADD A FEW CREASES TO THE CLOTHES.

Think about where your light source is coming from and add shading lines accordingly.

4 USING A 2B PENCIL OR HEAVIER, WORK UP THE DETAIL. REFINE THE FACIAL FEATURES, THEN ADD FRETS AND EXTRA PEGS TO THE GUITAR. DOUBLE UP THE GUITAR'S OUTLINE IN A FEW PLACES TO MAKE IT LOOK MORE 3D. ADD SHADING TO THE ROCK STAR'S CLOTHES AND DRAW LINES WHERE THE MATERIAL IS CREASED.

ROCK STAR!

5 GO OVER YOUR LINEWORK USING A BLACK PEN, THEN ADD COLOUR. USE A BRIGHTER COLOUR FOR THE GUITAR TO CONTRAST WITH YOUR ROCK STAR'S CLOTHES. TRY NOT TO PAINT EACH AREA OR OBJECT A SINGLE FLAT COLOUR. INSTEAD, USE PATCHES OF DARKER TONES FOR AREAS THAT ARE IN SHADOW.

Work out where the highlights will fall on your figure and add bands of white just inside the black outline.

Draw the outlines of a few heads and outstretched arms, then paint the entire area a flat, dark colour. It's better to keep the audience in silhouette so that all attention is focussed on your rock star!

BELTS

DESIGN A COOL FASHION BELT! SKETCH BASIC SHAPES THEN BUILD UP THE LOOK WITH COLOUR. AFTER TRYING THESE IDEAS, USE YOUR IMAGINATION TO COME UP WITH YOUR OWN DESIGNS!

Draw two long parallel lines for the belt with a ruler, then add a series of lines across the width for the keys. The buckle is made of two oval shapes.

Draw five long parallel lines with about 1 cm between each of them for the belt. Then draw a series of lines up and down it, also 1 cm apart, for the check pattern. Here, the buckle is made of two rectangles.

Draw two parallel lines. Inside these lines, draw a zig-zig pattern made up of triangle shapes, like this.

The buckle is made of two squares.

Draw double circles, varying between small and large along the belt. Link each loop with an oblong shape.

Sketch out the butterfly body first then draw the wings on each side. Draw two parallel lines coming off each side of the butterfly then add a pretty pattern to the belt.

Draw two light parallel lines to use as guidelines for your belt. Sketch parallel waves inside these guidelines. Erase any overlapping lines before adding colour.

SUPERHERO

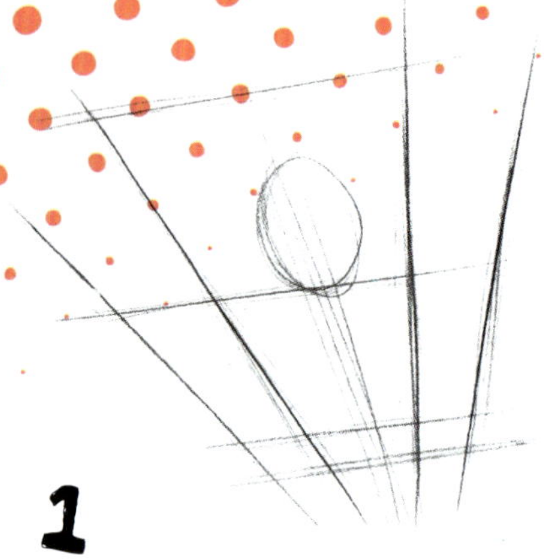

1

USING A HARDER PENCIL SUCH AS A 2H, LIGHTLY SKETCH SOME PERSPECTIVE LINES TO CREATE THE IMPRESSION OF THE SUPERHERO COMING TOWARDS US. ADD AN OVAL FOR HIS HEAD.

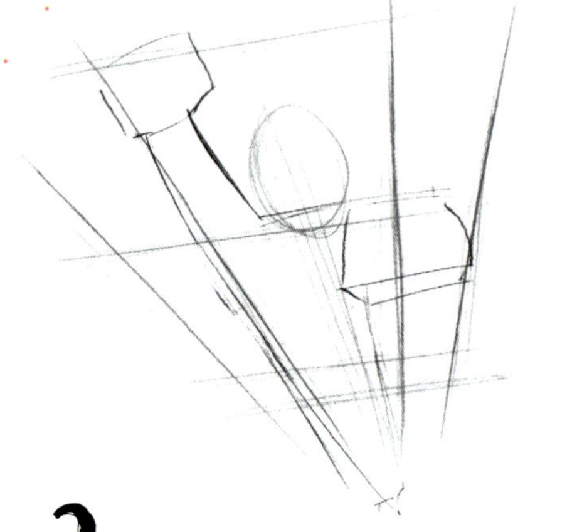

2

LOOSELY BLOCK OUT THE SHAPE AND PROPORTIONS OF THE FIGURE, USING YOUR GUIDES CAREFULLY. THE HANDS ARE THE CLOSEST THINGS TO US, SO THEY NEED TO LOOK QUITE BIG.

3

ROUGHLY SKETCH THE SHAPE OF THE BODY AND CAPE. THE FEET ARE A LONG WAY FROM US SO WILL BE A LOT SMALLER THAN YOU MIGHT THINK. IT'S IMPORTANT TO GET THE PERSPECTIVE RIGHT AT THIS STAGE, AS IT'S TRICKY TO ALTER LATER ON.

4

WORK ON THE DETAIL OF YOUR FIGURE'S BODY BY ADDING FINGERS, HAIR AND FACIAL FEATURES. IF YOU LIKE, YOU COULD TRY RAISING UP ONE OF THE KNEES FOR ADDED VISUAL INTEREST.

5

WORK ON THE TOP HALF OF THE FIGURE, ADDING DETAIL TO THE COSTUME. GIVE MORE DEFINITION TO THE MUSCLES AND LEGS. CHOOSE WHERE THE LIGHT SOURCE IS COMING FROM (TOP RIGHT IN THIS SKETCH) AND ROUGHLY SHADE SOME OF THE SHADOWY AREAS, SUCH AS JUST BELOW THE NECK AND HANDS.

If you find it difficult getting the hands exactly right, try placing a camera in a high spot and set the self-timer. Then strike a typical superhero pose and use your pic as reference!

6

USING A DARKER PENCIL SUCH AS A 4B, WORK ON THE FINER DETAIL AND THE SHADOWED AREAS. ADD SOME MOVEMENT LINES TO GIVE A SENSE OF SPEED.

Don't be afraid to shade large black areas where necessary. They will add visual impact to your superhero and help to bring out his impressive muscle tone!

7

COLOUR YOUR FIGURE IN BOLD COLOURS, USING INKS OR WATERCOLOURS. USE LIGHTER TONES FOR THE AREAS WHERE THE LIGHT IS HITTING THE FIGURE AND DARKER HUES FOR THE PARTS THAT ARE IN SHADOW.

CARTOON EXPLOSIONS

LIVEN UP YOUR DRAWINGS BY ADDING SOME NOISE! LEARN HOW TO DRAW COOL CARTOON EXPLOSIONS THAT LOOK THE WAY THEY SOUND.

BANG

1 USING A PENCIL, DRAW A STARBURST SHAPE, LIKE THIS. MAKE THE POINTS REALLY SPIKY AS YOU DRAW IN AND OUT.

2 DRAW THE LETTERS OF YOUR SOUND WORD, ZIG-ZAG FLASHES AND MOVEMENT LINES. GO OVER THE LINES IN HEAVY BLACK INK.

KA-BOOM

1 THIS CLOUD BURST SUGGESTS A SMOKY EXPLOSION. SKETCH THE SHAPE IN PENCIL FIRST TO BE SURE YOU ARE HAPPY WITH IT.

2 ADD LETTERING,THEN COLOUR THE BACKGROUND. OUTLINE THE CLOUD SHAPE WITH INK, VARYING THE LINE THICKNESS.

POW

1 THIS SHAPE IS GOOD TO SHOW IMPACT. DRAW A SERIES OF INWARD SWEEPING CURVES WITH SPIKY POINTS.

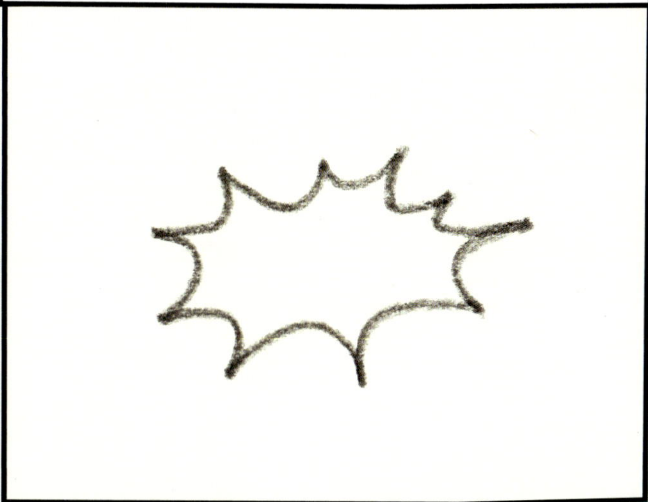

2 ADD A WORD, SOME CLOUD BURSTS, MOVEMENT LINES AND STARS. COLOUR WITH LINES COMING FROM THE CENTRE AND THEN INK OVER THE PENCIL LINES.

Use cloud shapes together with motion lines to make up smoke rings that show something moving at speed.

BLAST

1 DRAW THIS CLOUD SHAPE WITHOUT TAKING YOUR PENCIL OFF THE PAPER. THE SPIRAL OUTLINE SUGGESTS CHAOS!

2 ADD THE WORD AND MOVEMENT LINES BEFORE COLOURING THE BACKGROUND AND INKING OVER THE PENCIL LINES.

SPACE ROCKET

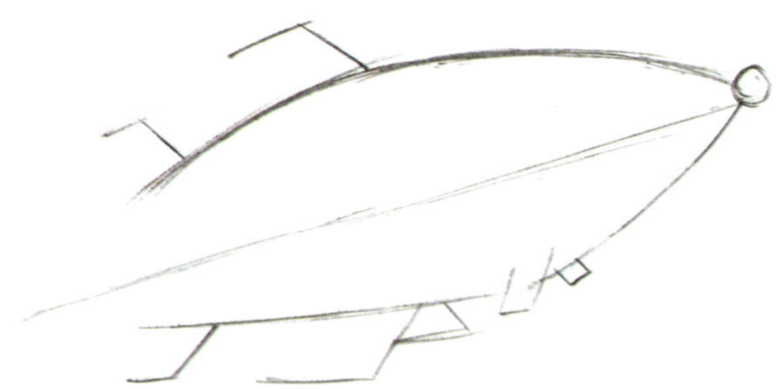

1 START WITH THE BASIC SHAPES OF THE ROCKET BODY AND THE LARGE OUTER FINS. THINK OF THE ROCKET AS AN AMERICAN FOOTBALL SHAPE. DRAW A GUIDELINE ALONG THE CENTRE TO HELP YOU.

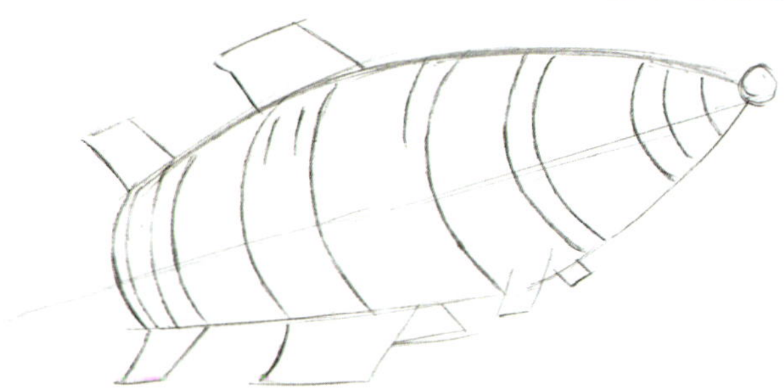

2 NOW DRAW A NUMBER OF LINES THAT FOLLOW THE CURVE OF THE ROCKET'S BODY AND DIVIDE IT INTO SECTIONS. THESE WILL BE THE PANELS AND HELP WITH POSITIONING OTHER ELEMENTS.

Space doesn't need to be all black! You can use all sorts of colours to brighten up your rocket design!

5 COLOUR THE ROCKET WITH METALLIC-COLOURED PAINTS. ADD SOME STRONG FLAMES OUT OF THE BOOSTER TO GIVE THE ROCKET EXTRA MOVEMENT.

3 ADD SOME LINES ALONG THE LENGTH OF THE ROCKET. REMEMBER THE SURFACE ISN'T FLAT AND CURVES INWARDS TOWARDS THE TIP. ADD PANELS, RIVETS AND A BOOSTER AT THE BACK.

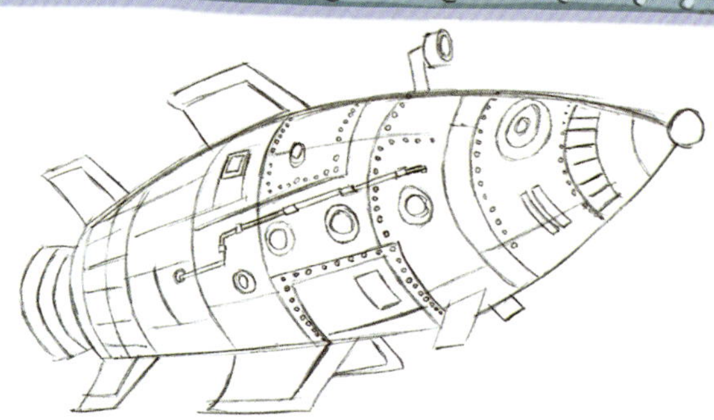

4 CONTINUE TO ADD DETAIL. DIVIDE THE BOOSTER UP INTO SECTIONS, PUT IN MORE RIVETS WHERE PANELS MEET AND ADD CIRCULAR FRAMES FOR THE PORTHOLES. RUB OUT GUIDELINES.

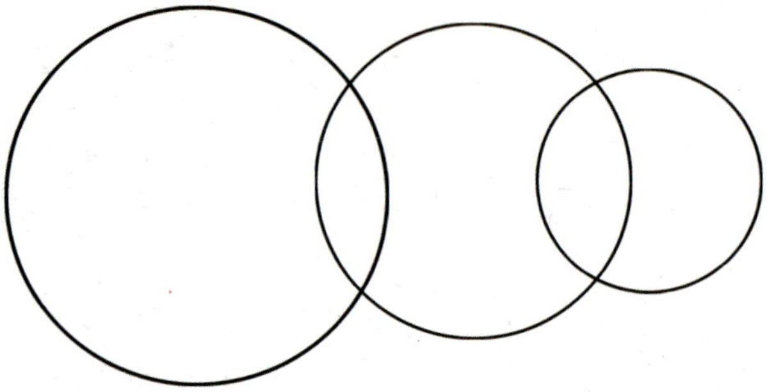

1 DRAW THREE OVERLAPPING CIRCLES. USE A SMALL ONE TO FORM THE SHAPE OF THE HEAD, A MEDIUM ONE FOR THE FRONT OF THE BODY AND A LARGE ONE FOR THE BACK PART OF THE ELEPHANT.

2 JOIN THE EDGES OF THE CIRCLES TO SKETCH THE OUTLINE OF THE ELEPHANT. DRAW IN LEGS, MAKING THE SHAPES NARROWER TOWARDS THE BOTTOM AND ADDING FEET. SKETCH LONG CURVES FOR A TRUNK.

ELEPHANT

5 DRAW A RECTANGULAR BLANKET WITH CURVED EDGING. SKETCH MORE CURVES FOR THE HAT AND TRUNK DECORATION. USE SWIRLS AND LEAF SHAPES TO MAKE THE HEADDRESS. ADD DETAIL TO THE TUSK, TAIL AND FEET TOO.

6 DRAW THE BASIC SHAPE OF THE CANOPY. SKETCH DIFFERENT-SIZED FLOWER SHAPES ON THE BLANKET, DOUBLING UP YOUR LINEWORK FOR SOME OF THEM. ADD MORE DECORATION TO THE ELEPHANT'S HEAD.

Try not to add too much detail to an area all in one go. Instead, gradually build up the detail across the whole drawing.

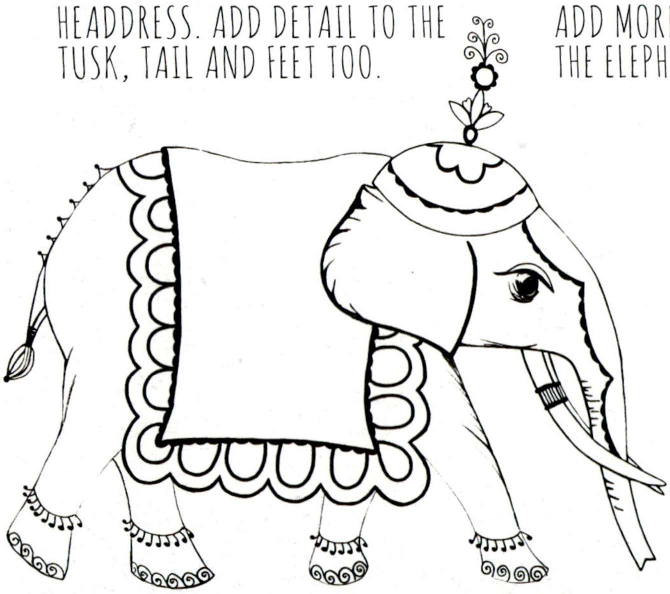

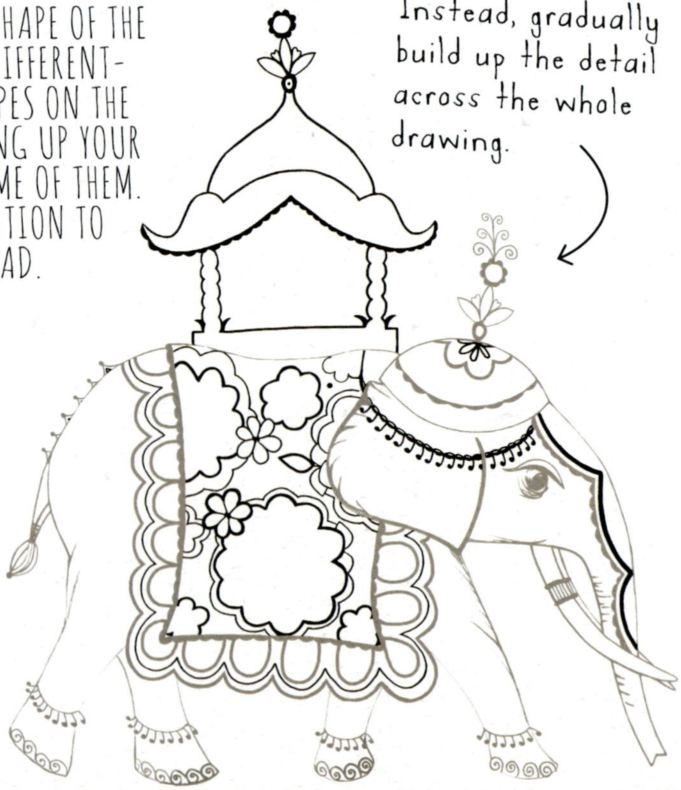

3 DRAW THE SHAPE OF THE EAR AND ADD A CIRCLE FOR THE EYE. USE SIMPLE CURVES FOR TWO TUSKS AND WAVY LINES FOR THE ELEPHANT'S TAIL.

4 ADD DETAIL TO YOUR ELEPHANT TO GIVE IT CHARACTER. SHOW FOLDS IN ITS SKIN BY DRAWING FINE LINES ON THE LEGS, TRUNK AND EAR. ADD MORE DETAIL TO ITS EYE AND GIVE IT SOME TOENAILS!

7 GO OVER YOUR LINEWORK IN PEN AND INK, THEN ADD THE FINE DETAILS. DRAW FLORAL PATTERNS ON THE CANOPY AND BUILD UP THE BLANKET DETAILS. DRAW SIMPLE LEAF PATTERNS ON THE HAT AND LEGS.

8 USE A WARM GREY TO PAINT THE ELEPHANT'S BODY, SUCH AS GREY WITH A LITTLE RED MIXED IN. CHOOSE BRIGHT COLOURS FOR THE DECORATIVE ELEMENTS TO MAKE THEM REALLY STAND OUT FROM THE ELEPHANT'S SKIN.

Adding more water to your paints will help give a wash-like effect.

STREET ART

TRY DRAWING SOME GRAFFITI ART – WHERE IT'S ALLOWED, OF COURSE! BEFORE YOU ATTEMPT A MORE DETAILED COMPOSITION, PRACTISE DRAWING THESE SIMPLE 3D SHAPES WITH A BLACK PEN OR INK.

Draw a star shape and add some lines coming away from three of the points, as shown. Create a 3D effect by making the star a lighter colour than its tail.

Draw a simple arrow and make it look 3D by adding lines underneath which follow the same basic shape.

A doughnut is basically an oval shape. Draw a hole in the middle and add some messy icing and perhaps a few sprinkles.

The ice lolly is simply a rectangular shape curved at the top. Draw a line below to achieve the 3D effect, and add a stick and a little shading.

This wafer cone is a semi-circle attached to a triangle. Use some simple crosshatching to create the cone texture, then add an ice-cream peak on top.

GRAFFITI AREA

COMBINE LOTS OF STARS AND ARROWS INTO ONE COMPOSITION. DRAW THEM IN DIFFERENT SIZES AND USE A VARIETY OF COLOURS. MAKE THEM FACE DIFFERENT DIRECTIONS TO ADD VISUAL INTEREST AND A SENSE OF MOVEMENT.

Vary the thickness of the outlines and try adding some circular shapes to break up all the straight lines.

Coloured inks are great for creating strong, vibrant tones. These colours work well with a heavy black outline.

DRAW FOOD SHAPES NEXT TO EACH OTHER AND ADD SOME SIMPLE CARTOON FEATURES AND A DRIPPY BACKGROUND. THINK OF OTHER INTERESTING JUNK FOOD YOU COULD ADD TO THE SCENE.

SKATEBOARDER

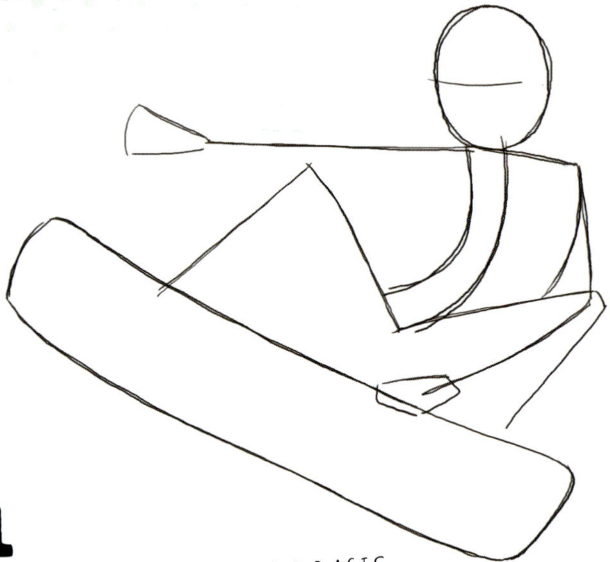

1

USING A PENCIL, DRAW A BASIC RECTANGULAR SHAPE FOR THE SKATEBOARD. SKETCH A ROUGH CIRCLE FOR THE BOY'S HEAD AND GUIDELINES FOR HIS BODY, ARMS, HANDS AND LEGS.

2

SKETCH IN THE SKATEBOARDER'S ARMS AND DRAW IN THE WHEELS ON THE BOTTOM OF THE BOARD.

3

ADD MORE DETAIL TO THE BOARD'S WHEELS AND GIVE YOUR FIGURE SOME ROUGH HANDS AND JEANS. DRAW TWO CURVED LINES FOR HIS SHOES.

The helmet should sit slightly above the top of the skateboarder's head.

4

DRAW A HALF CIRCLE ABOVE THE HEAD FOR THE SKATEBOARDER'S HELMET. SKETCH IN GUIDELINES FOR HIS T-SHIRT, BELT AND SHOES.

Make sure the boy is holding on to the board tightly!

Change the pose of the character by drawing both arms in the air!

5

FINISH THE SKETCH BY ADDING GLOVES AND FINGERS TO THE HANDS. SKETCH IN THE BOY'S EYES, NOSE AND MOUTH AND GIVE HIM HAIR, TOO. FINALIZE THE DETAILS ON THE HELMET AND BOARD.

Use shading and lines within your colour for depth and movement.

6

ADD FINAL DETAILS TO YOUR DRAWING THEN RUB OUT ANY STRAY LINES FROM THE ORIGINAL SKETCH. ADD COLOUR! USE DIFFERENT SHADES OF THE SAME COLOUR ON THE CLOTHES TO GIVE THE PICTURE SOME DEPTH.

Give your board an exciting design underneath, like these bright flames. See pages 68 and 69 for some more ideas.

PIZZA

FEELING HUNGRY? DISCOVER HOW EASY IT IS TO DRAW YOUR OWN PIZZA WITH SIMPLE SHAPES!

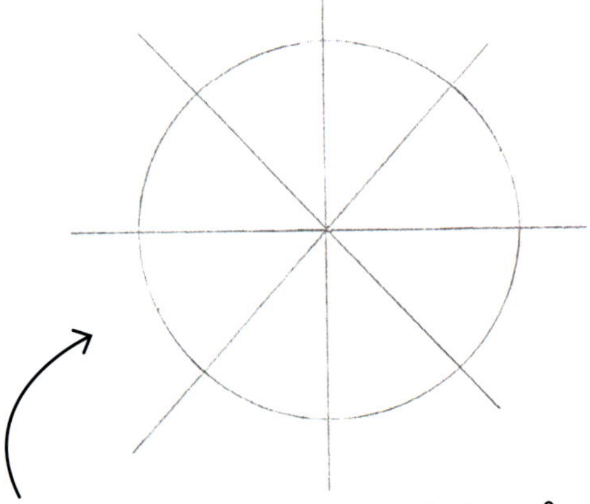

Draw out a large circle. It helps if you use a compass to give you a centre point. Draw four lines through the centre of the pizza, like this, to divide it into eight slices.

TOPPINGS

ADDING SLIGHTLY BROADER INK LINES GIVES YOUR PIZZA ILLUSTRATION MORE DEPTH.

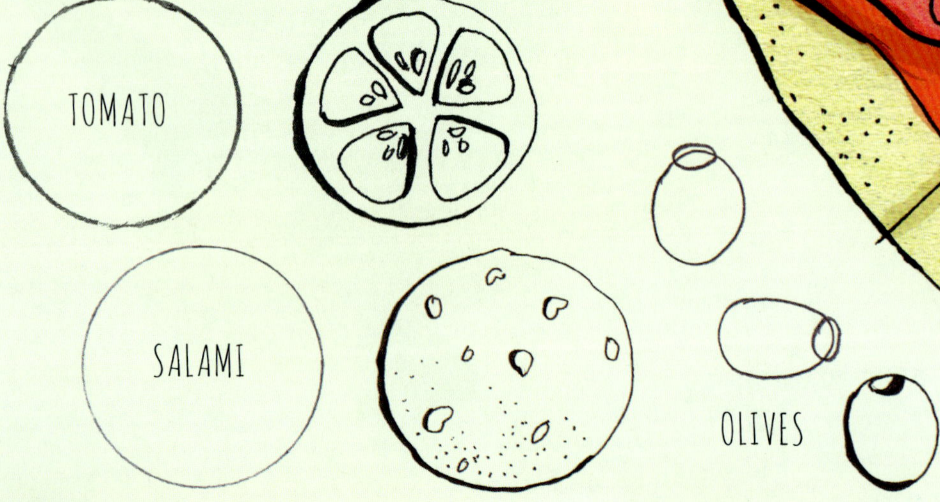

SLICE

1

TO DRAW A 3D SLICE, SKETCH AN ANGLED TRIANGLE SHAPE FOR SIMPLE PERSPECTIVE, LIKE THIS.

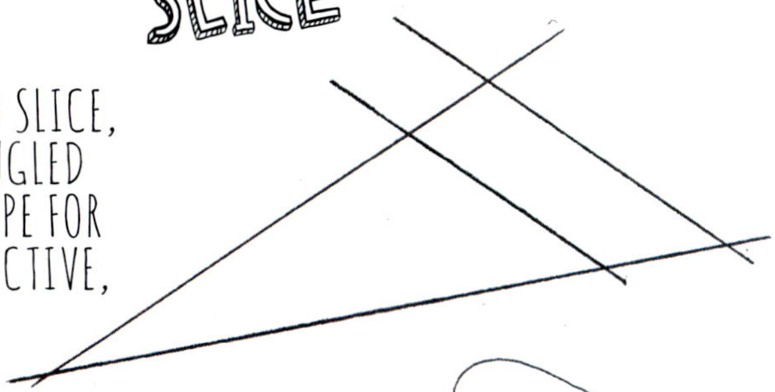

2

ADD DEPTH WITH ANOTHER LINE UNDERNEATH TO GIVE THE SLICE SOME THICKNESS.

3

GIVE THE CRUST A WAVY EDGE AND ADD SOME TOPPINGS AND MELTING CHEESE DRIPPING DOWN.

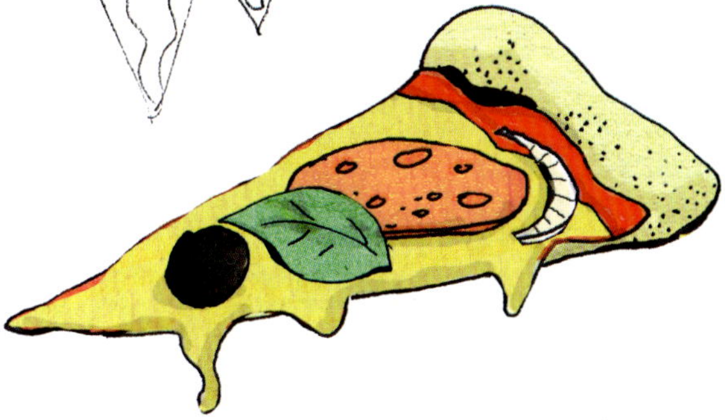

Have fun with the colour! Spread the toppings out and don't put all the same colours next to each other to balance out the drawing.

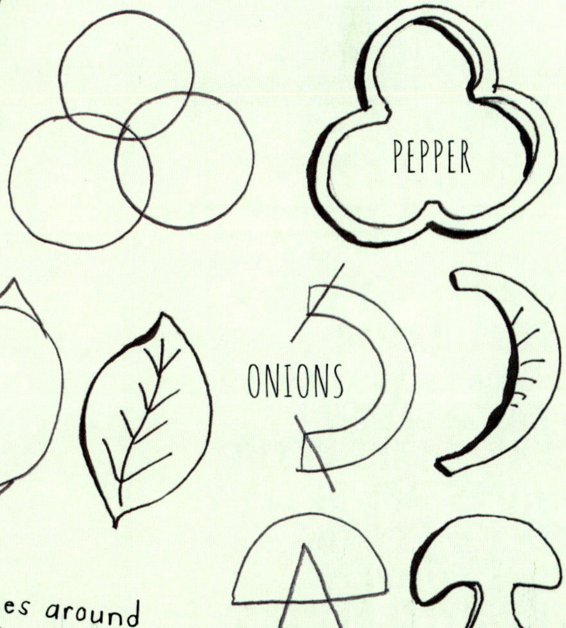

Add irregular lines around the edge to create the wobbly and authentic shape of a pizza crust.

GEOMETRIC PATTERNS

CREATE PATTERNS USING BASIC GEOMETRIC SHAPES. START WITH SIMPLE REPEATING SHAPES AND BUILD UP TO SOMETHING MORE COMPLEX. TRY OVERLAPPING SHAPES OR USING MIRROR IMAGES.

Circles

ADD REPEATED CIRCLES AROUND LOTS OF DIFFERENT-SIZED CIRCLES. COLOUR EACH RING, OVERLAPPING FOR EFFECT.

Hearts

MIRROR-IMAGE HEARTS MAKE UP A COOL PATTERN. COLOUR THE GAPS IN BETWEEN TO EMPHASIZE THE DIAMOND SHAPE.

Zig-zag

DIVIDE ZIG-ZAGS BY COLOURING ONE SIDE LIGHT AND ONE DARK.

CUSTOMIZE STUFF

WORK OUT SOME FANCY PATTERNS ON PAPER, THEN APPLY THE BEST ONES TO YOUR FAVOURITE SNEAKERS, CLOTHES OR PENCIL CASE USING FABRIC PENS.

Ovals

BUILD UP THE PATTERN BY ADDING OVALS INSIDE OVALS. START AT THE BOTTOM AND WORK TO THE TOP.

Diamonds

BUILD UP A DIAMOND PATTERN WITH CRISS-CROSS DOTTED LINES INSIDE SOLID ONES TO ADD TEXTURE.

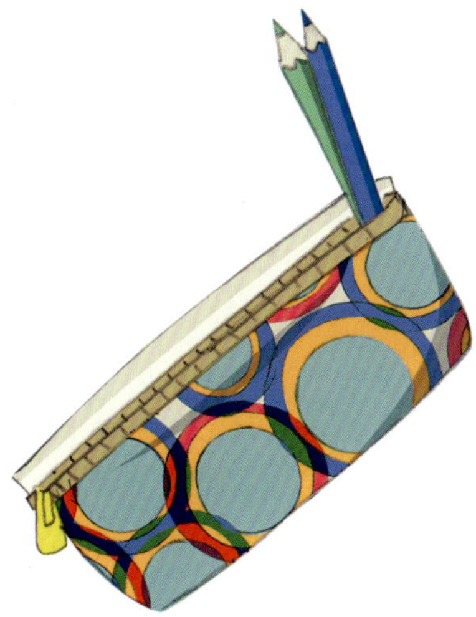

Wavy

TRY VARIATIONS OF WAVY LINES WHERE GAPS ARE WIDER OR THINNER.

T-REX

1

DRAW THE BASIC SHAPE OF THE T-REX WITH A PENCIL. THE DINOSAUR IS MADE UP OF CIRCULAR AND OBLONG SHAPES, AS SHOWN.

2

ADD BASIC SHAPES FOR THE NECK, EYE, ARMS, LEGS AND THE TIP OF THE TAIL. USE THE SHAPES FROM STEP ONE TO HELP YOU PLOT WHERE EACH PART NEEDS TO BE DRAWN.

Gently rub a pencil over the areas you want to shade to create different skin tones and shadow.

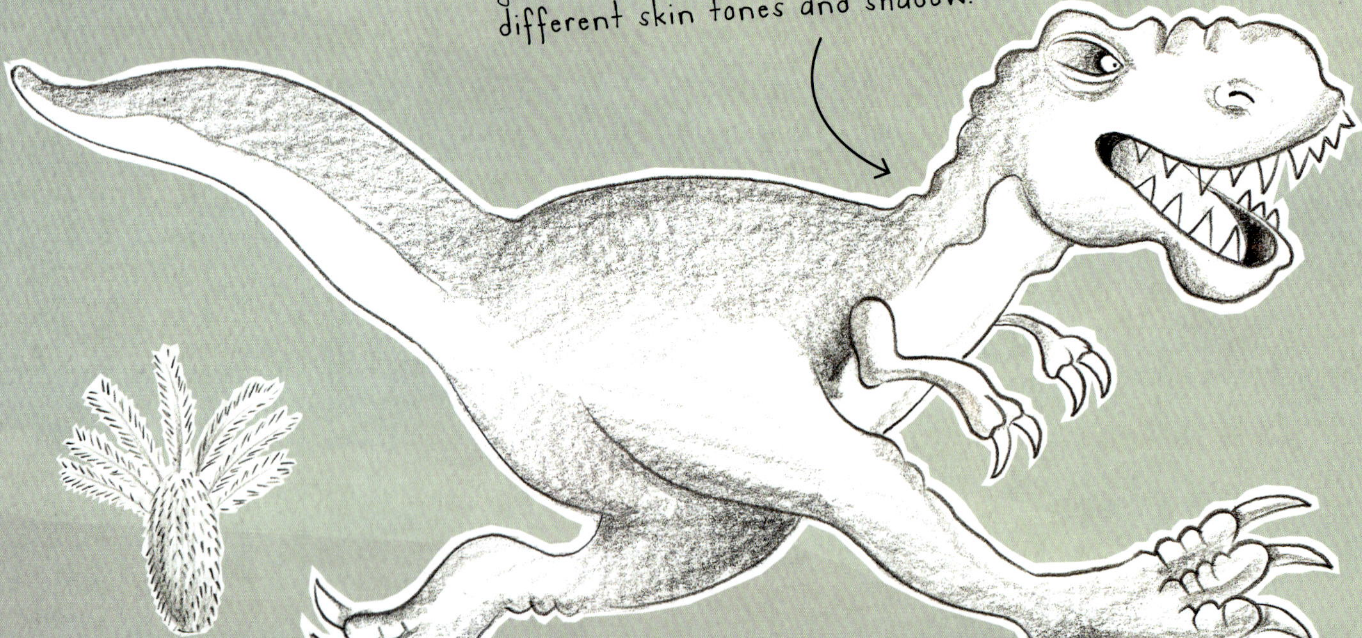

5

ADD SHADING TO YOUR DINO. LEAVE CERTAIN AREAS WHITE TO HELP TO SHOW THE DIFFERENT SKIN TONES.

3

SKETCH IN THE OUTLINE OF THE DINO'S BODY. IT HAS SMALL RIDGES ON THE NOSE, NECK, LEGS AND TOES. SKETCH THE OUTLINE WITH A FAINT LINE TO BEGIN WITH THEN GO OVER WITH A HEAVIER, MORE CONFIDENT LINE.

4

DRAW IN THE OTHER FEATURES OF THE DANGEROUS BEAST. GIVE IT A BIG EYE AND SOME NOSTRILS. TO MAKE IT LOOK EXTRA SCARY, MAKE SURE IT HAS REALLY RAZOR-SHARP TEETH AND CLAWS!

6

FINISH WITH SOME COLOUR. ADD LOADS OF DIFFERENT MARKS USING TRIANGLE SHAPES AND DOTS TO CREATE A PATTERN FOR THE SKIN. LEAVE THE TEETH WHITE AND GIVE YOUR T-REX A BIG RED TONGUE.

MOTORBIKE STUNT RIDER

1

SKETCH SIMPLE SHAPES AS GUIDES. USE CIRCLES FOR THE HEAD, WHEELS AND MOTOR AND RECTANGLES FOR THE BODY, LEGS, ARMS AND BIKE.

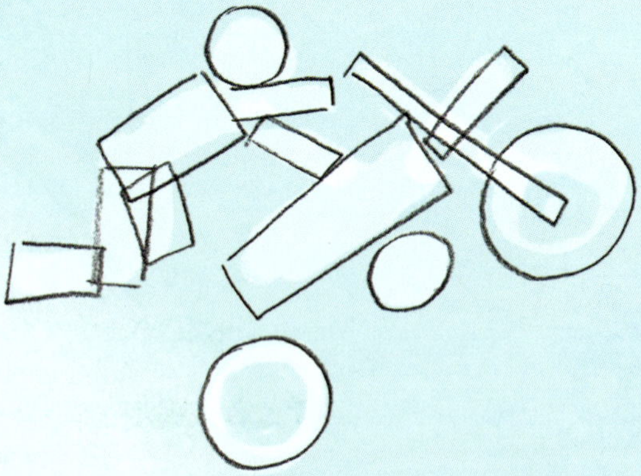

2

BEGIN JOINING THE DIFFERENT SHAPES TOGETHER. ADD MUD GUARDS, A SEAT, CHAIN AND FRAME TO BUILD UP THE MOTORBIKE. ADD HANDS AND FEET TO THE RIDER.

3

START ADDING SOME DETAIL. DRAW THE HELMET AND ADD RIMS TO THE OUTSIDES OF THE WHEELS AND AXLES IN THE CENTRES OF THE WHEELS.

Look for pictures of motorbikes in magazines for inspiration and to understand the shape. Each make of stunt bike will have different details.

4

GO OVER YOUR LINE TO START SMOOTHING OUT THE CURVES. ADD DETAIL TO THE RIDER'S CLOTHES, SPOKES TO THE BIKE WHEELS AND DETAIL TO THE MOTORBIKE FRAME AND TANK.

5

NOW ADD SOME COLOUR! FINISH THE DETAILS OF THE MOTORBIKE IN BLACK. ADD TREAD TO THE MOTORBIKE TYRES.

Design some cool, bright gear for the stunt rider.

MAD HATS

1

START WITH A FLATTENED OVAL TO FORM THE BRIM OF THE HAT. IF YOU ARE ADDING IT TO A CHARACTER, THINK OF THE ANGLE YOU WANT THE BRIM ON THE HEAD.

2

ADD AN ALMOST HALF CIRCLE FOR THE DOME OF THE HAT. ADD A LINE FOLLOWING THE CURVE OF THE BRIM TO MAKE A HATBAND. THIS WILL BE THE RIBBON WHERE THE HAT DECORATIONS WILL BE FIXED.

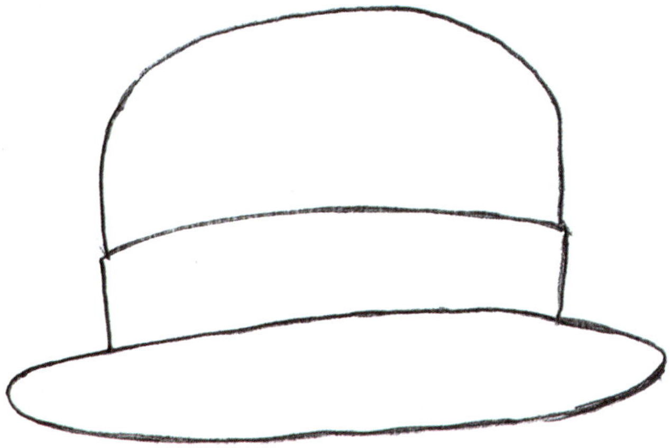

Remember to check the proportions of the dome against the head so that it looks as though it fits comfortably.

A rounded dome like this makes a hat called a bowler hat.

3

TO CREATE A FEATHER, DRAW A CURVED OVAL WITH POINTED ENDS. ADD THE CENTRE LINE, THEN SMALL LINES TO BUILD UP THE TEXTURE.

4

ADD COLOUR USING A VARIETY OF MATERIALS TO BUILD UP TEXTURE AND INTEREST. FOR EXAMPLE, FIRST APPLY A WATERCOLOUR WASH, THEN ADD SOME LOOSER PENCIL LINES, WITH SOFT PASTEL OR CHARCOAL OVER THE TOP.

Add the feather to the hatband like this.

5

FINALLY, APPLY AN INK OUTLINE WITH A BRUSH. EXPERIMENT WITH THICK AND THIN LINES FOR SOME OF THE FEATHERY TRIMMINGS. ADD A SOFT SHADOW BELOW THE BRIM WITH PENCILS OR PAINT.

Draw a shaped grid like this to create a net veil that adds mystery to your character.

EXPERIMENT WITH THE SHAPES OF THE DOME AND THE SIZE OF THE BRIM. TRY OUT FEATHERS, FLOWERS, INSECTS, EVEN FOOD – GO WILD!

FANCY TOP HAT

PIANO BOWLER HAT

Build on the basic bowler hat shape with a cool twist of piano keys.

CUPCAKE HAT

HAUNTED HOUSE

1 BREAK DOWN THE DRAWING INTO SMALLER PIECES. FIRST, DRAW A SET OF UNEVEN RECTANGLES FOR THE TWO FLOORS OF THE HOUSE, AND TWO ROOFS.

2 SKETCH THE BITS OF THE HOUSE THAT JUT OUT FROM THE BUILDING AND THE FRONT DOOR. USE A MIXTURE OF TRIANGULAR AND ROUNDED, UNEVEN SHAPES.

3 ADD THE WINDOWS. USE DIFFERENT-SHAPED ONES TO MAKE THE HOUSE LOOK RICKETY AND CREEPY. USE CIRCLES AND RECTANGULAR SHAPES. ADD DETAIL TO THE CHIMNEY, DOOR AND ROOF.

4 SKETCH IN LINES FOR THE TILES ON THE ROOFS, GARGOYLES TO MAKE THE HOUSE LOOK EXTRA SCARY, SOME GHOSTS AND A SET OF CREEPY HANDS.

5 USE A DARK COLOUR SCHEME FOR THE HAUNTED HOUSE BUT PAINT THE WINDOWS REALLY BRIGHT SO THEY STAND OUT. ADD A SINISTER LIGHTNING STRIKE TO THE PICTURE AND A GREY, CLOUDY SKY. CREEPY!

MANGA IS A STYLE OF JAPANESE COMIC AND CARTOON.

MANGA GIRL

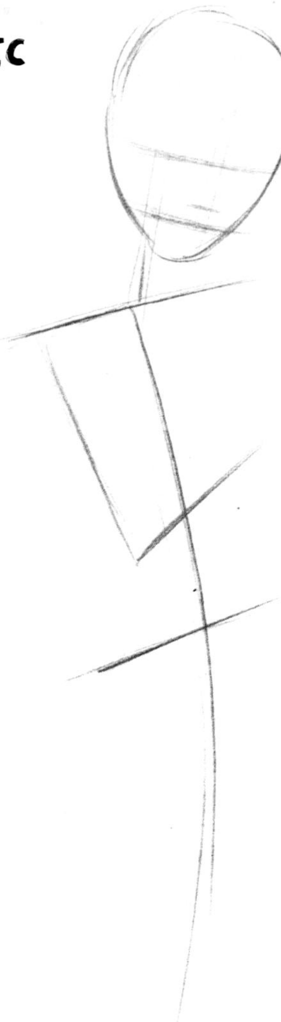

1

FIND A PHOTO OF A CUTE, COOL GIRL FOR INSPIRATION. USE A HARD PENCIL TO DRAW SOME GUIDELINES TO GET THE FEEL OF THE POSE.

2

SKETCH THE SHAPE OF THE FIGURE. MAKE HER HEAD BIG AND EMPHASIZE THE HAIR. THE LEGS AND FEET CAN BE QUITE DELICATE TO MAKE HER MORE DOLL-LIKE.

3

START DRAWING THE HANDS AND FACE. THE EYES SHOULD BE BIG AND STAND OUT. SKETCH THE OUTLINE FOR THE CLOTHES. ADD JEWELLERY FOR EXTRA INTEREST.

EYES

Manga eyes are great fun to draw, so go crazy! Work in light spots to make the pupils shine. Try adding big eyelashes too!

4

USE A SOFT PENCIL TO WORK UP THE DETAIL AND SHADOWS. YOU DON'T NEED MUCH DETAIL FOR THE NOSE AND MOUTH WITH MANGA DRAWINGS. ADD SOME FRECKLES AND HAIR TEXTURE.

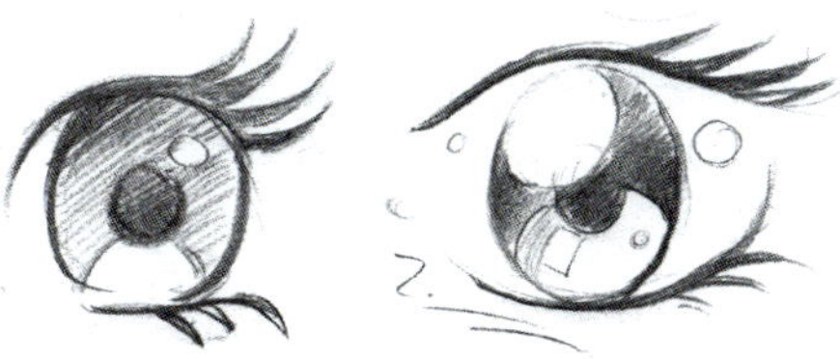

5

ACID GREENS AND ELECTRIC PINKS ARE GREAT VIBRANT COLOURS TO BRING YOUR MANGA CHARACTER TO LIFE. USE A DARKER TONE TO CREATE THE SHADOWS THAT WILL GIVE THE FIGURE DIMENSION.

HAIRSTYLES

Manga hairstyles are wild, so don't hold back! Try the hairstyles below or experiment with some creations of your own.

URBAN BRIDGE

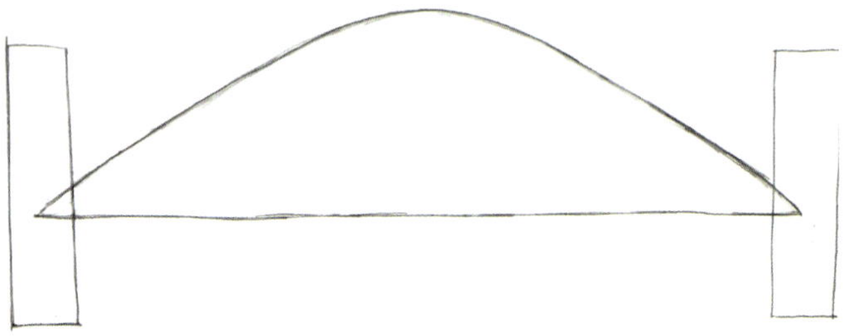

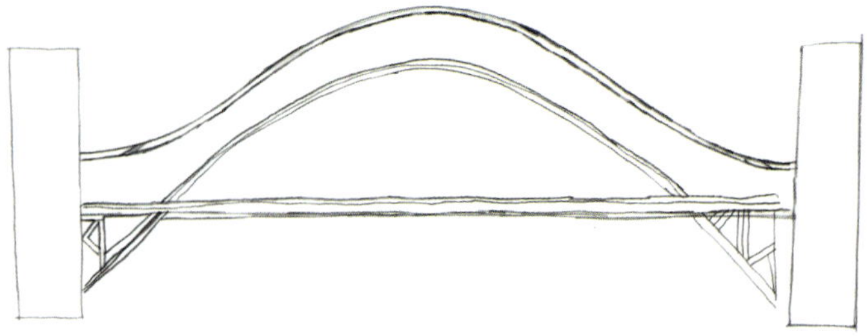

1 DRAW A WIDE TRIANGLE SHAPE WITH THE TOP POINT ROUNDED OFF. ADD AN OVERLAPPING RECTANGLE SHAPE AT BOTH ENDS.

2 DRAW MORE CURVES ABOVE AND BELOW YOUR GUIDE ARCH. LEVEL OFF THE TOP CURVE ENDS. ADD MORE HORIZONTAL LINES ALONG THE BOTTOM OF THE TRIANGLE FOR THE ROAD AND ADD SETS OF DIAGONAL LINES FOR THE FRAMEWORK BELOW. RUB OUT ANY UNWANTED GUIDELINES.

Use dark lines and shadows to make certain elements of your drawing fade into the background. Here, the blackened bars help the red ones in the foreground to pop.

3 DRAW A SEQUENCE OF CRISS-CROSSING BARS TO FILL THE GAP BETWEEN THE TWO CURVED SHAPES. ADD A LITTLE SHADING HERE AND THERE TO CREATE A 3D EFFECT.

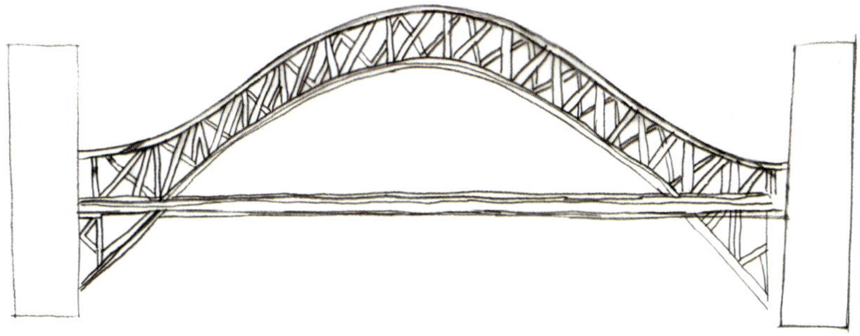

4 TURN THE RECTANGLES INTO BUILDINGS BY ADDING WINDOWS AND STONEWORK DETAIL. SKETCH ROUGH OUTLINES OF A COUPLE OF TREES BEHIND. ADD SOME TOWER BLOCKS BELOW BY DRAWING A FEW VERTICAL RECTANGLES. THEN ADD ROUGH SQUARE SHAPES FOR WINDOWS.

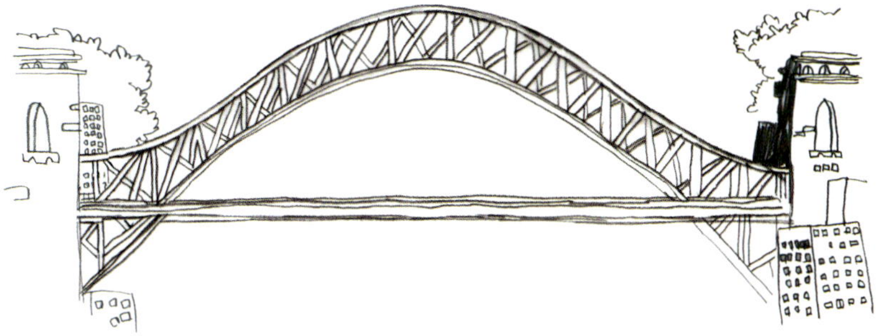

Draw a few leaves here and there, then paint a yellowy-green wash. Draw some jaggedy, inky lines for leafless branches.

5 GO OVER YOUR OUTLINES IN PEN AND INK, KEEPING THE LINEWORK LOOSE AND SCRATCHY TO CREATE AN URBAN FEEL. DRAW MORE BUILDINGS IN THE DISTANCE. PAINT THE BRIDGE A BRIGHT COLOUR TO MAKE IT STAND OUT.

CARTOON WILD ANIMALS

CARTOON ANIMALS ARE EASIER TO DRAW THAN YOU THINK! CHECK OUT THESE SUGGESTIONS THEN GO WILD WITH YOUR PENCIL AND PAINTS.

NOSES

DIFFERENT ANIMALS HAVE DIFFERENT NOSE SHAPES – TRIANGLES, TRUNKS OR EVEN JUST TWO DOTS FOR NOSTRILS, LIKE ON A HIPPO.

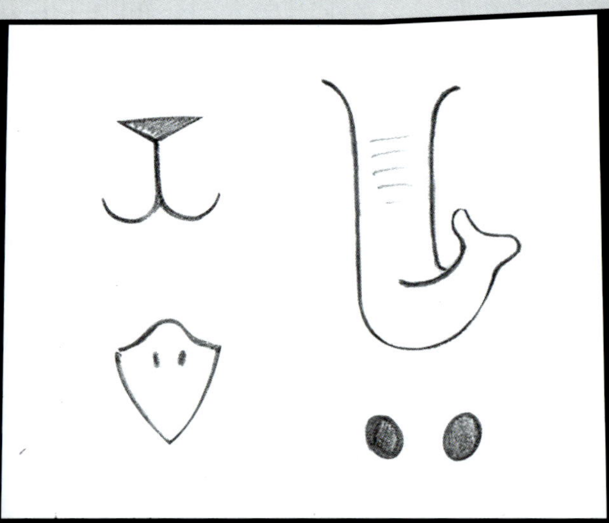

EARS

WHETHER THEY'RE ROUND AND FUZZY OR WIDE AND FLAPPY, ALWAYS LOOK AT HOW HIGH ON THE HEAD THE EARS SHOULD BE.

FEET

WHAT KIND OF FEET DOES YOUR CARTOON ANIMAL NEED? TRY OUT THESE SIMPLE SHAPES. DON'T FORGET TO ADD MARKS FOR TOES!

EYES

START WITH CIRCLES, THEN ADD STRAIGHT EYELID LINES TO GIVE YOUR CARTOONS DIFFERENT EXPRESSIONS. USE LITTLE SEMI-CIRCLES TO ADD GLINTS TO THE EYES TOO.

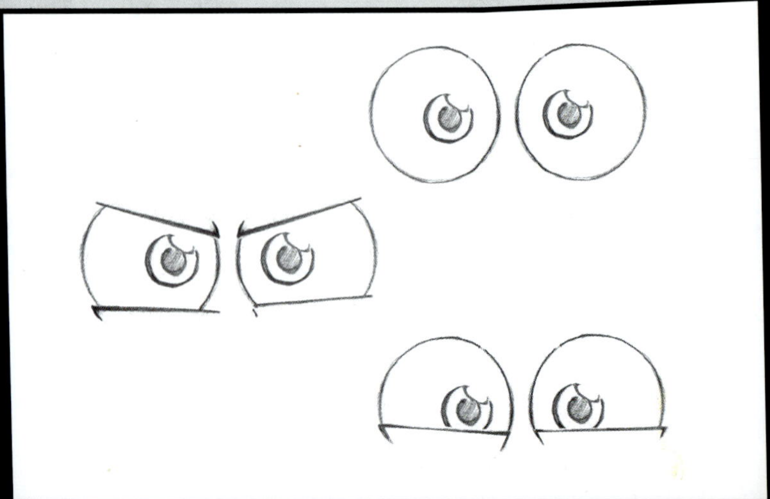

Find some pictures for inspiration and look at what features are unique to that animal. Then exaggerate them!

Use jagged lines to show a furry beard, and light lines inside for the fur texture.

JETPACK

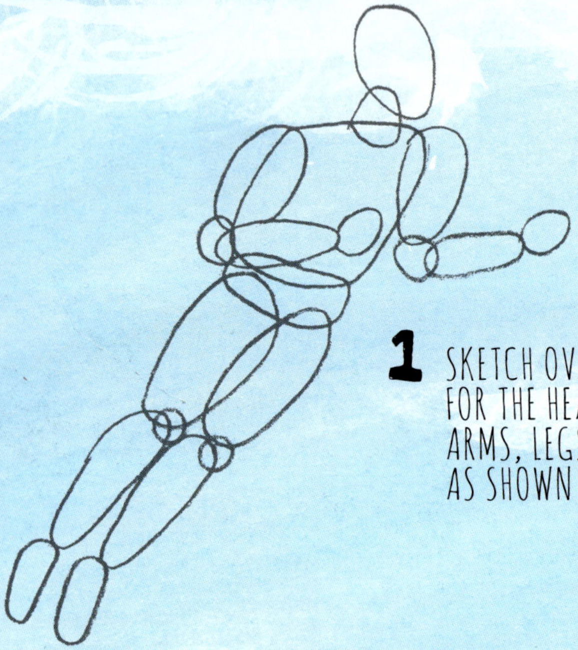

1 SKETCH OVAL SHAPES FOR THE HEAD, TORSO, ARMS, LEGS AND FEET, AS SHOWN HERE.

Drawing 3D shapes can be tricky to get right the first time. That's why we start with a pencil!

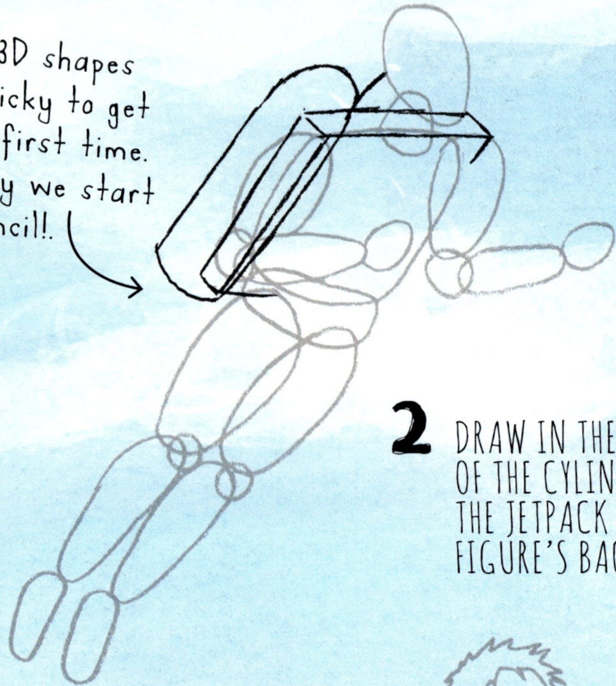

2 DRAW IN THE SHAPE OF THE CYLINDERS FOR THE JETPACK ON THE FIGURE'S BACK.

3 SKETCH OUT THE DETAIL OF THE JETPACKER'S COSTUME AND START DRAWING IN HIS FEATURES, TOO.

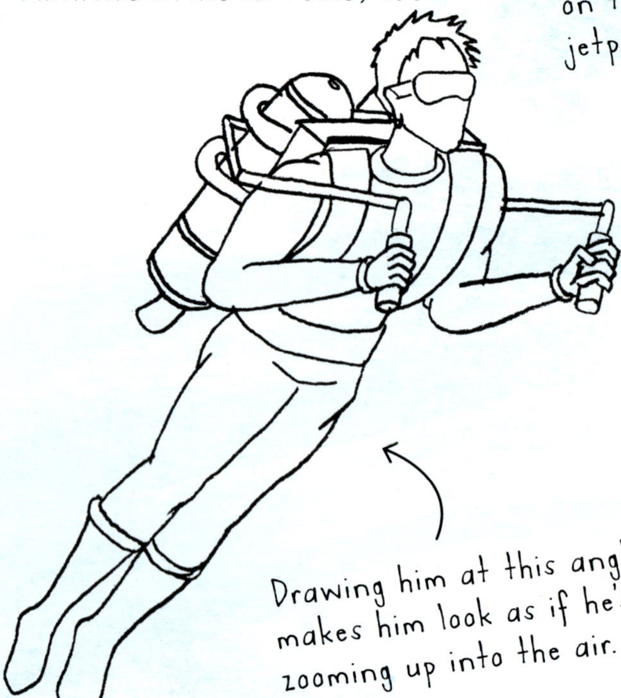

Drawing him at this angle makes him look as if he's zooming up into the air.

Make sure your figure is holding on tightly to the jetpack controls!

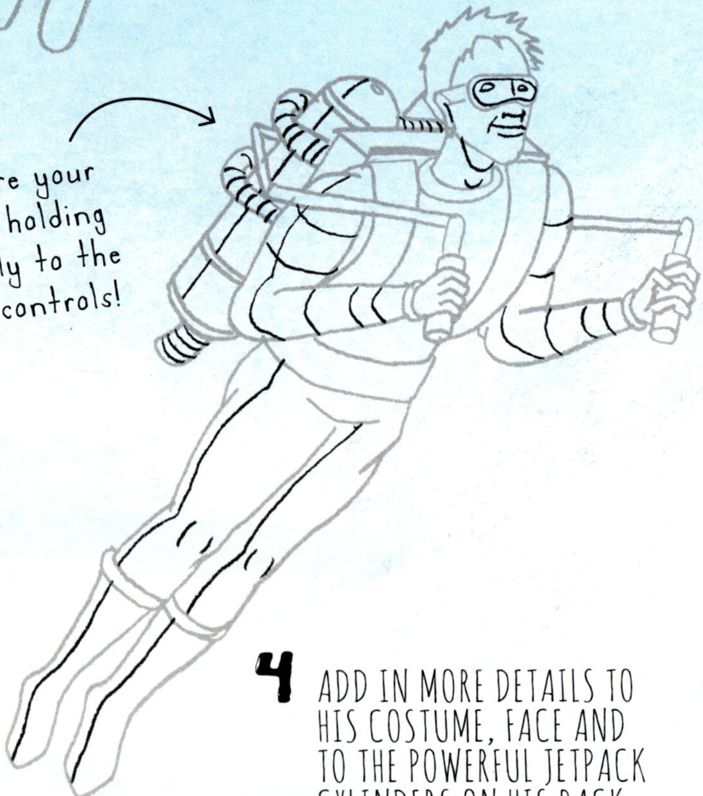

4 ADD IN MORE DETAILS TO HIS COSTUME, FACE AND TO THE POWERFUL JETPACK CYLINDERS ON HIS BACK.

5 ADD SHADING TO THE EDGES OF THE LIMBS AND BODY TO GIVE THE PICTURE A MORE DRAMATIC FEEL.

6 ADD BRIGHT COLOURS TO THE JETPACKER'S COSTUME TO MAKE HIM STAND OUT FROM THE BLUE SKY BEHIND HIM.

MONSTER PLANT

1

DRAW A SQUARE POT, WITH AN OVAL AT THE TOP. FOLLOW THE CURVE OF THE OVAL TO GIVE YOUR POT DEPTH.

2

LIGHTLY DRAW THREE CURVING GUIDELINES COMING FROM THE POT. DRAW PARALLEL LINES EITHER SIDE OF THE GUIDELINES TO MAKE THE PLANT STALKS. USE OVALS OR CIRCLES AT THE END OF EACH STALK TO MAKE MONSTER-HEAD SHAPES.

3

DRAW ROOTS BURSTING OUT OF CRACKS IN THE POT. THE ROOTS SHOULD BECOME THINNER, ENDING IN A SHARP POINT.

4

DRAW FANGS AND GROSS LIQUID DRIBBLING OUT OF THE MOUTH. ADD SOME BULGING EYEBALLS OR EYES.

5

FINISH THE PLANT WITH WATERCOLOUR PENCILS. BLEND YELLOWS AND GREENS TOGETHER. MAKE THE STALKS DARKER AT THE EDGES TO CREATE THE EFFECT OF A CYLINDER. THEN USE BLACK TO GIVE THE MONSTER PLANT A HEAVY OUTLINE.

World's TALLEST BURGER

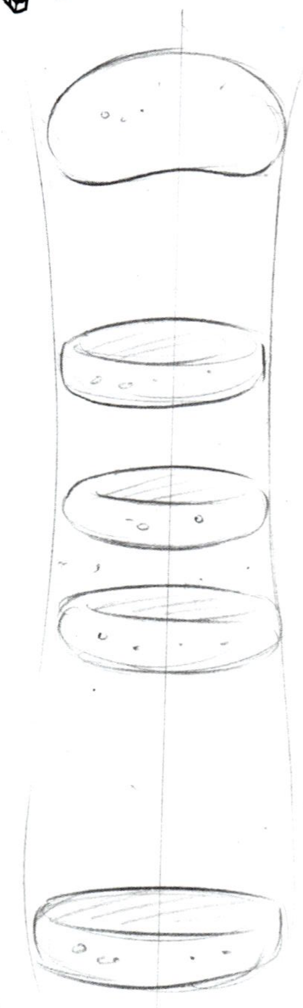

1

USING A 2H PENCIL, DRAW THE ROUGH OUTLINE OF YOUR HUGE MULTI-LAYERED BURGER! MAKE THE SHAPE SLIGHTLY NARROWER IN THE MIDDLE TO GIVE YOUR FINAL DRAWING ADDED VISUAL INTEREST. USE ROUGH ELLIPSES AND CURVED SHAPES FOR THE LAYERS OF BREAD.

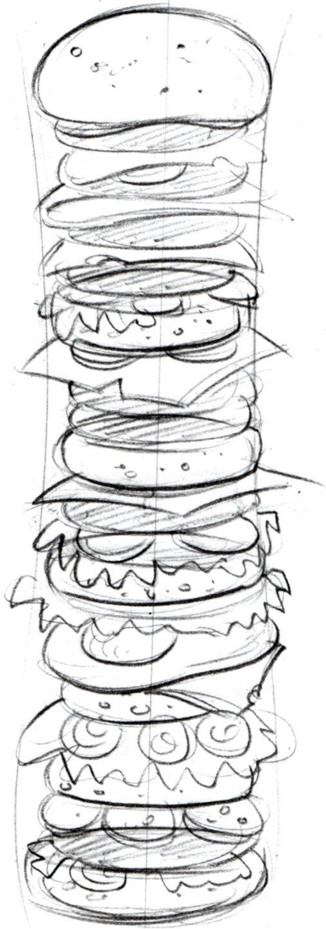

2

ADD LAYERS OF FILLING! USE WAVY LINES FOR LETTUCE LEAVES AND STRAIGHTER EDGES FOR CHEESE SLICES. USE ROUND SHAPES FOR SLICES OF TOMATO, ONION AND PICKLES. EXAGGERATE THE SIZES OF THE DIFFERENT FILLINGS AND HAVE THEM HANG OVER THE SIDES SO THEY'RE CLEARLY VISIBLE.

3

USING A SOFTER PENCIL SUCH AS A 2B, GIVE YOUR FILLINGS MORE DETAIL AND DOUBLE UP ON THE OUTLINES IN PLACES TO MAKE THE FILLINGS LOOK 3D. DECIDE WHERE THE LIGHT IS COMING FROM AND ADD SHADING LINES FOR THE AREAS THAT ARE IN SHADOW.

To create a sense of movement in your picture, vary the thickness of your linework and keep the colouring loose. It doesn't matter if some areas of colour accidentally cross over a line!

4

GO OVER YOUR LINEWORK WITH A BLACK PEN. A THICK, HEAVY OUTLINE WILL CREATE MORE OF A GRAPHIC-NOVEL EFFECT. COLOUR YOUR DRAWING, USING DARKER TONES FOR THE SHADED AREAS, WITH ADDED WHITE BANDS FOR THE HIGHLIGHTS.

Circular patterns

MAKE USE OF THE EASY-TO-DRAW CIRCLE SHAPE TO COME UP WITH PATTERNS THAT LOOK MORE COMPLICATED THAN THEY ARE! USE THEM TO DECORATE YOUR THINGS OR DRAWINGS.

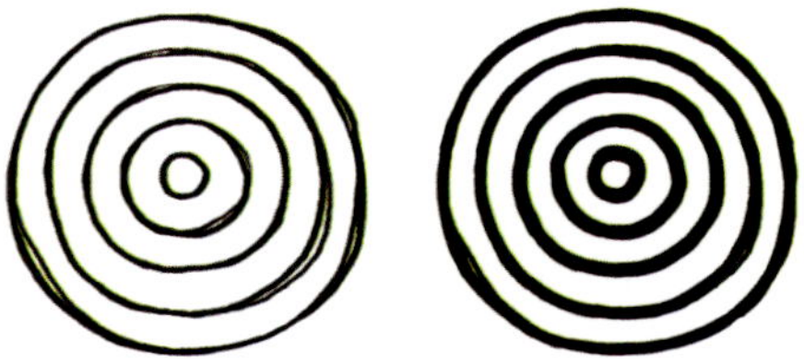

One simple circular pattern option is to draw lots of circles inside each other. Use thick and thin lines for the rings.

MAKE A COMBINATION PATTERN BY DRAWING YOUR PATTERNS ONE ON TOP OF THE OTHER, VARYING THE THIN AND THICK LINES.

For a colour option, choose different tints for each ring of the pattern. Try colours that work well together until you find combinations that you like.

MIX THE TWO DIFFERENT COLOUR CIRCLES PATTERNS THAT YOU HAVE CREATED TO MAKE A LARGER DYNAMIC COLOURED PATTERN.

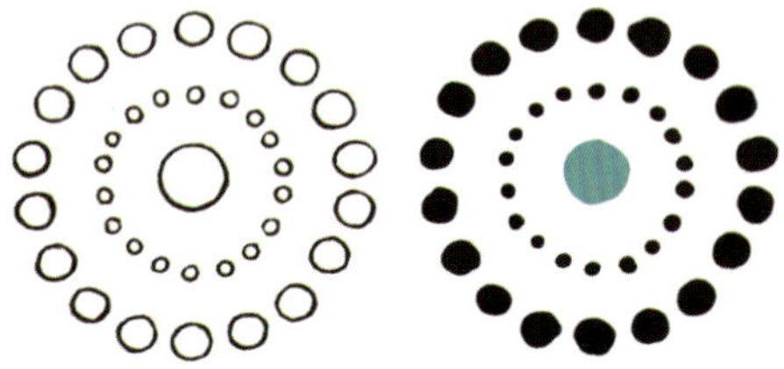

Or, try drawing tiny circles around your centre circle. Experiment with outlines and solids, or circles of different sizes. Add colour or not!

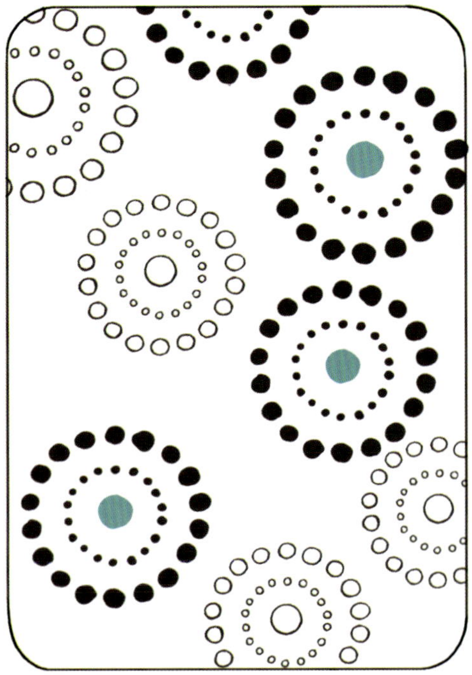

MAKE A PATTERN BY MIXING UP THE OUTLINE SHAPES AND SOLID COLOUR SHAPES. THEY DON'T ALL HAVE TO BE THE SAME SIZE.

RADIAL

WITH A PENCIL, DRAW TWO BASIC CIRCLES INSIDE EACH OTHER. ADD LEAF SHAPES OR TEAR DROPS AROUND THE OUTSIDE, THEN ADD COLOUR!

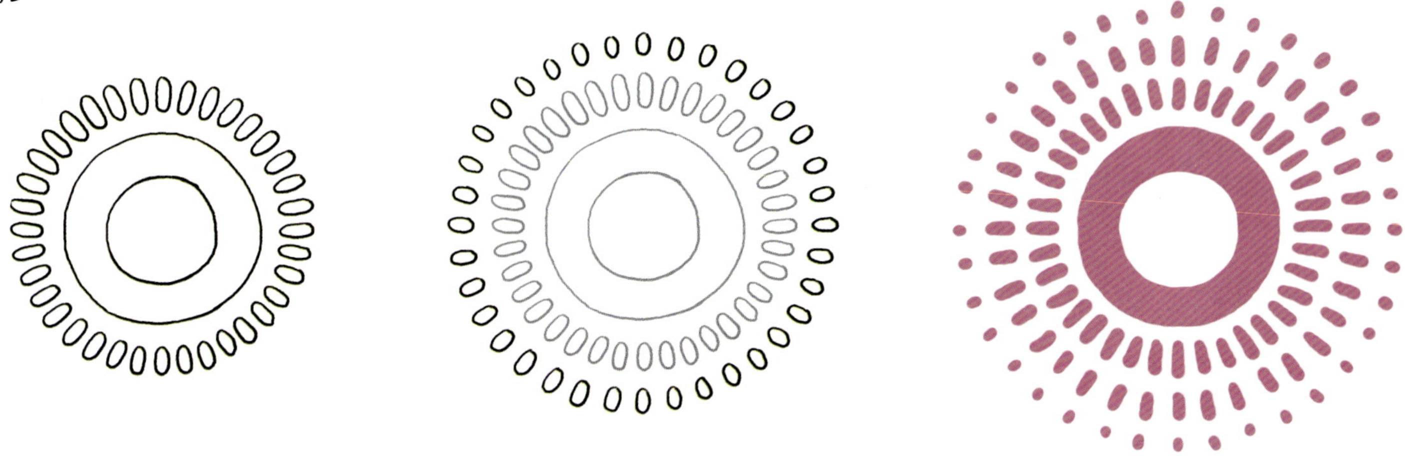

GEOMETRIC

DRAW AN INNER CIRCLE, THEN AN OUTER CIRCLE. DIVIDE THE CIRCLE IN HALF, THEN QUARTERS, THEN AGAIN TO END UP WITH 12 SECTIONS LIKE A CLOCK. DRAW A ZIG-ZAG LINE IN EACH CIRCLE. EXPERIMENT WITH COLOURS.

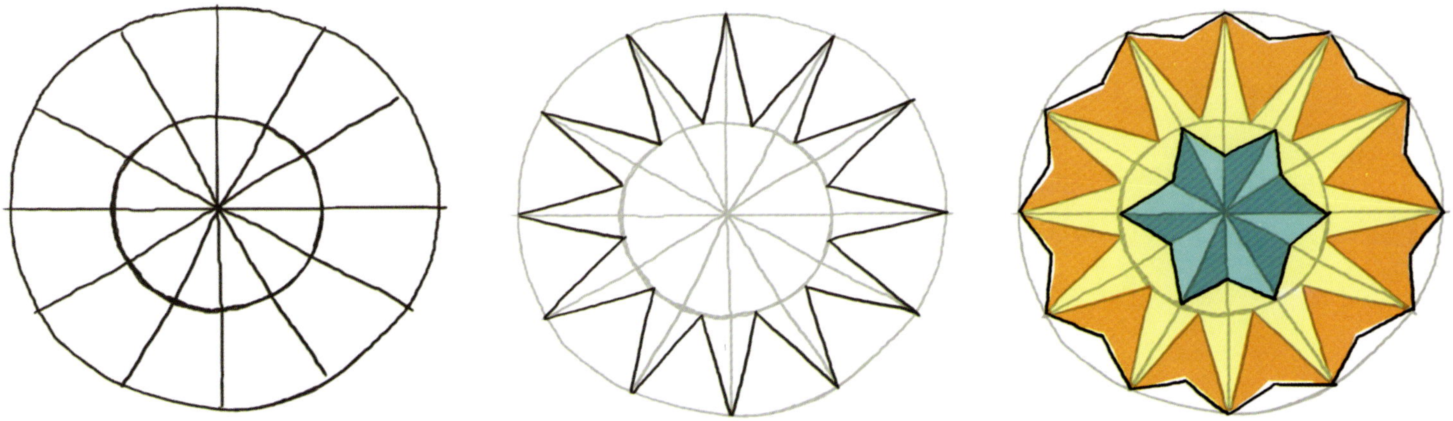

ORNAMENTAL

DRAW A CIRCLE AND DIVIDE IT INTO SIX. ADD SOME LEAF SHAPES ON THE DIVIDING LINES. EXPERIMENT WITH OTHER SHAPES USING THE DIVIDING LINES AS GUIDES TO MAKE UP A UNIQUE PATTERN.

ZOMBIE

1

USE A PENCIL TO DRAW A SIMPLE STICK FIGURE. SKETCH THE BASIC SHAPE OF ONE HAND REACHING OUT.

2

SKETCH IN THE SHAPE OF THE ZOMBIE BODY, BIT BY BIT.

3

ADD DETAIL TO THE ZOMBIE'S FACE, BODY AND CLOTHING. GIVE HIM AN UNNATURAL POSE.

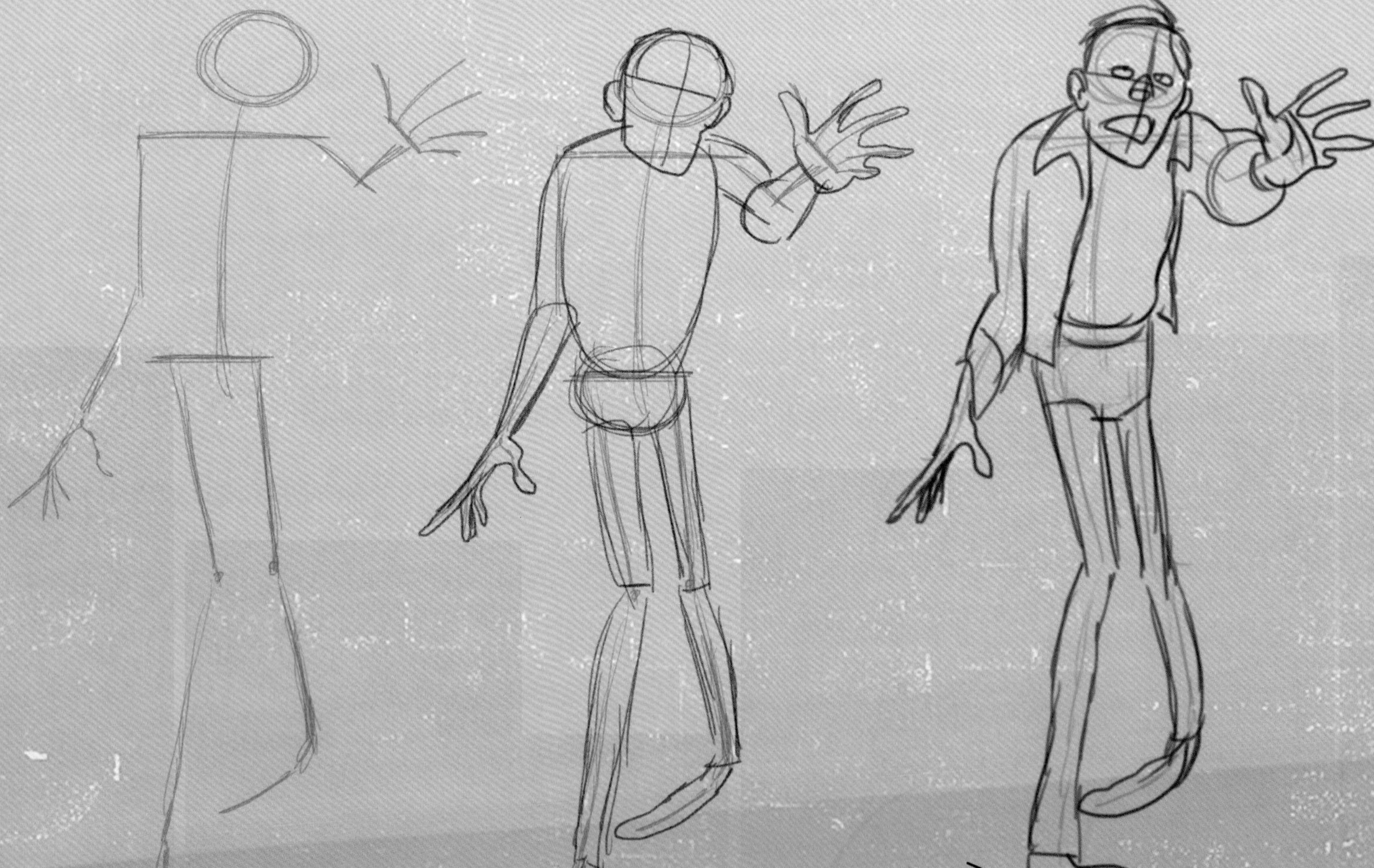

As your sketch takes shape, use darker lines to create the outline you'll go with for your monstrous figure.

4

DRAW IN MORE ZOMBIE DETAIL. GIVE HIM BIG, DARK SHADOWS AROUND HIS EYES, HORRIBLE SKIN AND RIPS IN HIS SHABBY CLOTHING.

5

USE COLOUR TO BRING YOUR ZOMBIE BACK TO LIFE. THREE DIFFERENT TONES OF THE SAME COLOUR (DARK FOR THE SHADOWS, MEDIUM FOR THE NEUTRAL AREAS AND LIGHT FOR HIGHLIGHTS) WILL MAKE THE FIGURE LOOK 3D – LIKE HE'S COMING RIGHT AT YOU!

Create the texture on the zombie's dirty jeans by starting with a dark, flat blue colour and then adding lighter strokes of blue, leaving plenty of creepy shadows.

SWEET MACHINE

DRAW A COMPLICATED-LOOKING, GADGETY, MAGICAL SWEET MACHINE BY BREAKING IT DOWN INTO DIFFERENT PARTS.

1 USE A PENCIL TO CREATE A SIMPLE CYLINDER SHAPE. DRAW A SMALL CIRCLE FOR A PRESSURE GAUGE. LINES FOLLOWING THE FORM OF THE CYLINDER BASE WILL GIVE THE EFFECT OF METAL PANELLING ON YOUR MACHINE.

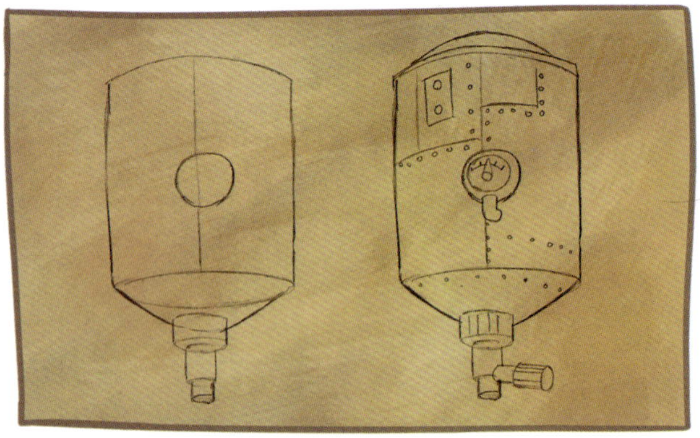

Add containers and levers to make the machine look more complex!

2 DRAW LIQUID SPILLING OUT OF A TAP USING LOOSE WOBBLY LINES. ADD CIRCLES AROUND THE LIQUID TO GIVE THE IMPRESSION THAT IT'S BUBBLING AND SPLASHING. SHADE THE FUNNEL FOR A 3D LOOK.

For the control panel, split the front face of the box into smaller squares and rectangles and draw lots of even smaller button shapes onto them.

3 SKETCH ANOTHER CYLINDER SHAPE UNDER THE MACHINE'S FUNNEL.

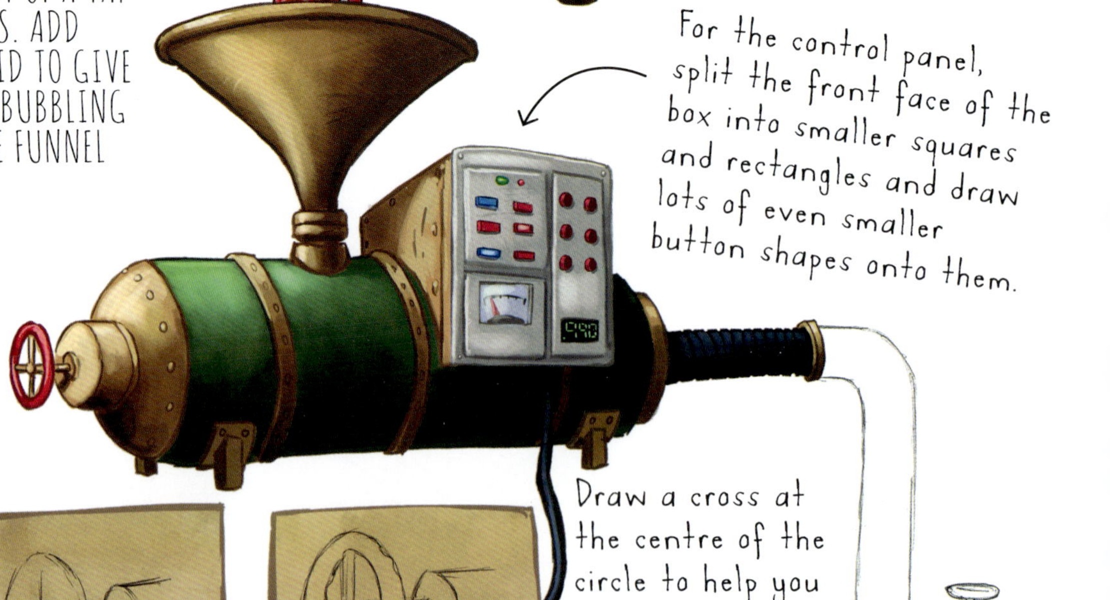

To draw a valve, start with a cylinder then draw another, thinner cylinder sticking out from it. Draw a big circle on top of it.

Draw a cross at the centre of the circle to help you position the arms of the valve that join the outer ring.

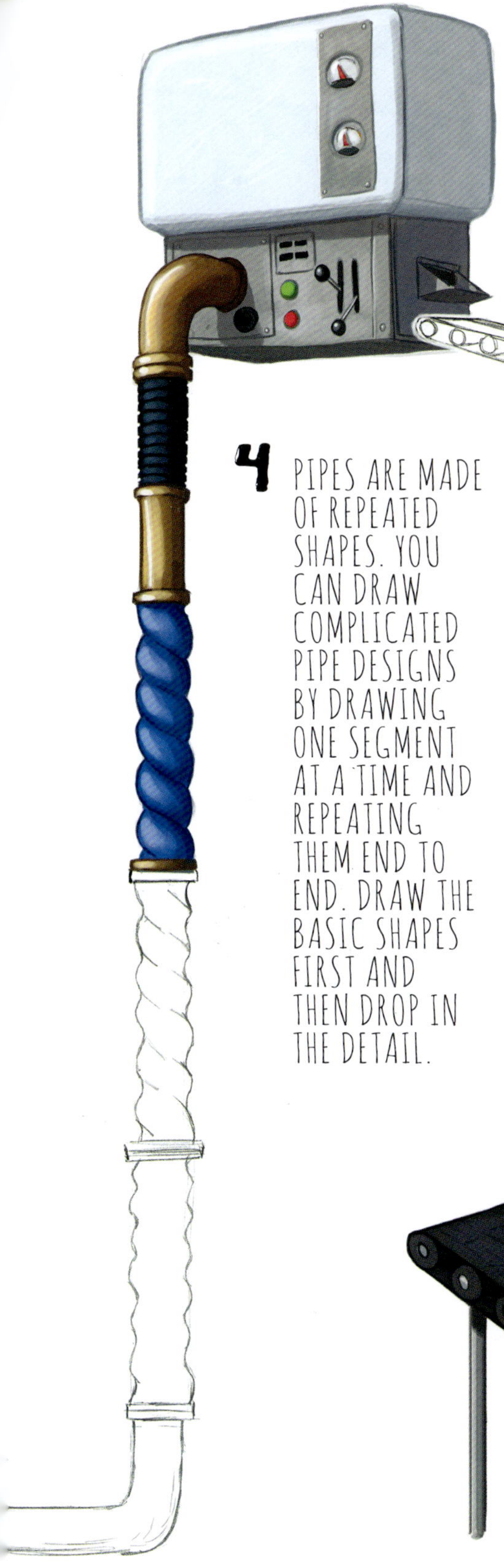

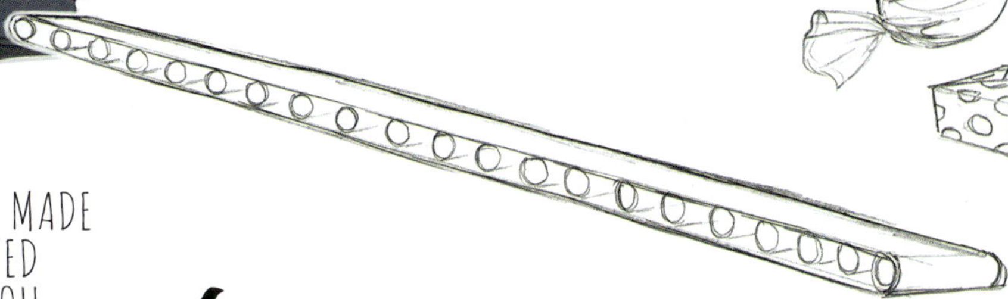

5 TO DRAW A SIMPLE CONVEYOR BELT, START WITH A SMALL CIRCLE SHAPE AT BOTH THE START AND THE END OF WHERE YOU WANT YOUR CONVEYOR BELT TO BE, THEN JOIN THEM WITH A PAIR OF STRAIGHT LINES.

What sweets will your machine produce? Here are some ideas!

4 PIPES ARE MADE OF REPEATED SHAPES. YOU CAN DRAW COMPLICATED PIPE DESIGNS BY DRAWING ONE SEGMENT AT A TIME AND REPEATING THEM END TO END. DRAW THE BASIC SHAPES FIRST AND THEN DROP IN THE DETAIL.

6 DRAW A PARALLEL HORIZONTAL LINE ON TOP, THEN JOIN THE TWO SETS OF LINES WITH SHORT HORIZONTAL LINES TO CREATE A 3D BELT SHAPE. NOW DRAW IN THE REST OF THE CIRCLES ALONG THE LENGTH OF THE SHAPE.

A simple jar can be drawn by starting with a cylinder shape and filling it up with different-shaped sweets.

SHARK!

QUICK-DRAW SHARK

Why not draw a 3D shark bite on the edge of your page?

1 DRAW A CURVED TRIANGULAR SHAPE FOR THE FIN AND TWO LARGE OVALS TO FORM THE SHARK'S MOUTH.

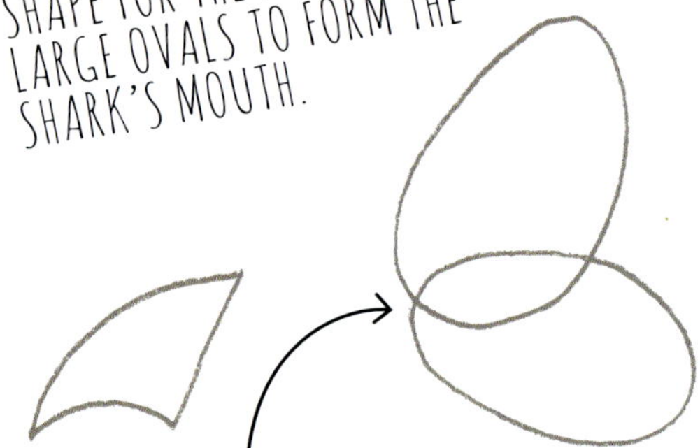

Draw the two ovals overlapping each other.

2 SKETCH THE SHARK'S BODY AT AN ANGLE, AS IF IT'S JUMPING OUT OF THE WATER. DRAW CURVED SHAPES FOR THE MOUTH AND TONGUE, THEN ADD AN EYE.

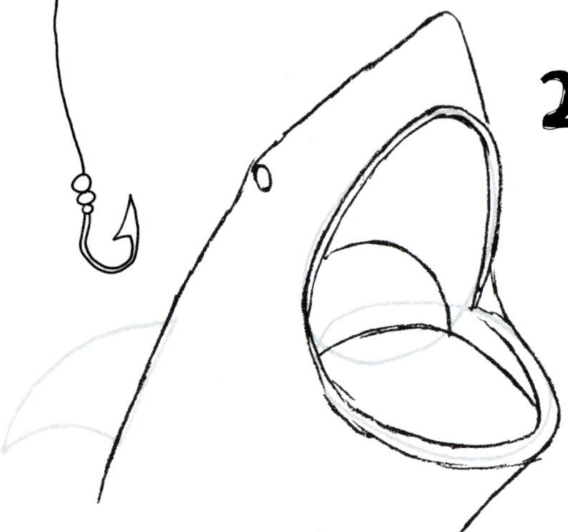

This shading technique uses lots of curved and straight lines. Draw them closer together for the darker areas, such as the inside of the shark's mouth.

3 DRAW MORE LINES AND CURVES ON THE SHARK'S BODY TO MAKE IT LOOK MORE 3D. ADD IN EXTRA LINES AROUND THE EYES AND MOUTH.

4 GIVE YOUR SHARK LOTS OF TRIANGULAR-SHAPED TEETH. ADD SHADING TO EMPHASIZE THE CURVED SHAPE OF THE BODY, WITH HEAVIER SHADING FOR THE INSIDE OF THE MOUTH. DRAW A BIG WATER SPLASH WITH WAVY LINES.

Great white shark

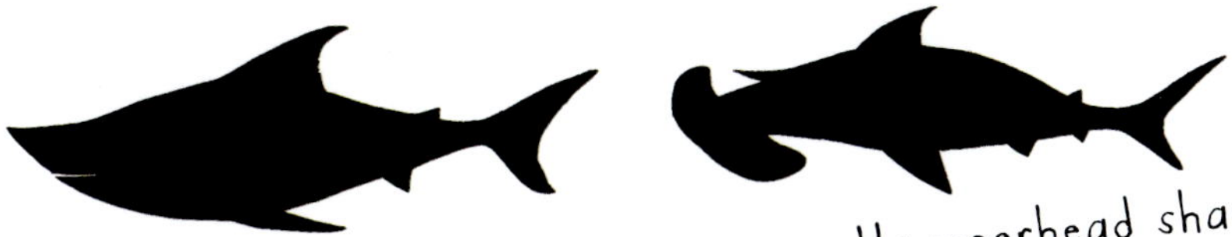

Hammerhead shark

5 TO COLOUR YOUR SHARK, USE A DEEP RED FOR THE INSIDE OF ITS MOUTH. THIS WILL CONTRAST WELL WITH BOTH THE PALE AND DARK BLUE TONES USED ON THE BODY. ADD SOME EXTRA DETAILS, SUCH AS STARTLED TROPICAL FISH!

To achieve a watery effect, paint larger areas with a single watercolour wash, adding random blobs and patches of contrasting tones.

SKYSCRAPERS

1

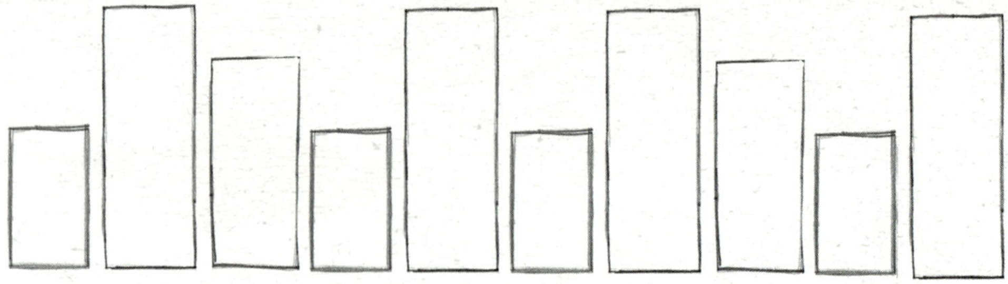

USING A PENCIL, DRAW A SERIES OF BLOCKS IN A ROW TO FORM A SKYLINE.

2

ADD EXTRA SHAPES TO YOUR BLOCKS TO MAKE THE BUILDINGS MORE INTERESTING.

3

ADD SOME GUIDELINES TO HELP YOU DRAW DETAILS SUCH AS WINDOWS AND ORNATE DECORATION.

4

USING A FINE-LINE PEN, DRAW OVER YOUR PENCIL LINES AND FILL IN THE DETAILS OF THE BUILDINGS. RUB OUT THE PENCIL LINES WHEN YOU HAVE FINISHED.

5

ADD A WASH OF COLOUR OVER YOUR BUILDINGS USING WATERCOLOUR PAINTS.

Gather some inspiration from pictures of real buildings.

BASKETBALL PLAYER

You could use an image of a real basketball player to help you get the pose right.

1

USING A 2H PENCIL, ROUGHLY SKETCH A STICK FIGURE FOR YOUR BASKETBALL PLAYER. DRAW AN ARM POINTING IN THE AIR AND MAKE ONE LEG MORE BENT THAN THE OTHER FOR A JUMPING POSE. EVEN AT THIS INITIAL STAGE, TRY AND DRAW A FIGURE THAT LOOKS LIKE IT'S IN MOTION.

2

SKETCH THE BASIC OUTLINE AND PROPORTIONS OF YOUR FIGURE, USING THE STICK LINES AS A GUIDE. NOTICE HOW THE MUSCLES BULGE OUT MORE ON THE LEG THAT'S BENT.

3

WORK ON THE BODY PARTS, USING CURVED LINES FOR THE MUSCLE SHAPES. ADD THE FINGERS, HAIR AND FACIAL FEATURES AND DRAW IN CLOTHING, THINKING ABOUT HOW THE POSE WILL AFFECT THE WAY THE CLOTHES HANG.

Draw a circle for the basketball and sketch curved shapes for the markings. A little shading here and there will make it look more 3D.

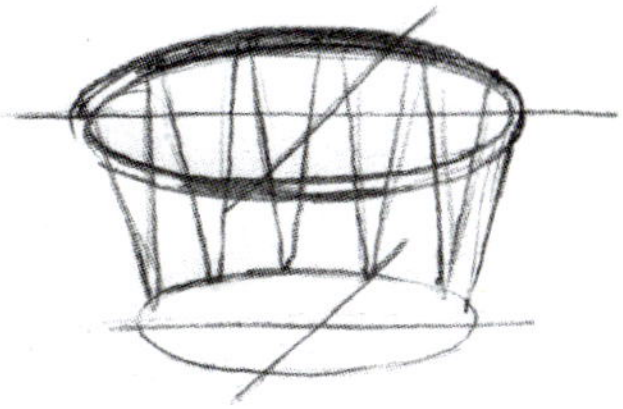

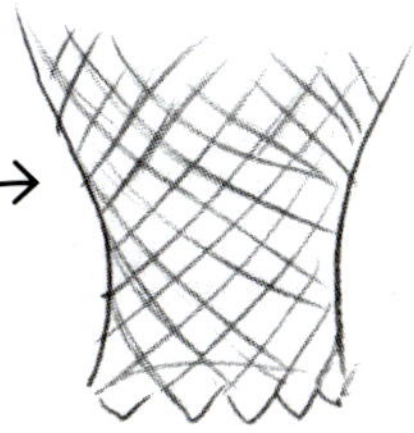

When drawing the basket, use simple crosshatch strokes for the mesh part of the net. The top third of the basket is actually more of a zig-zag shape - a bit like a row of shark's teeth!

4

USING A HEAVIER PENCIL SUCH AS A 4B, REFINE YOUR LINEWORK EVEN MORE. SKETCH SERIES OF SLANTED LINES FOR THE SHADOWS, USING SUBTLE SHADING TO BRING OUT THE MUSCLE TONE. ADD DETAIL TO YOUR PLAYER'S TRAINERS AND DRAW A FEW MORE CREASES ON HIS CLOTHES.

5

GO OVER YOUR LINEWORK WITH A BLACK PEN. USE A THICKER LINE FOR THE OUTSIDE OF HIS BODY, WITH A THINNER LINE FOR FINE DETAILS SUCH AS THE CREASES IN HIS CLOTHING. WHEN COLOURING YOUR PICTURE, USE A RANGE OF TONES FOR EACH AREA, ADDING SUBTLE HIGHLIGHTS AND EXTRA SHADOWS TO CREATE DEPTH.

VOLCANO

1

DRAW A PYRAMID SHAPE (WITH THE TOP CUT OFF) IN PENCIL. USE INK TO DRAW JAGGED LINES TO GIVE THE VOLCANO TEXTURE.

2

USING INK, DRAW THICK LINES ON THE VOLCANO SIDES. ADD TREES, ROCKS, FLEEING DINOS AND LAVA.

3

PAINT DARK ORANGES AT THE BOTTOM OF THE LAVA AND WORK UP TO THE BRIGHTER COLOURS FOR THE LAVA ERUPTING.

4

PAINT THE REST OF YOUR PICTURE, ADDING SHADOWS AND HIGHLIGHTS FOR DRAMATIC EFFECT.

WEIRD BEARDS

BEARDS ARE SIMPLE TO DRAW, BUT YOU CAN HAVE PLENTY OF FUN INVENTING ALL SORTS OF STRANGE STYLES.

1 DRAW A CURVED SHAPE FOR THE TOP OF THE HEAD AND ADD AN EAR TO EACH SIDE. SKETCH A SIMPLE OUTLINE OF A BEARD WITH AN ADJOINING MOUSTACHE.

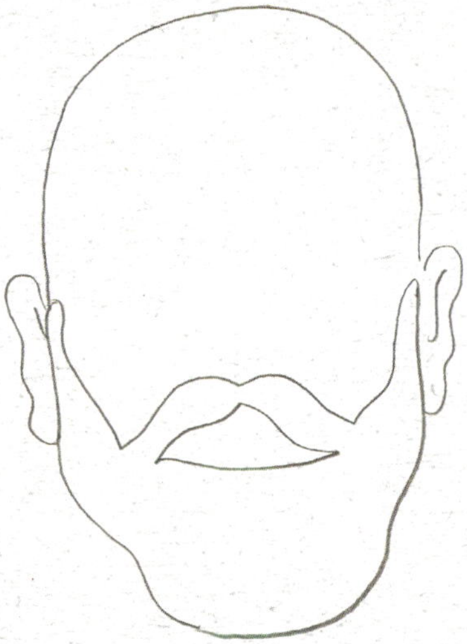

2 FOR AN EASY WAY OF DRAWING HAIR, SIMPLY FILL THE BEARD AREA WITH LOTS OF VERTICAL, WAVY LINES. USE SHORTER LINES TO FILL IN THE MOUSTACHE AREA.

Drawing the lines closer together will make your beard look darker.

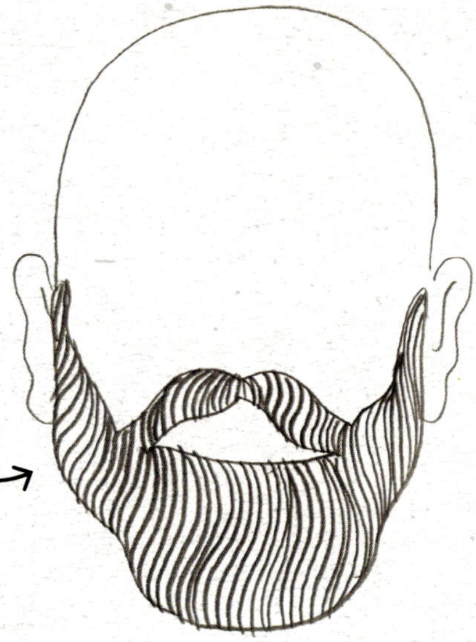

TO GET THE EFFECT OF A DENSE, WAVY BEARD, DRAW LOTS OF REPEATED CURVES IN LONG, WINDING ROWS.

Try adding something unexpected in your weird beard, such as a pair of birds!

DRAW LOTS OF LITTLE SPIRALS FOR A LONG, CURLY BEARD.

You could experiment with other simple doodles and try using them for different beard textures.

TRY DRAWING SOME OF THESE WEIRD BEARDS, OR INVENT YOUR OWN!

BEARD GALLERY

PENCIL STROKES

DRAW SHORT, SIMPLE LINES FANNING OUTWARDS TO EACH SIDE TO CREATE A BUSHY BEARD.

THE BRUSH

THE CHECKS

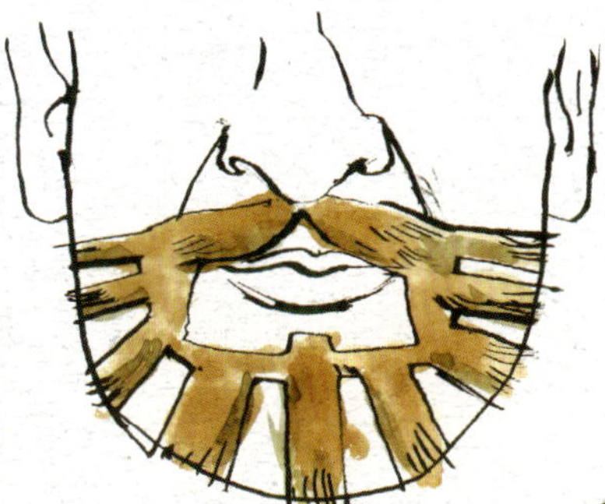

THE OCTOPUS

TWISTS AND CURLS

TRY DRAWING A BEARD THAT LOOKS MORE LIKE A BIG, CURLY MOUSTACHE. ADD WAVY LINES FOR TEXTURE.

THE WAVE

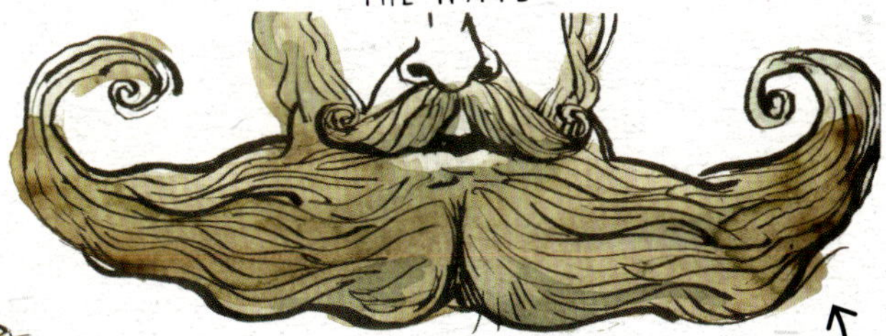

When colouring, use different colour tones to add depth.

THE MAD MAJOR

THE RING MASTER

This builds on the Mad Major style, but the curls are tighter, like waxed loops!

LONG

ALTHOUGH A PLAITED BEARD LOOKS COMPLICATED, IT'S JUST A SUCCESSION OF SIMPLE SHAPES, WITH ADDED LINES FOR TEXTURE.

LONG PLAIT

Draw lots of linked curved shapes like this:

Then fill them in.

SPEEDBOAT

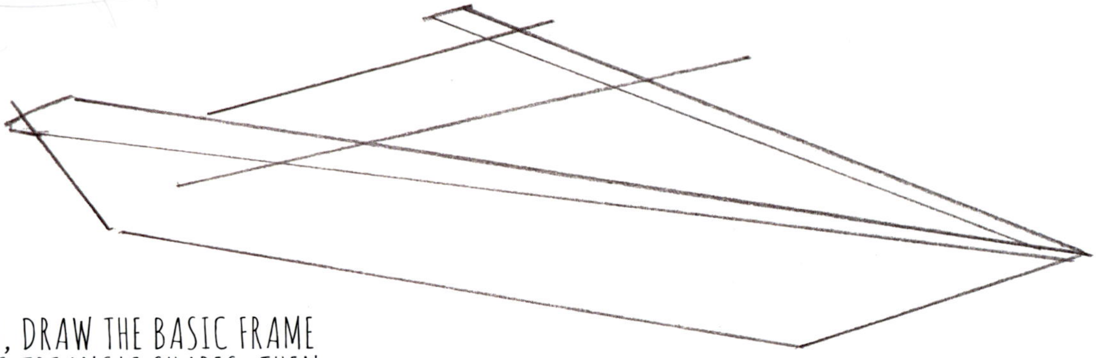

1

WITH A RULER, DRAW THE BASIC FRAME WITH TWO BIG TRIANGLE SHAPES, THEN DRAW IN THE BOTTOM OF THE BOAT. ADD TWO DIAGONAL LINES TO SHOW WHERE THE GLASS SCREEN WILL GO.

If the people's hair is flying about, it will look like the boat is really speeding through the water!

2

DRAW IN MORE OF THE STRUCTURE OF THE BOAT, ADD SOME CURVES AND USE THE DIAGONAL LINES TO DRAW IN THE WINDSCREEN.

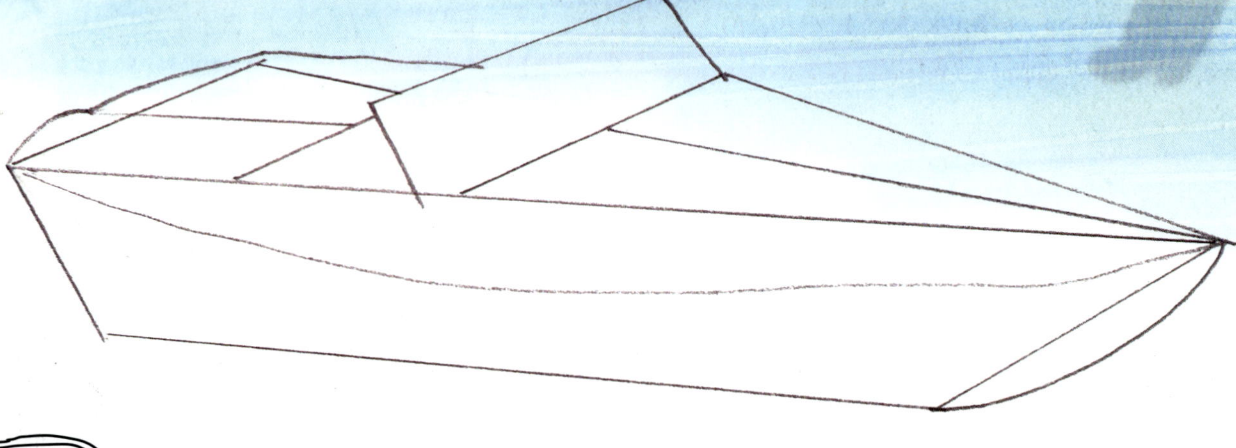

3

RUB OUT THE LINES YOU DON'T NEED, AND ADD SOME CURVES AND DETAILS. ROUGHLY SKETCH IN WHERE THE PEOPLE WILL SIT IN THE SPEEDBOAT, A STEERING WHEEL AND MOTOR.

4

DRAW IN SOME SPIKY WAVES. THESE ARE MEANT TO LOOK LOOSE AND SPLASHY SO DON'T WORRY ABOUT BEING TOO PRECISE. ADD IN THE PEOPLE'S FEATURES AND A REFLECTION LINE ON THE WINDSCREEN.

5

FINISH BY COLOURING UP THE PICTURE. BE PRECISE WITH THE COLOUR OF THE BOAT AND LOOSE WHEN COLOURING THE WAVES.

Add little splash marks loosely coloured in to really give the sense of the boat's speed!

Frames

TRY DRAWING FRAMES FOR YOUR PICTURES USING SIMPLE SHAPES TO BUILD UP PATTERNS.

FOR A ZIG-ZAG PATTERN, DRAW TWO LONG PARALLEL LINES, THEN DRAW ZIG-ZAG LINES BETWEEN THEM. BUILD UP A COMPLEX PATTERN BY ADDING DETAIL AND SHADING LINES IN THE TRIANGLES YOU'VE CREATED.

THIS PATTERN IS SIMILAR TO THE ONE ABOVE, BUT THIS TIME USE CONSECUTIVE CURVES AND REMOVE THE TOP LINE TO GIVE A DIFFERENT, ROUNDED STYLE. ADD DETAIL INSIDE THE CURVES FOR SOPHISTICATION.

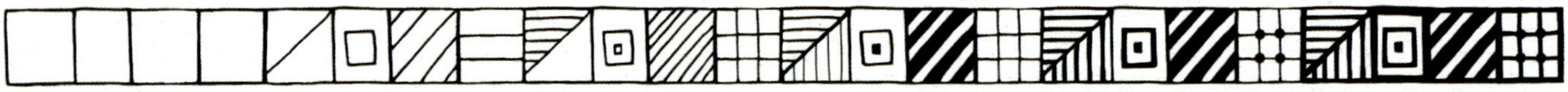

FOR ANOTHER INTERESTING PATTERN, DIVIDE THE SPACE BETWEEN THE PARALLEL LINES INTO SMALL SQUARES. TRY DIFFERENT PATTERNS IN EACH ONE, OR REPEAT SOME OF THE DESIGNS TO BUILD UP A BIGGER PATTERN.

The top and bottom panels of a frame could share the same pattern. Add variety by drawing a different pattern for the two side panels. Try mixing soft curves and sharp zig-zags for this striking frame.

Try using the same pattern in all four corners of your frame to make it look well balanced. Vary the patterns in the spaces between. Colour a frame like this with washed tones of the same colour.

Round

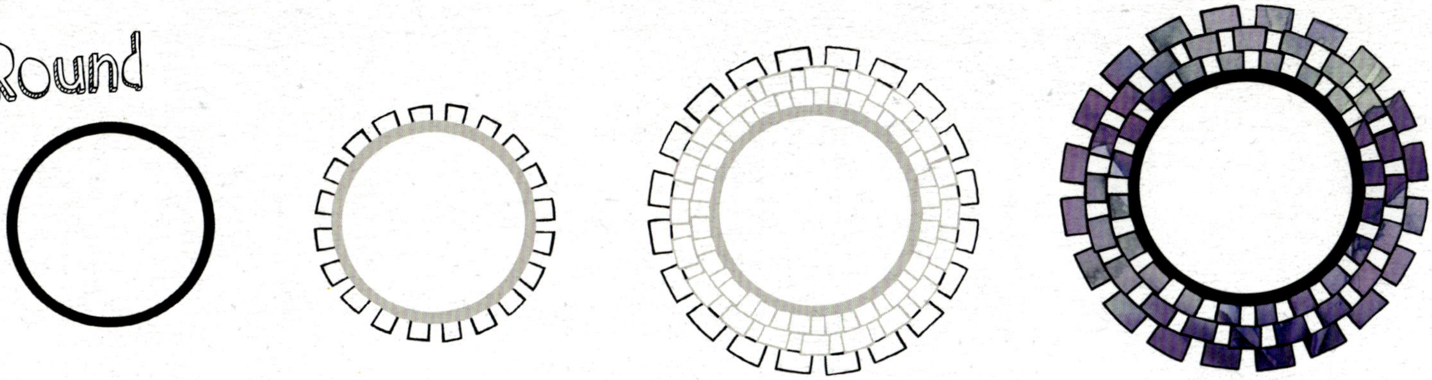

Start by drawing a thick circle. Add squares around the outside, leaving spaces in between. On the next layer add squares building on the spaces in the first layer. Do the same for the third layer. Mix different tones of watercolour paints to colour the squares, leaving white space in between.

Oval

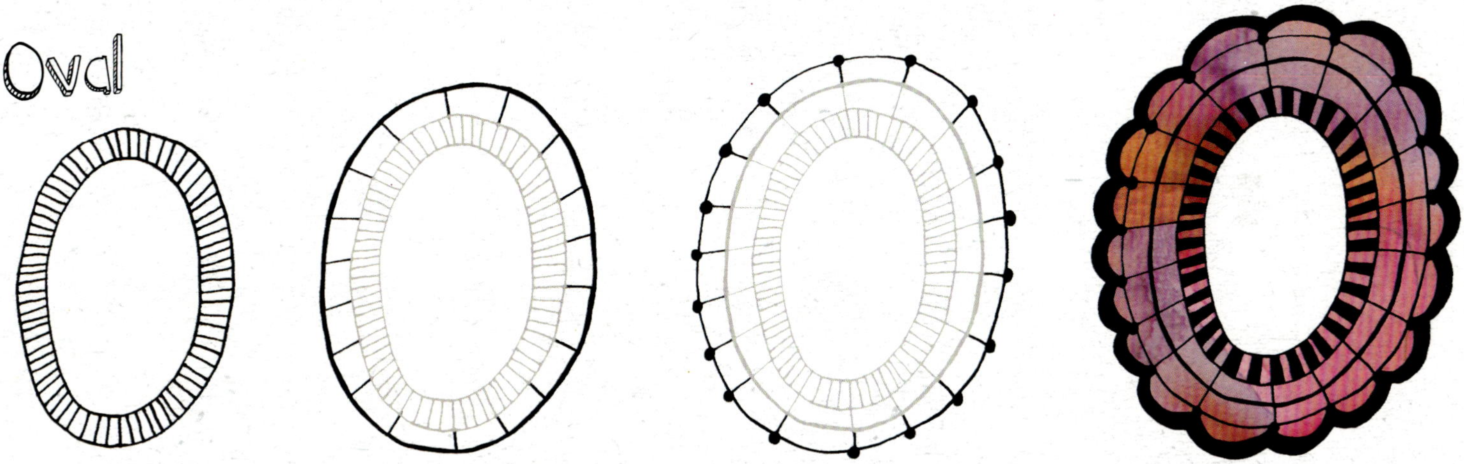

Draw an oval shape with a larger oval around the outside. Draw lines close together inside. Add larger ovals and divide them up into equal sections, as shown. Add curves around the outside of the frame, looping from line to line. Colour with watercolour paints and varying tones.

Star

To make a star-shaped frame draw two interlocking triangles, one on top of the other. Add larger stars around the outside. In light pencil, draw curves around the outside. Paint the frame. When it's dry, ink over the lines varying the thickness to make it interesting. Add pretty detail!

CARICATURES

1

THIS LAD HAS SPIKY HAIR AND A FIRM JAWLINE AND CHEEKBONES. LET'S EXAGGERATE THESE! START WITH SOME GUIDELINES FOR THE EYES AND NOSE, THEN USE A LIGHT PENCIL TO SKETCH IN THE BASIC HEAD SHAPE AND FEATURES.

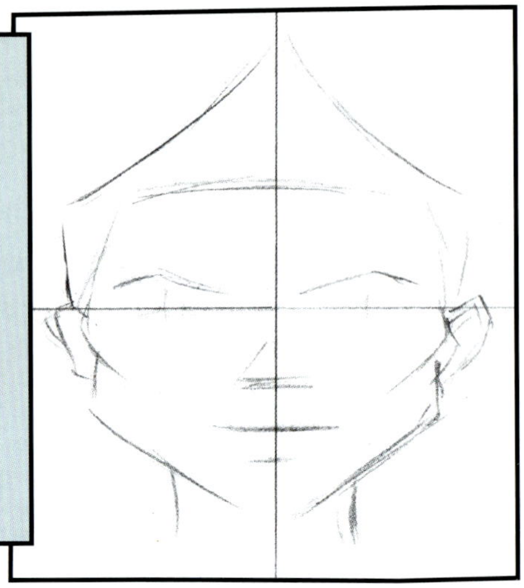

1

THIS GIRL'S HAIR SWEEPS OVER ONE EYE, MAKING THE OTHER EYE LOOK HUGE. SHE ALSO HAS FRECKLES AND AN OVAL FACE. USING GUIDELINES, LIGHTLY SKETCH AN EXAGGERATED OVAL HEAD SHAPE AND HAIR.

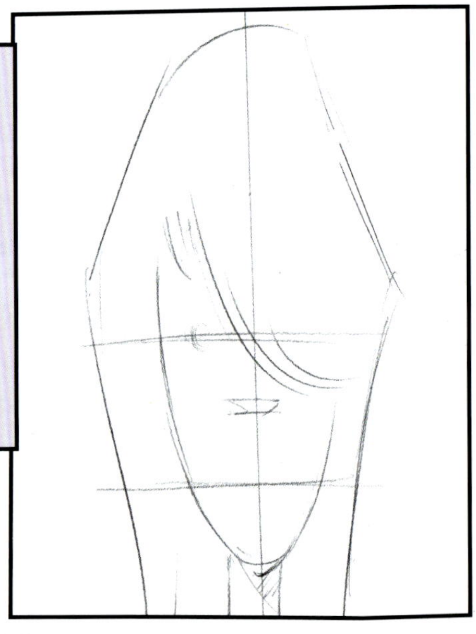

1

THIS GUY'S KEY FEATURES ARE HIS GLASSES AND HEAD SHAPE. THE GLASSES DIVIDE HIS HEAD IN TWO, EMPHASIZING HIS FOREHEAD AND EARS. MAP SOME GUIDELINES AND SKETCH IN THE MAIN SHAPES.

A CARICATURE IS A PICTURE THAT EXAGGERATES CERTAIN FEATURES FOR COMICAL EFFECT. START WITH A PHOTO OR SKETCH OF A PERSON, THEN EXAGGERATE THE FEATURES THAT STAND OUT - MAYBE A DISTINCTIVE NOSE OR WACKY HAIRSTYLE!

2

USE A SOFTER PENCIL TO START ADDING IN SOME OF THE DETAIL. LOOK AT THE SHAPE OF THE EYES, NOSE AND MOUTH, AND SLIGHTLY EXAGGERATE THEM.

3

KEEP REFERRING BACK TO THE PHOTO. USE COLOUR TO BRING THE CARICATURE TO LIFE!

2

MAKE HER EYE SHAPE SLIGHTLY BIGGER, SEPARATE OUT THE EYELASHES AND SKETCH IN FRECKLES. YOU CAN MAKE THE HAIR MORE SHAGGY TO EMPHASIZE THE STRAIGHT STYLE.

3

YOU ARE PLAYING UP THE HAIR, SO MAKE IT COLOURFUL, WITH A DRAMATIC STREAK. ADD COLOUR TO THE FACE TOO.

2

ADD DETAIL TO THE FACE AND SHADE IN THE DARKER AREAS, EMPHASIZING HIS FOREHEAD. LEAVE WHITE HIGHLIGHTS, PARTICULARLY ON THE GLASSES.

3

BRING OUT THE CARICATURE, WITH COLOUR, USING GREYS, BLACKS, BLUES AND WHITE HIGHLIGHTS.

CROCODILE

1 SKETCH OUT THE BASIC SHAPE OF THE CROCODILE'S BODY WITH A LIGHT, SHARP PENCIL. ADD ROUGH CIRCLE SHAPES FOR THE THREE LEGS YOU'LL SEE.

2 DRAW AN OVAL SHAPE FOR THE HEAD BEFORE ADDING IN THE OPEN MOUTH. SKETCH IN THE ROUGH DETAIL OF THE MOUTH AND ADD SOME FEET FOR THE BEGINNING OF THE CLAWS.

3 SKETCH OUT THE OUTLINE OF THE CROCODILE. DRAW TWO LINES RUNNING PARALLEL ALONG HIS BACK. USING A GRID SYSTEM, DRAW A GUIDE FOR THE SCALES ON THE LIMBS AND BODY.

4 ADD THE EYES, CLAWS, TEETH AND BACK SCALES, MAKING SURE THE SCALES FOLLOW THE CONTOUR OF THE BODY. MARK SMALL CURVES FOR SCALES ON THE FEET AND BACK.

5 USING THE GRID AGAIN, ROUND OFF THE SQUARES AND FILL IN THE GAPS WITH SHADES OF PENCIL. TO CREATE A SOFT, EVEN TONE, ANGLE YOUR PENCIL AND USE GENTLE SWEEPING MARKS. PUSH HARDER FOR HEAVIER TONES.

Applying shading to the crocodile's body gives a fantastic feeling of scaly texture across the whole picture.

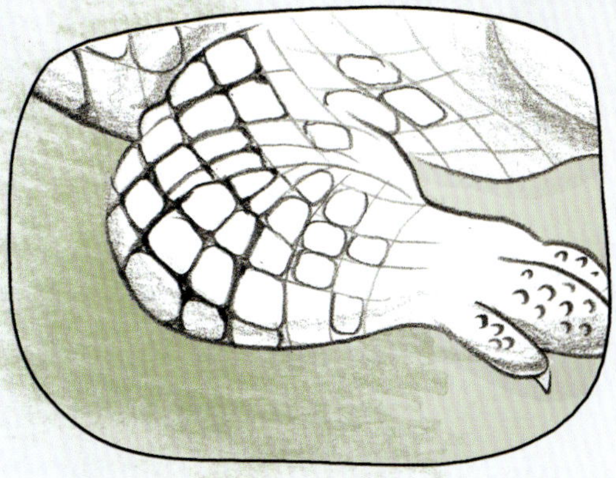

6 FINISH OFF YOUR DRAWING WITH COLOUR. ADD TONES OF GREEN AND SKIN MARKS ACROSS THE BODY WITH SMALL CIRCLES AND DOTS.

Draw in a suitably swampy background for your croc.

TORNADO

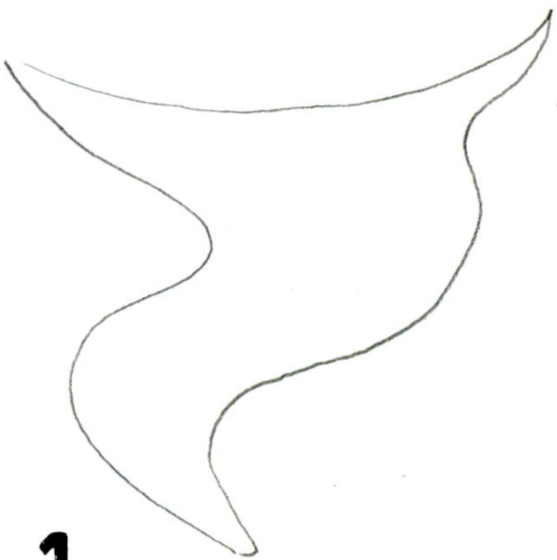

1

DRAW THE OUTLINE OF YOUR TORNADO USING WAVY LINES. THINK ABOUT HOW A TORNADO TWISTS FROM SIDE TO SIDE, WIDENING OUT TOWARDS THE TOP.

2

ADD AN OVAL AT THE TOP OF THE TORNADO. THIS WILL GIVE YOUR DRAWING A 3D EFFECT AND IT WILL SEEM AS IF YOU'RE ABLE TO LOOK DOWN INTO THE TORNADO FROM ABOVE!

Scratchy pen-and-ink linework helps to create a feeling of movement. Blotches of colour that aren't perfect will also add to the sense of chaos!

3

ADD LOTS OF CURVED LINES TO SUGGEST MOVEMENT. DRAW THEM AT VARYING ANGLES AS YOU MOVE UPWARDS, FOLLOWING THE TWISTING SHAPE OF THE TORNADO. ADD THE OUTLINES OF SOME SIMPLE OBJECTS.

4

ADD MORE CURVED LINES, DRAWING THEM CLOSE TOGETHER IN THE AREAS THAT NEED TO LOOK LIKE THEY'RE IN THE SHADE. SKETCH MORE OBJECTS AND ADD DETAIL TO THE FIRST ONES. ADD LEAVES AND CLOUDS, THEN USE SOME SCRATCHY LINEWORK FOR THE GROUND.

MONSTER

PIECE TOGETHER DIFFERENT IMAGINATIVE BODY PARTS TO CREATE A MOB OF MASHED-UP MONSTERS!

1

START WITH THE MONSTER'S BODY. USE A SIMPLE CIRCLE, BENDING THE LINES A LITTLE, THEN ADD MONSTER DETAIL ON TOP, SUCH AS SPIKES OR STRIPES.

2

FOR THE LEGS, TRY TENTACLES, LEGS WITH WEBBED FEET LIKE A BIRD, BIG HAIRY ONES WITH GIANT CLAWS OR ANYTHING ELSE YOU CAN THINK OF. GO WILD!

3

SIMILARLY FOR THE HANDS, THERE ARE SO MANY POSSIBILITIES! TRY SIMPLE CLAWS, A BIG HAIRY HAND WITH SHARP NAILS OR EVEN A CLAW LIKE A SEA CREATURE.

Attach the hands directly to the body, or draw long wavy lines for arms.

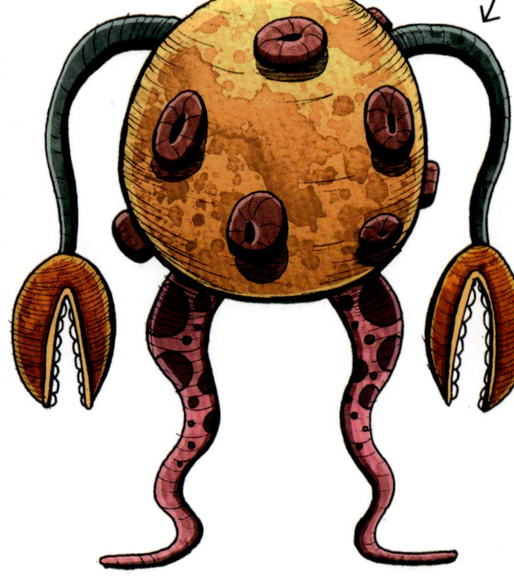

MASH-UP

4

FOR INTEREST, GIVE YOUR MONSTER SOMETHING OTHER THAN TWO EYES – TRY ONE LARGE ONE IN THE MIDDLE OF THE HEAD, PUT A FEW ON LITTLE STALKS OR DRAW ON LOADS!

Draw a head with a similar texture to the body so that it looks connected.

5

THE MOUTH SHOULD BE QUITE BIG TO MAKE THE MONSTER LOOK SCARY. AND DON'T FORGET THE TEETH! THE SHARPER THE TEETH, THE SCARIER THE MONSTER!

6

ADD MASSIVE HORNS COMING OUT OF THE SIDE OF THE MONSTER'S HEAD OR MAYBE SMALLER ONES ON THE FRONT. DON'T FORGET YOU DON'T HAVE TO STOP AT JUST TWO!

FERRIS WHEEL

1

DRAW TWO OVAL SHAPES TO FORM THE MAIN STRUCTURE OF THE WHEEL. THIS DRAWING USES PERSPECTIVE, SO THE WHEEL WILL LOOK ELLIPTICAL RATHER THAN PERFECTLY ROUND.

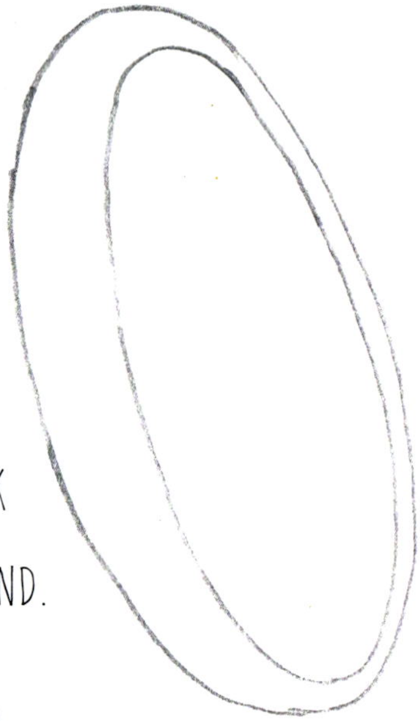

2

DRAW TWO PARALLEL GUIDELINES THROUGH THE CENTRE OF THE WHEEL. USE THEM TO POSITION TWO MORE ELLIPSES. THEN DRAW PERSPECTIVE LINES RADIATING OUT FROM THE LARGER ELLIPSE.

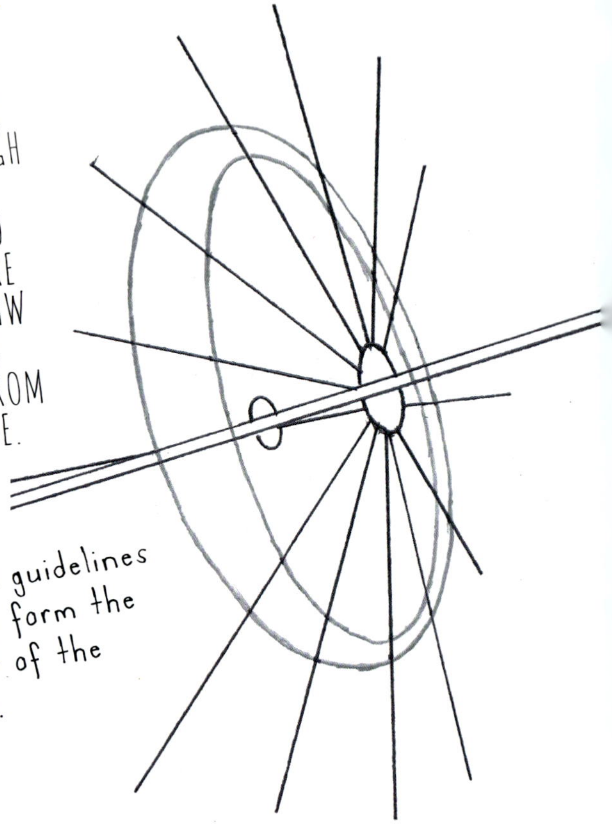

These parallel guidelines will also help form the central pivot of the Ferris wheel.

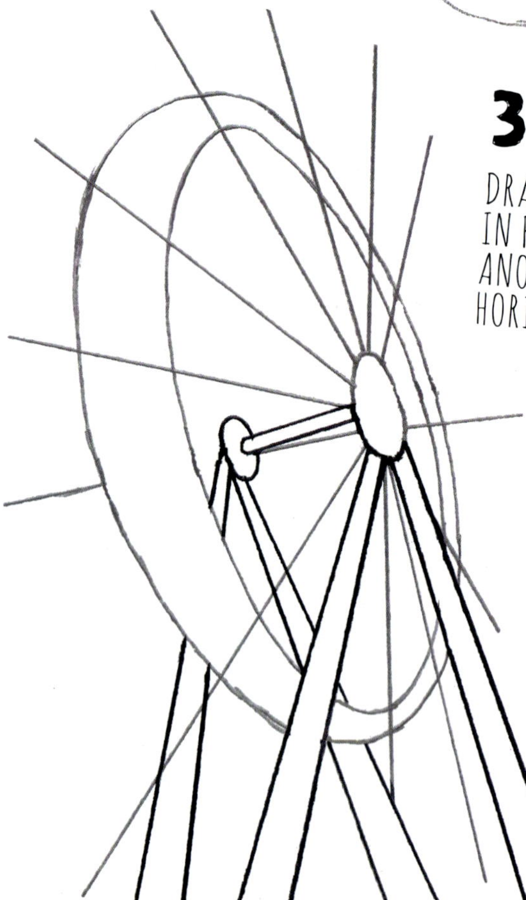

3

DRAW A TALL A-SHAPED BASE IN FRONT OF THE WHEEL, WITH ANOTHER BEHIND IT. ADD A HORIZONTAL CROSS BAR.

Don't worry about wobbly lines or other imperfections. They'll add to the feeling of movement!

4

LIGHTLY SKETCH SPOKES RADIATING OUT FROM THE SMALLER ELLIPSE. ADD A CURVE TO THE LARGER ELLIPSE TO MAKE IT LOOK 3D. THEN USE SIMPLE ELLIPSES TO FORM THE SHAPES OF THE BASKETS AND PASSENGERS.

5

ADD LOTS OF CIRCLES AND ELLIPSES FOR THE LIGHTS, THEN DRAW IN A FEW HUMAN FIGURES. AT THIS LOW ANGLE, IT'S REALLY ONLY THEIR HEADS THAT WOULD BE VISIBLE. COLOUR YOUR FERRIS WHEEL USING BRIGHT, CONTRASTING TONES.

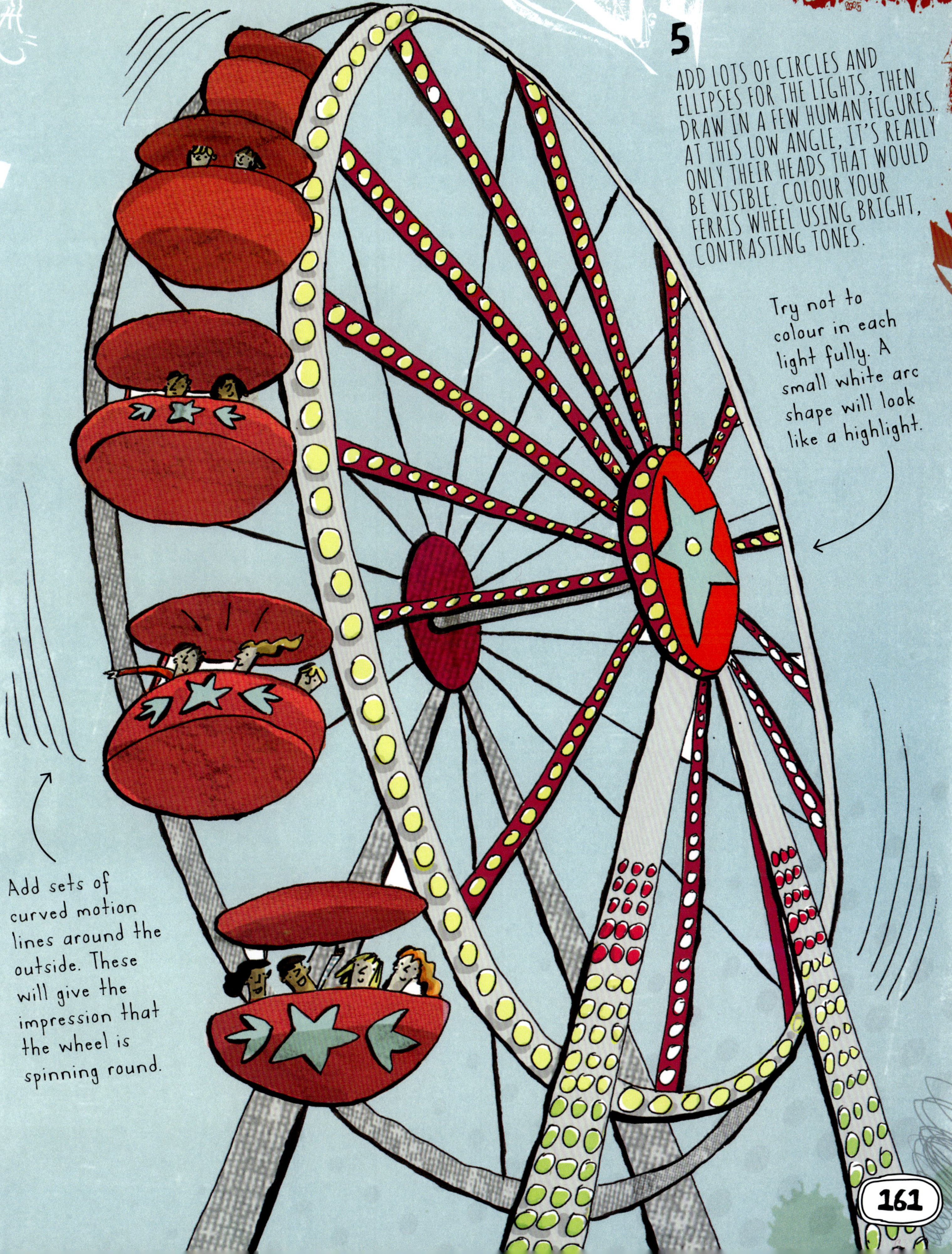

Try not to colour in each light fully. A small white arc shape will look like a highlight.

Add sets of curved motion lines around the outside. These will give the impression that the wheel is spinning round.

SCAREDY CAT

1 DRAW AN EGG-SHAPED BODY, CONTINUING THE TOP CURVE TO FORM THE CAT'S REAR LEG. ADD SIMPLE SHAPES FOR THE FRONT LEGS AND TAIL. DRAW A CIRCLE FOR THE MOUTH AND A RECTANGLE FOR THE HEAD.

2 DRAW ROUGH TRIANGULAR SHAPES FOR THE CAT'S CHEEKS AND WHISKERS, AND CIRCLES FOR ITS FEET, TOES AND EYES. USE THE CURVED LINE RUNNING THROUGH THE FACE TO HELP YOU POSITION AN OPEN MOUTH.

For a more subtle fur texture, apply pressure at the start of each pencil stroke, easing off as your pencil flicks sharply upwards.

3 WORK ON THE FACIAL DETAILS, ADDING TEETH, WHISKERS AND A TONGUE. DRAW IN THE TOES AND CLAWS. THEN SKETCH LOTS OF PARALLEL LINES ALONG THE OUTLINE OF THE CAT'S BODY TO SUGGEST FUR STANDING ON END!

Small details will help make your scaredy cat look even more afraid. Draw large ovals for its wide eyes, adding raised eyebrows just above the head. Make the mouth wide open, and use zig-zags for the whiskers.

4 DRAW IN THE BODY FUR BY USING SWEEPING PENCIL STROKES IN AN UPWARD DIRECTION. USE SMALLER STROKES TO ADD SOME STRIPES.

5 NOW USE CONTRASTING PENCIL CRAYON COLOURS. THIS PICTURE USES GREEN AND BROWN TONES, WITH CERTAIN AREAS LEFT WHITE, SUCH AS THE EYES AND HIGHLIGHTS ON THE MOUTH AND PAWS. ADD MOVEMENT LINES TO ADD TO THE 'SCAREDY-CAT' EFFECT!

CYBORG

1

DRAW A STICK FIGURE TO SHOW THE BASIC POSE AND PROPORTIONS. SKETCH A SLIGHT CURVE FOR THE BACK AND HORIZONTAL LINES FOR THE HIPS AND SHOULDERS. ADD ARMS AND LEGS AND AN OVAL SHAPE FOR THE HEAD.

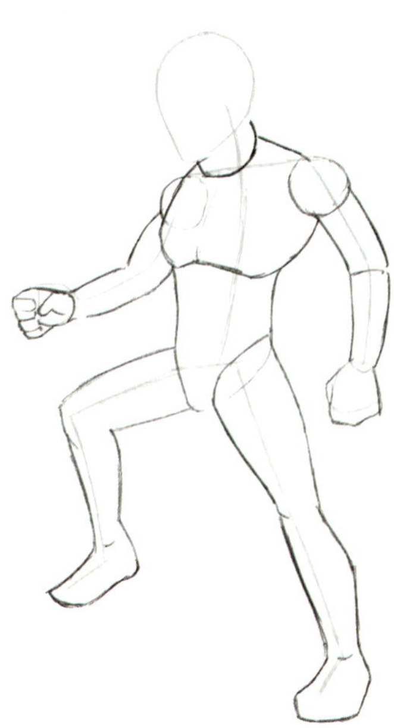

2

TO FLESH OUT THE LIMBS, DRAW CYLINDERS AROUND THE STICK LINES, MAKING THE LINES CURVE OUTWARDS TO SUGGEST BULGING MUSCLES. ADD IN THE CHEST MUSCLES, PLUS A CIRCLE TO SUGGEST A PUMPED-UP SHOULDER!

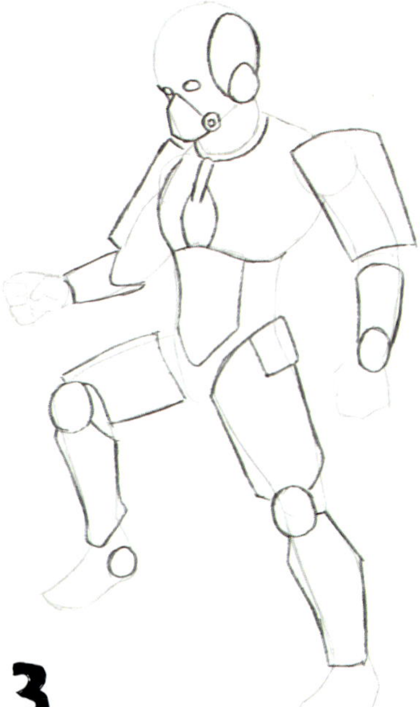

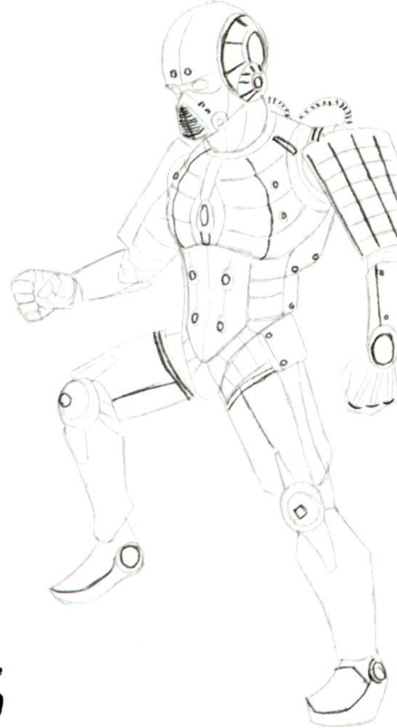

3

RUB OUT THE STICK LINES. DRAW THE CYBORG'S ARMOUR BY SKETCHING SHAPES THAT MIMIC THE BODY PARTS UNDERNEATH, BUT LARGER TO GIVE THE IMPRESSION OF WEIGHT AND THICKNESS. USE CIRCLES FOR THE WRIST, KNEE AND ANKLE JOINTS.

4

WORK ON THE ARMOUR DETAIL. ADD CIRCULAR LIGHTS AND DRAW CURVED LINES ON THE CHEST AND SHOULDER AREAS. CREATE A SCI-FI FEEL BY ADDING TUBING AND MORE ELABORATE KNEE JOINTS. ADD MORE DETAIL TO THE MASK AND HELMET.

5

REFINE THE DETAIL FURTHER. DRAW RIVETS ON THE ARMOUR, LINES ON THE MASK AND A CRISS-CROSS PATTERN ON THE SHOULDER PLATE. ADD LINES TO DIVIDE PARTS OF THE ARMOUR INTO SMALLER SECTIONS, SUCH AS THE HELMET AND UPPER LEG AREAS.

6

PAINT YOUR CYBORG WITH COOL COLOURS. TO MAKE THE CYBORG LOOK METALLIC, USE NARROW BANDS OF DIFFERENT TONES, ESPECIALLY FOR THE HIGHLIGHTS, TO SHOW LIGHT REFLECTING OFF A SHINY SURFACE.

Draw rocks using a mix of smooth and angular lines to form spiky peaks. Add plenty of shadows for dramatic contrast.

Add small, dark lines to the armour to suggest wear and tear.

FUNKY CAKE

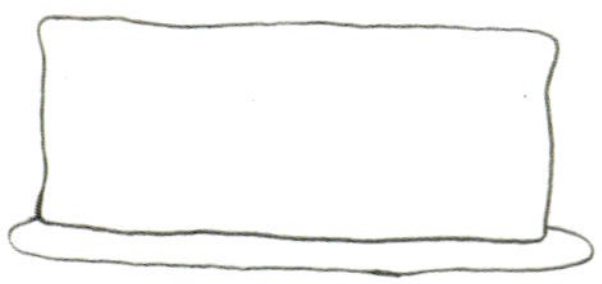

1 DRAW A SIMPLE, SLIGHTLY CURVED RECTANGLE FOR THE CAKE BASE. ADD THE EDGE OF A PLATE BENEATH.

2 REPEAT THE RECTANGLE SHAPE AS MANY TIMES AS YOU LIKE. IF YOU'RE FEELING HUNGRY AND EXTRA CREATIVE, MAKE IT A REALLY TALL CAKE!

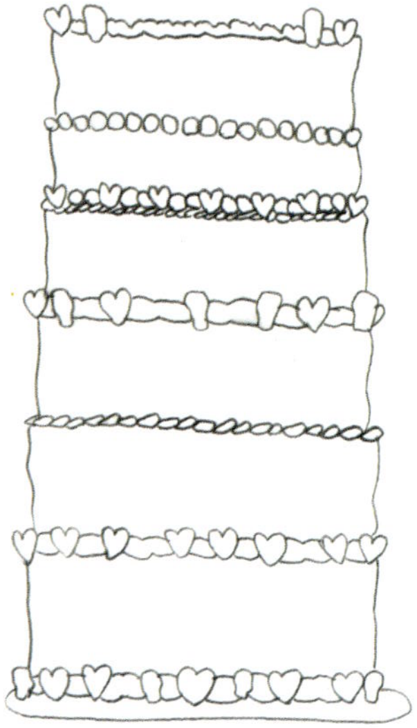

3 DRAW IN THE DECORATION BETWEEN THE LAYERS. TRY HEARTS AND SKULLS OR ANYTHING YOU FANCY. LITTLE CIRCLE PATTERNS MAKE GREAT ICING.

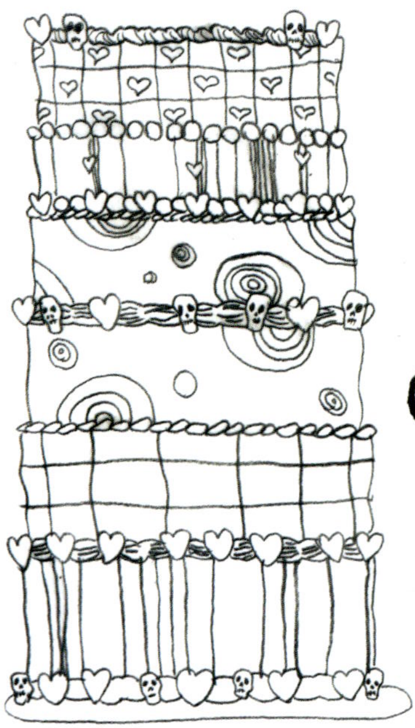

4 ADD MORE DETAIL, SUCH AS A CHECK PATTERN OR REPEATED VERTICAL LINES. THE MORE DETAIL YOU ADD, THE MORE INTERESTING THE CAKE WILL BE.

Colour in your cake with limited colours. Check out magazines or websites to find the best looks!

ROBOT

1

USING A LIGHT PENCIL, DRAW SQUARES AND RECTANGLES TO BEGIN THE ROUGH SHAPES OF YOUR ROBOT. INCLUDE A HEAD, BODY, ARMS, LEGS AND FEET.

2

DRAW THE EYES AND JOIN UP THE SQUARES TO MAKE THE ROBOT LOOK MORE SOLID. ADD SHAPES ON THE FEET TO ADD DIMENSION TO THE ROBOT.

3

START ADDING SOME DETAIL. USE SIMPLE SHAPES FOR A FACE, HEADPHONES AND ANTENNAE. ADD CLAW HANDS TO THE ARMS AND DETAIL TO THE LEGS.

4

ADD DETAILS SUCH AS DOTS FOR RIVETS AND PANELS WITH DIALS TO MAKE THE ROBOT LOOK MORE MECHANICAL. GO OVER THE OUTLINE.

5

NOW ADD COLOUR – GREY AND PALE BLUE ARE GOOD TO SHOW METAL. ADD SOME LIVELY COLOURS LIKE ORANGE AND YELLOW FOR CONTRAST.

PICTURES IN LIGHTS

1 DRAW A BASIC CITY SKYLINE OF DIFFERENT-SHAPED BUILDINGS WITH WHITE CHALK OR PAINT ONTO A PIECE OF BLACK CARD OR PAPER, LIKE THIS.

2 DRAW SMALL WHITE AND YELLOW RECTANGLES TO LIGHT UP ALL THE BUILDINGS AND MAKE YOUR CITY LOOK BRIGHT AND BUSY.

Use bright chalk, paint or gel pens to bring your picture to life. Black paper makes an easy night sky!

3 USE LINES, SWIRLS AND DOTS COMING OUT OF A CENTRAL POINT TO MAKE FIREWORKS. TRY DIFFERENT DESIGNS BEFORE ADDING THEM TO YOUR PICTURE.

4 USE BRIGHT COLOURS TO FILL THE NIGHT SKY WITH YOUR FIREWORK DESIGNS. ADD A FEW BRIGHT STARS INTO THE PICTURE TOO.

CARTOON CUTE ANIMALS

LEARN TO DRAW DIFFERENT FEATURES THEN HAVE FUN PUTTING THEM TOGETHER TO CREATE YOUR OWN CUTE CARTOON ANIMALS.

TAILS

THINK SHAGGY AND WAGGY OR THIN AND CURLY – TAILS CAN ADD A LOT OF CHARACTER TO YOUR ANIMALS!

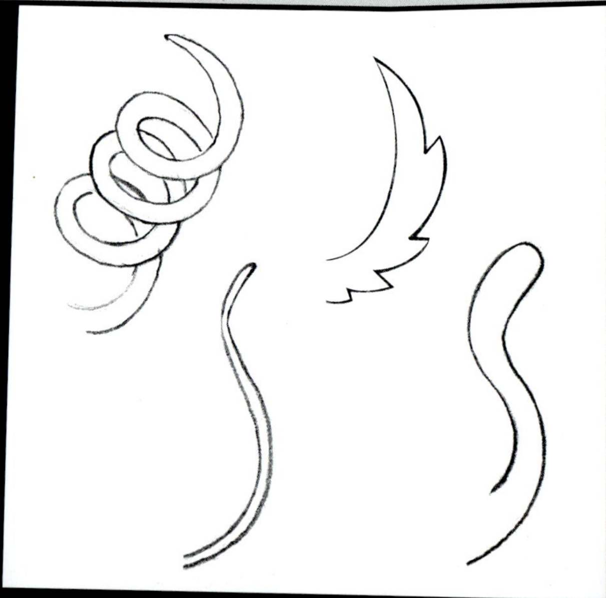

PAWS

HERE ARE SOME SIMPLE SHAPES YOU CAN USE FOR PAWS AND HOOFS. BIG PAWS RELATIVE TO A BODY CAN EMPHASIZE THE CARTOON FEEL.

NOSES

TRY AN UPSIDE-DOWN TRIANGLE FOR A NOSE AND SIMPLE LINES FOR A MOUTH. USE PENCIL STROKES FLICKING OUTWARDS FOR WHISKERS.

EYES

EXPERIMENT WITH DIFFERENT-SHAPED EYELIDS – THE SLANT OF THE LINE CAN MAKE YOUR CHARACTER LOOK MEAN, CROSS OR SAD. USE A SMALL CIRCLE FOR AN EYE GLINT.

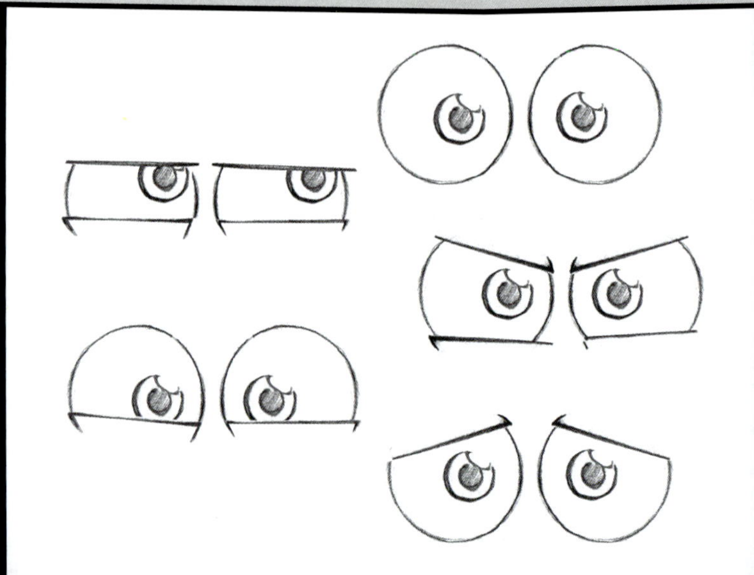

Add dark colours and shadows to give dimension to the cartoon figures.

Cartoon characters are just that - cartoons! They don't need to look real, so you can use realistic colours, but try wacky ones too!

SURFER

1 DRAW A VERTICAL ELLIPSE WITH POINTED ENDS FOR THE SURFBOARD. DRAW STICK LINES FOR THE SURFER'S LIMBS, HIPS, SHOULDERS AND TORSO. FOR THE CROUCHING POSITION, DRAW THE LEGS BENT AT THE KNEES, WITH THE UPPER BODY LEANING FORWARDS SLIGHTLY. ADD A CIRCLE HEAD.

2 FLESH OUT YOUR FIGURE'S BODY PARTS, USING SAUSAGE SHAPES FOR HIS LIMBS. DRAW CIRCLES FOR HIS KNEE JOINTS AND ADD ROUGH SHAPES FOR HIS HANDS.

3 SKETCH THE POSITIONS OF THE FACIAL FEATURES AND ADD AN OUTLINE FOR THE HAIR. DRAW THE SHAPE OF THE BAGGY SURF SHORTS, THEN ADD FINGERS.

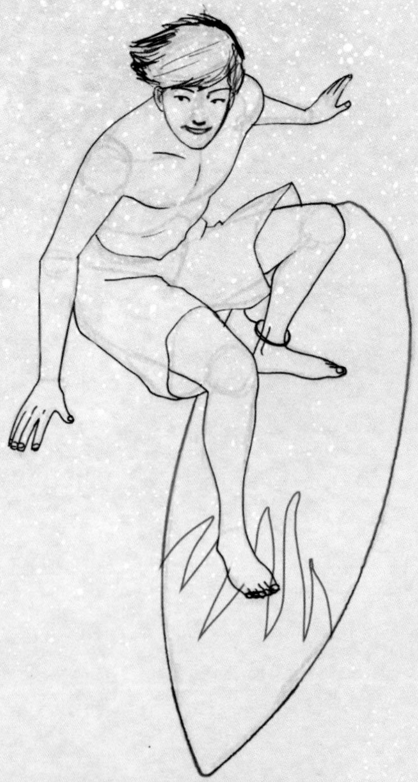

4 REFINE THE SURFER'S BODY AND FACIAL FEATURES AND DRAW IN THE TEXTURE OF HIS HAIR. ADD A FLAME DESIGN TO THE SURFBOARD USING WOBBLY ZIG-ZAG LINES. RUB OUT ANY GUIDELINES.

5 PAINT YOUR SURFER'S SKIN USING A FLAT BROWN COLOUR. THEN USE PALER HUES ON TOP TO BRING OUT HIS MUSCLE TONE, WITH BANDS OF WHITE FOR HIGHLIGHTS. GIVE HIM A NECKLACE AND BRACELET, AND PAINT A FLOWERY DESIGN ON HIS SHORTS. COLOUR THE FLAMES RED FOR DRAMATIC IMPACT.

Add sea spray by dipping an old toothbrush in white paint. Then run your finger along the bristles to flick tiny dots of paint onto the picture.

Choose a simple but striking colour scheme. Here, the red flames contrast well with the green of the surfer's shorts.

Paint the background with a big brush. Use watercolour washes in different shades of blue, starting with a lighter tone first, before merging in slightly darker areas.

COOL SHADES

TRY SKETCHING A SIMPLE PAIR OF GLASSES, THEN GET CREATIVE AND VARY THESE FOR SOME OF YOUR OWN COOL DESIGNS.

1 SKETCH TWO ROUNDED LENS SHAPES, THEN DRAW AN EXTRA LINE AROUND EACH ONE TO CREATE THE FRAMES. ADD A BRIDGE WHERE THE SHADES SIT ON THE NOSE, PLUS AN EXTRA BAR ABOVE THAT, IF YOU WANT.

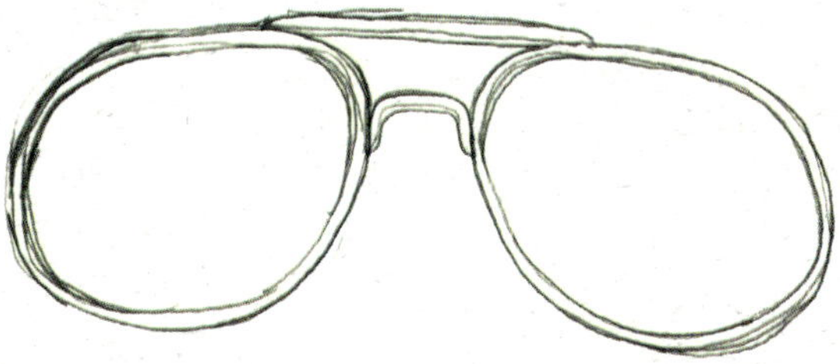

2 DRAW THE ARMS OF YOUR GLASSES. THEY WILL BE PARTIALLY VISIBLE THROUGH THE SHADES, SO ADD A CROSSHATCH EFFECT ON THE LENSES, LEAVING CERTAIN AREAS WHITE TO GIVE THE EFFECT OF REFLECTIONS ON THE GLASS.

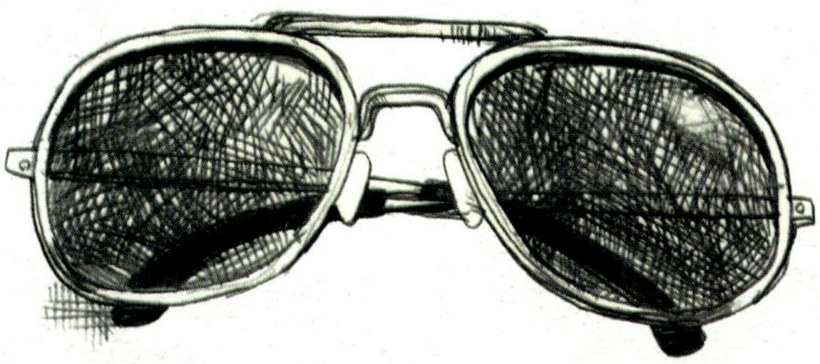

3 TRY DRAWING THE SAME PAIR OF GLASSES FROM A SIDEWAYS PERSPECTIVE WITH THE ARMS STRAIGHTENED OUT, LIKE THIS. THE LENS AND ARM NEAREST TO US WILL NEED TO LOOK SLIGHTLY BIGGER.

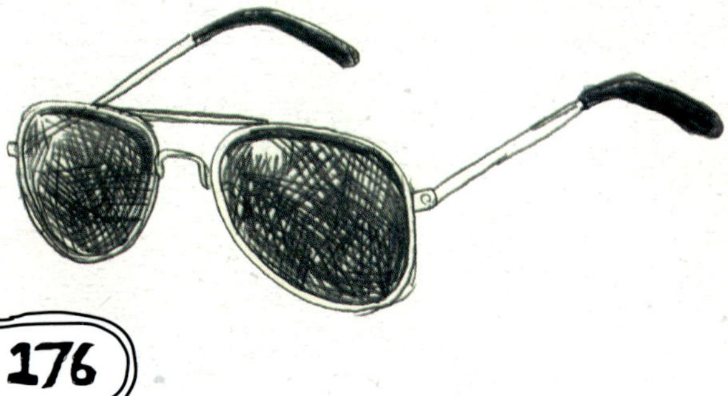

NOW THINK ABOUT HOW YOUR SHADES WILL LOOK ON SOMEONE'S FACE. HOW REFLECTIVE OR TRANSPARENT WILL THEY BE?

You could draw your shades as flat, black circles. Add narrow bands of white for reflections.

When drawing shades in profile, the nearer lens will look more like an ellipse. The other will only be partially visible.

To draw highly reflective glasses, add white, wavy bands on top of a dark base colour.

SHADES CAN BE PLAIN OR PATTERNED, AND CAN COME IN ALL SORTS OF SHAPES AND SIZES...

STANDARD SHAPE

STANDARD FRAMES ARE BASICALLY SQUARES WITH CURVED EDGES. EXPERIMENT WITH DIFFERENT SHAPES, CHOOSING HEAVY BLACK FRAMES, OR EVEN ONES WITH AN UNUSUAL STRIPED EFFECT!

SECRET AGENT

STRIPY

PATTERNED SHADES

A SIMPLE REPEATED MOTIF IS GOOD FOR DECORATING YOUR FRAMES, SUCH AS THESE THIN LINES. YOU COULD ALSO TRY GIVING YOUR FRAMES A MOTTLED PAINT EFFECT.

HALF-PATTERNED FRAMES

PATTERNED LENSES

SHAPED FRAMES

PLAY AROUND WITH DIFFERENT SHAPES AND STYLES. FROM POINTY EDGES TO LOVE HEARTS, THEY CAN BE ANY SHAPE YOU LIKE.

DIAMANTÉ BLING

LOVE HEARTS

POP IDOL

SQUARE

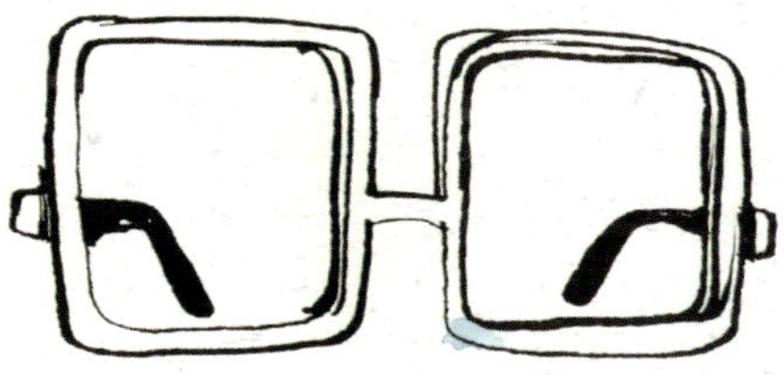

STARS

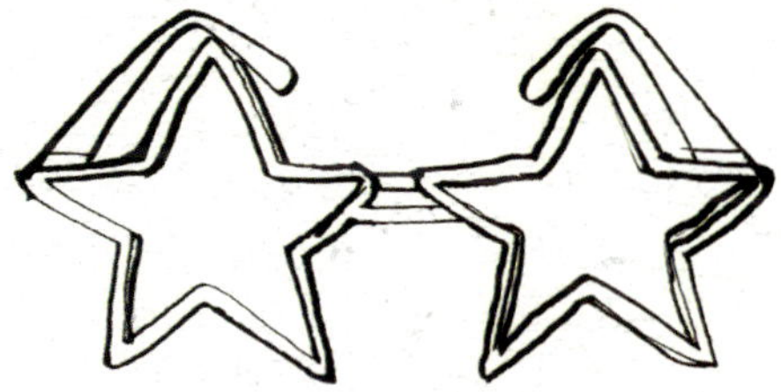

STATEMENT SHADES

EVEN A BASIC STYLE OF FRAME CAN BE LIVENED UP BY ADDING QUIRKY DETAILS OR A REFLECTIVE PATTERN TO THE LENSES.

WACKY WINDSCREEN WIPERS

SKI CHIC

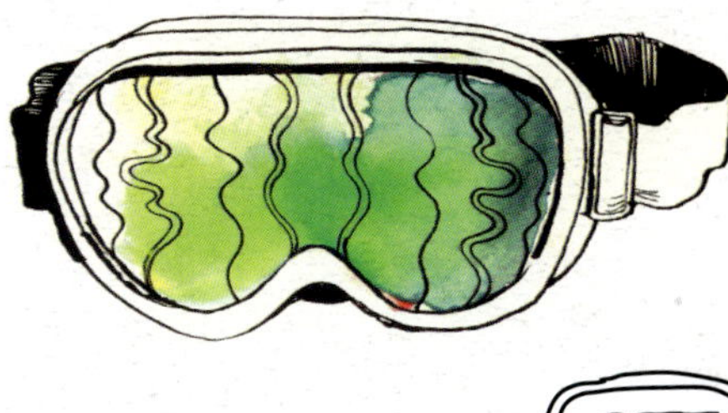

FRANKENSTEIN'S MONSTER

1

DRAW BASIC GUIDE SHAPES FOR THE MONSTER'S HEAD, BODY, LEGS AND HANDS.

2

USE SAUSAGE SHAPES TO BUILD UP HIS FEET AND LIMBS. ADD THE FINGERS, DRAWING SMALL CIRCLES AT THE END OF EACH ONE.

Draw sausage shapes for the ears and eyebrows, adding round and triangular shapes for the other facial features.

3

POLISH THE OUTLINE OF THE MONSTER AND DRAW SOME CLOTHES. ADD MORE DETAIL TO THE HANDS AND HEAD.

4

SHADE THE PARTS OF YOUR MONSTER THAT ARE IN SHADOW. USE MORE SHADING FOR THE CREASES IN HIS CLOTHES AND ADD SOME TO HIS FACE TO EMPHASIZE HIS SCARY EYES!

Use a fine point for this shading technique. Make areas look darker with rows of horizontal or vertical lines.

5

WHEN COLOURING YOUR MONSTER, MAKE HIS GREEN SKIN LIGHTER THAN THE OTHER COLOURS IN ORDER TO DRAW OUR ATTENTION TO THE SCARIER PARTS OF HIS BODY. FOR THE CLOTHES, USE TONES THAT WORK WELL WITH GREEN, SUCH AS DARK BLUE AND PURPLE.

Add highlights to your monster's hands and face. These light bands of colour contrast dramatically with the black lines, emphasizing the scary effect.

Add a simple brick wall behind the monster and use pale tones to help him stand out from the page.

Woodland Animals

1

STARTING WITH A LIGHT PENCIL, DRAW CIRCLES FOR A SQUIRREL'S HEAD, LEG AND NUT. SKETCH IN EARS, ARMS, LEGS AND A BUSHY TAIL.

2

ADD THE NOSE, EYE AND WHISKERS. BUILD THE SHAPE BY SMOOTHING OUT THE CURVES. ERASE ANY GUIDELINES.

3

USE DIFFERENT TONES OF THE SAME COLOUR TO SHADE IN THE FUR. THIS WILL CREATE THE EFFECT OF VOLUME. NOTICE WHERE THE FUR IS DARKER OR LIGHTER.

ANIMAL FUR

Use short pencil strokes, mixing different tones of the main colour. The direction of the strokes should follow the shape of the animal.

1

DRAW THE FOX'S SHAPE USING CIRCLES AND TRIANGLES. ADD A BEAN SHAPE FOR THE BODY, THEN ADD THE LEGS. NOTICE THE WAY THE BACK LEGS BEND.

1 TO DRAW A DEER, USE CIRCLES FOR THE HEAD AND KNEES AND RECTANGLES FOR THE NECK, BODY AND LEGS.

2 USING THE SHAPES AS A GUIDE, SMOOTH AND SOFTEN THE OUTLINE OF THE SHAPE. ADD EARS, NOSE, AN EYE, MOUTH AND TAIL.

3 ERASE THE GUIDELINES AND ADD SOME COLOUR. BLEND DIFFERENT BROWN PENCILS TO CREATE THE FUR AND ADD STROKES OF WHITE PAINT FOR THE DOTS. USE BLACK INK FOR THE FINAL DETAILS AND HOOVES.

2 DRAW AROUND YOUR GUIDELINES TO SMOOTH OUT THE FOX SHAPE. ADD DOTS FOR THE EYES AND NOSE. DRAW THE TAIL LIKE THE SHAPE OF A LETTER S.

3 ERASE ANY GUIDELINES, THEN USE COLOURED PENCILS TO DRAW THE FUR, FOLLOWING THE DIRECTION OF THE FOX'S SHAPE. ADD THE EYES, NOSE, MOUTH AND WHISKERS TO GIVE THE FOX PERSONALITY.

Add mushrooms to create a colourful scene. Use a rounded triangle for the cap and a rectangle for the stalk. Draw circles for spots then colour it all in.

MOUNTAIN BIKE

1 DRAW A LARGE CIRCLE FOR THE BACK WHEEL. SKETCH A SIMPLE 'H' SHAPE LEANING BACKWARDS NEXT TO IT. THIS FORMS THE BASIC SHAPE OF THE BIKE'S FRAME.

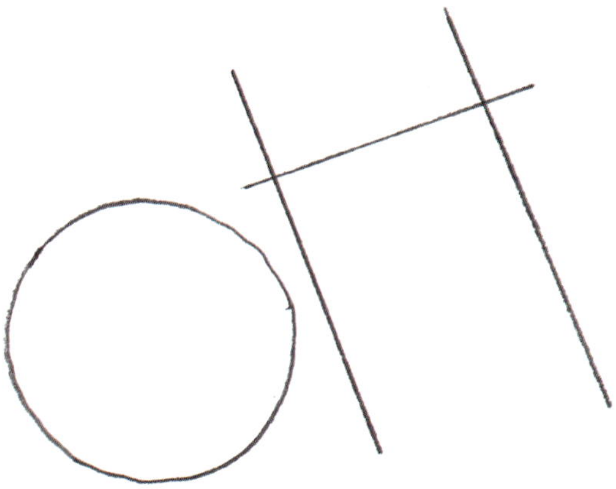

2 DRAW THE FRONT WHEEL BY ADDING ANOTHER CIRCLE THE SAME SIZE AS THE FIRST ONE. SKETCH A SMALLER CIRCLE FOR THE CHAIN WHEEL, THEN ADD A DIAGONAL LINE FROM THE CENTRE OF THIS WHEEL TO THE FRONT PART OF THE FRAME.

The two spokes of the 'H' frame need to go through the centre of both the front wheel and chain wheel.

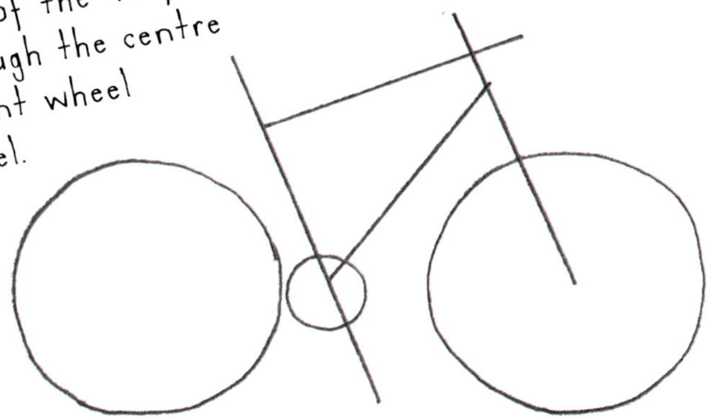

3 ADD SMALL ELLIPSES FOR THE SEAT AND HANDLEBARS, WITH LITTLE RECTANGLES TO MARK THE POSITIONS OF THE PEDAL. SKETCH ANOTHER CIRCLE FOR THE REAR CHAIN WHEEL.

4 FOLLOWING YOUR GUIDES, DRAW TWO PARALLEL LINES FOR EACH PART OF THE BICYCLE FRAME. SKETCH A LARGER CIRCLE AROUND EACH WHEEL SHAPE, AND ADD SMALLER ONES FOR THE GEAR SYSTEM. DRAW SETS OF PARALLEL LINES FOR THE SPOKES.

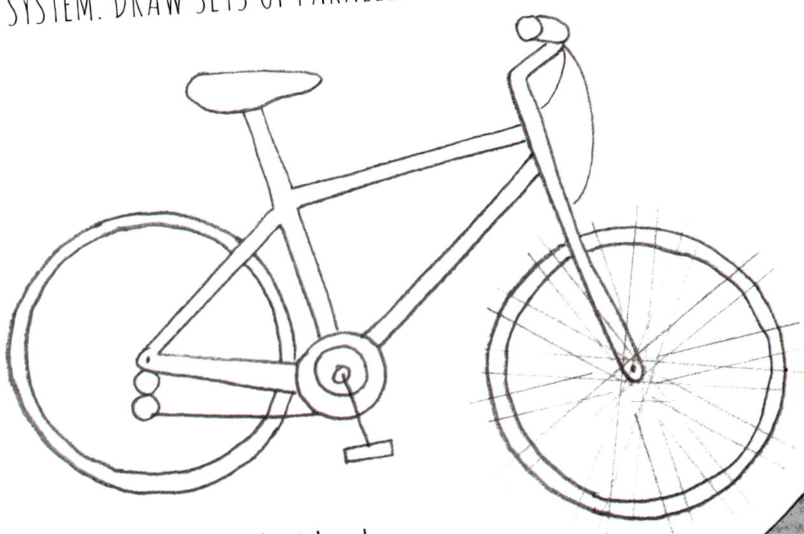

Use a ruler to draw the spokes for a professional-looking bike.

Don't worry if the spoke lines are incomplete. The faintness of the linework suggests that the spokes are very thin.

5 RUB OUT ANY LINES THAT AREN'T NEEDED. REFINE THE SPIKY SHAPE OF THE CHAIN WHEEL AND ADD OTHER DETAILS, SUCH AS THE WAVY BIKE CHAIN AND BRAKE CABLES AND PADS BETWEEN THE HANDLEBARS AND FRONT WHEEL.

6 GO OVER YOUR LINEWORK IN PEN AND INK. CHOOSE A BRIGHT COLOUR FOR THE FRAMEWORK TO CONTRAST WITH THE DARK TYRES. ADD MARKINGS TO THE FRAME FOR EXTRA VISUAL INTEREST.

Add a simple background in a contrasting tone to make your bike stand out from the page.

Try using a fine paintbrush and black Indian ink to add shadows and depth to your bike.

Straight patterns

IT IS AMAZING HOW MANY PATTERNS YOU CAN INVENT USING THE HUMBLE LINE! DOODLE SOME LINES AND SEE WHAT YOU COME UP WITH.

Lines and stripes

SIMPLE HAND-DRAWN VERTICAL LINES CAN MAKE A SURPRISINGLY SOPHISTICATED DESIGN. TRY THIN AND THICK STYLES OF STRIPES AND THEN COMBINE THEM. HAVE A COUPLE OF DIFFERENT-SIZED PENS AND BRUSHES TO HAND TO FIND WHAT WORKS BEST.

Draw pinstripes with a fine pen or brush.

A flat brush will make wide stripes.

The two styles combined look fab!

Use tonal colours of different widths.

Draw contrasting horizontal stripes.

Combine them to make a plaid pattern!

CHANGING THE DIRECTION, WIDTH AND COLOUR OF THE LINES ADDS TO THE VARIETY OF PATTERNS YOU CAN ACHIEVE. OVERLAPPING COLOURS CAN ADD TO THE PATTERN IN SURPRISING WAYS.

BUILDING UP CRISS-CROSS DIAGONALS IN DIFFERENT LINE WIDTHS CAN LOOK QUITE ORGANIC. TRY COMBINING TWO SIMPLE PATTERNS ON TOP OF EACH OTHER. TRY THIS WITH INK ON ABSORBENT PAPER TO GET A FUZZY EDGE TO THE LINES.

Mix up the width and direction.

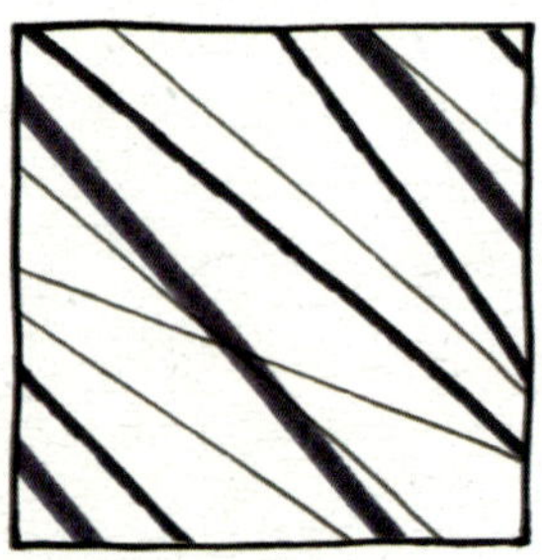

Change the corner-to-corner direction.

Lay one pattern on top of the other.

Zig-zags

ADD A SPLASH OF ZINGY COLOUR TO BLACK AND WHITE TO CREATE A LIVELY ZIG-ZAG PATTERN.

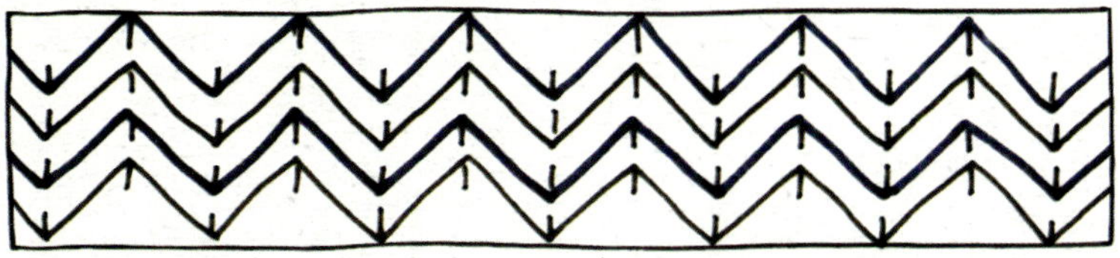

Dotted lines help keep the zig-zags symmetrical.

Experiment with thin and thick zig-zags.

Alternate between zig-zags in ink and paint.

Use your imagination to combine new patterns you have invented.

Grid squares

WORKING ON SQUARED PAPER CREATES A REGULAR, MOSAIC EFFECT.

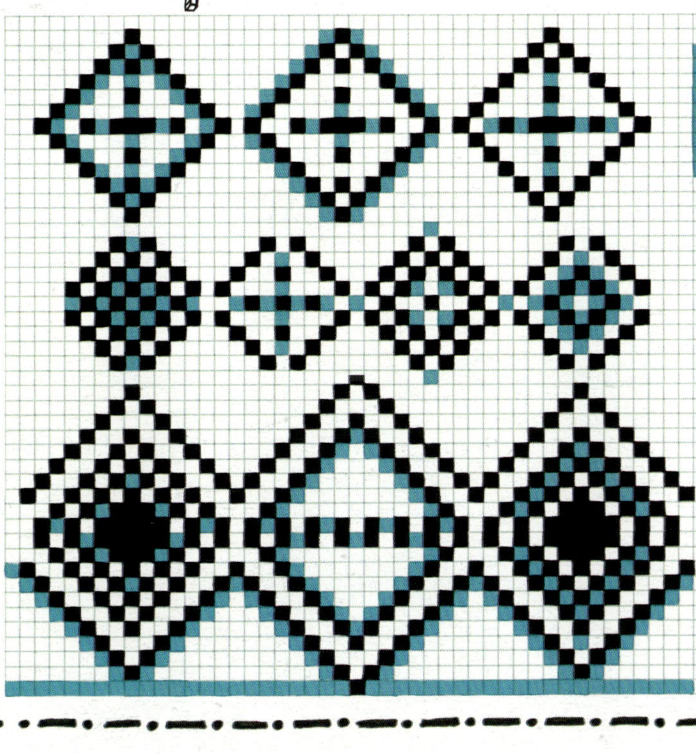

Using two colours, block in the squares to make diamond shapes. Experiment with different variations. Think of the squares you haven't coloured as part of the pattern too. When you have a couple of designs, try combining them.

TWISTY TREE

1 DRAW AN OUTLINE OF THE TREE. THEN, MOVING UPWARDS FROM THE ROOTS, DRAW LOTS OF SWEEPING, WAVY, SOMETIMES OVERLAPPING LINES. NOTICE THAT THE BRANCHES ARE THICKEST WHERE THEY MEET THE TRUNK. USE SINGLE LINES FOR TWIGS.

2 ADD MORE DETAIL TO THE TRUNK. FOR THE BARK TEXTURE, SKETCH LOTS OF PARALLEL LINES THAT ARE SLIGHTLY CURVED IN PLACES, FOLLOWING THE OVERALL SHAPE OF THE TREE. ADD EXTRA SWIRLS AND OTHER SHAPES TO MAKE THE BARK LOOK MORE INTERESTING.

3

ADD MUSHROOMS AND FUNGI AROUND YOUR TREE. DRAW CYLINDER SHAPES FOR STALKS, WITH EITHER A CIRCULAR OR CONICAL SHAPE ON TOP. DECORATE WITH LITTLE LUMPS AND USE SHADING LINES TO ADD DEPTH.

4

FOR A REALISTIC EFFECT, DRAW SOME OF YOUR BRANCHES SPLITTING OFF INTO TWO OR MORE SMALLER ONES. DON'T OVERDO THIS THOUGH! USE THIN, CROOKED LINES.

5

ONLY DRAW THE INDIVIDUAL LEAF SHAPES THAT ARE CLOSE TO THE VIEWER. FOR LEAVES THAT ARE MORE DISTANT, SIMPLY DRAW THE OUTLINE OF A BIG CLUMP OF LEAVES AND ADD A FEW VAGUE LEAF SHAPES HERE AND THERE FOR TEXTURE.

MANGA BOY

THIS IS A VERY JAPANESE STYLE OF DRAWING! SEE PAGES 120 AND 121 FOR A COOL MANGA GIRL.

1

USING A LIGHT PENCIL, LOOSELY SKETCH OUT SOME GUIDELINES TO GET THE FEEL OF THE MANGA BOY'S POSE. ANGLE THE SHOULDERS AND HEAD TO GIVE HIM SOME ATTITUDE.

2

SKETCH THE OUTLINE SHAPE OF THE FIGURE. EXAGGERATE THE FEATURES SLIGHTLY, SO MAKE THE HEAD A BIT BIGGER THAN NORMAL. GO OVER YOUR LINES UNTIL YOU'RE HAPPY WITH THE PROPORTIONS.

3

START WORKING ON THE OUTLINE OF THE HANDS, HAIR AND FACE. ADD IN THE BASIC OUTLINE FOR THE HOODY, JEANS AND SNEAKERS. THE CLOTHES ARE PART OF THE MANGA CHARACTER.

EYES

You don't need too much detail for manga facial features. Experiment with line shapes to get the right expression for your character's eyes.

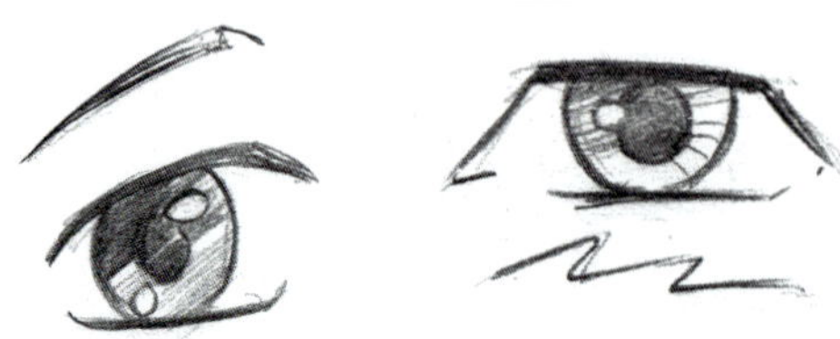

The hair covers a good portion of the face, so have only one eye clearly peeping through.

HAIRSTYLES

Manga hair is great fun to draw. Think cool and spiky! Work in the hair to give it a layered feel.

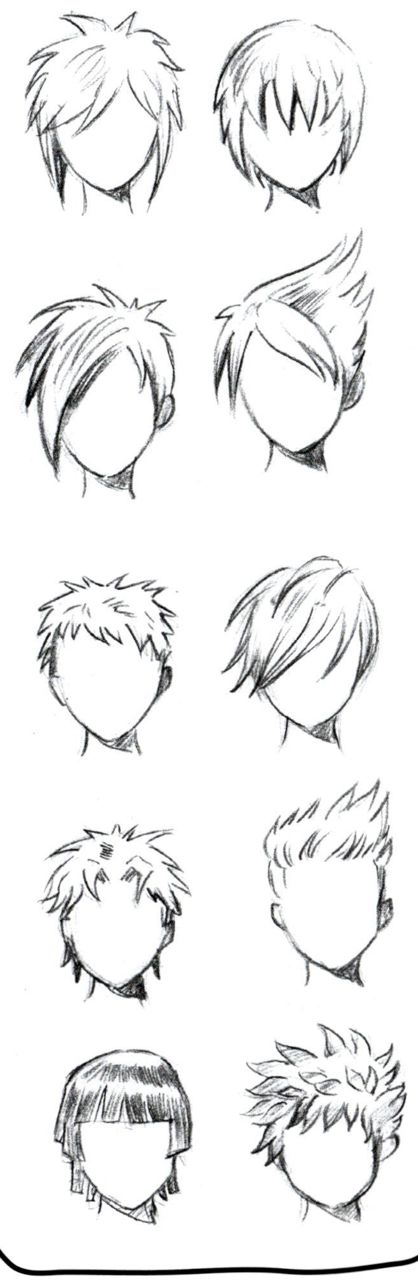

4

USE A SOFT PENCIL TO WORK IN DETAIL. THINK ABOUT WHERE THE LIGHT IS COMING FROM (TOP RIGHT HERE) TO ADD SHADOWS – DON'T BE SCARED TO PUT IN LARGE BLACK AREAS.

5

MANGA ILLUSTRATIONS ARE USUALLY COLOURED UP ON A COMPUTER, BUT YOU CAN USE THICK MARKER PENS TO MIMIC THE GOOD FLAT COLOURS THAT YOU SEE IN BOOKS AND ANIMATION.

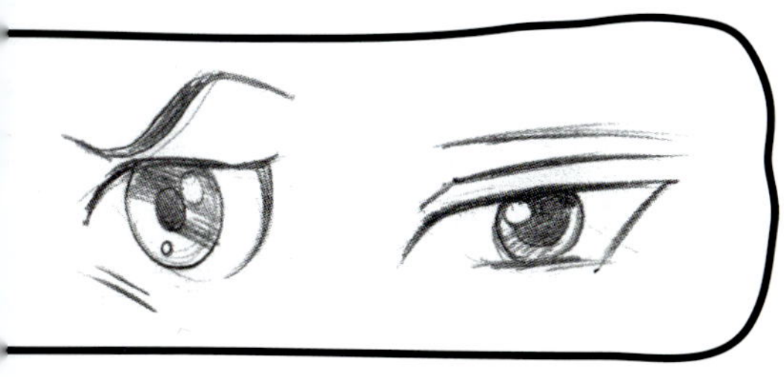

SUBMARINE

1 DRAW A LARGE OVAL WITH A SLIGHTLY POINTED TIP. ADD A CURVED FIN AT THE BACK AND ANOTHER CURVED SHAPE AT THE FRONT. SKETCH A LONG LINE RUNNING ALONG THE MIDDLE.

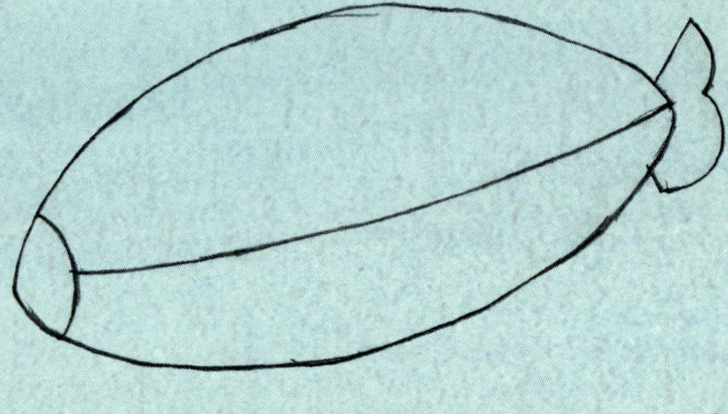

2 DRAW EXTRA ROUNDED SHAPES ON THE TOP OF YOUR SUB, ADDING A CURVED FIN ON THE NEAR SIDE. DRAW TWO WINDOWS ON THE SIDE, MAKING ONE ELLIPTICAL TO REINFORCE THE SENSE OF PERSPECTIVE.

3 ADD THREE RECTANGULAR FUNNELS AT THE REAR, EACH WITH A CONE SHAPE ON TOP. DRAW CURVED LINES FOR THE PROPELLERS. SKETCH THE OUTLINE OF THE BRIDGE WITH A CURVED PERISCOPE ON TOP. ADD MORE CURVED LINES AT THE FRONT.

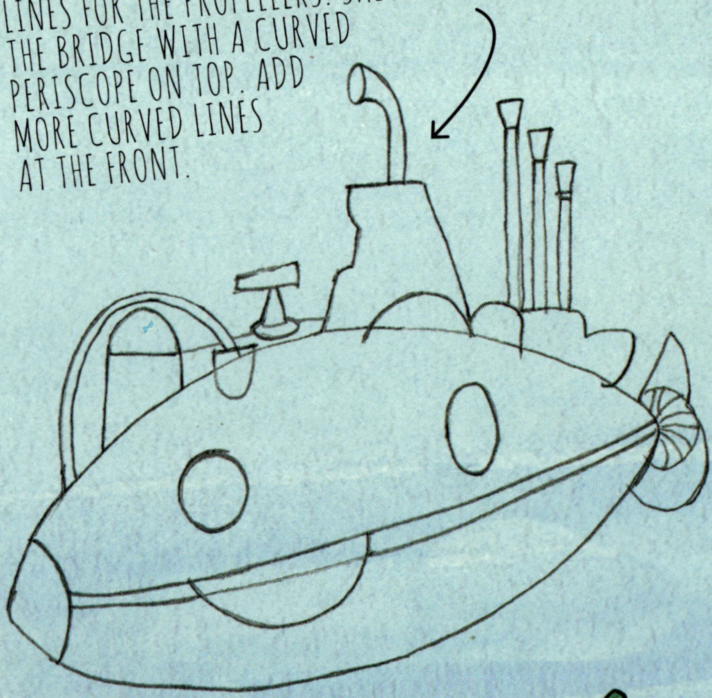

4 WORK ON THE FINE DETAIL. DRAW EXTRA LINES AND CIRCLES ON THE WINDOW FRAMES, THEN ADD SWIRLS AND COILS TO THE FRONT FOR AN OLD-FASHIONED, DECORATIVE EFFECT. DRAW CURVED, DOTTED LINES ON THE BODY TO SUGGEST IT'S BEEN RIVETED TOGETHER.

5 GO OVER YOUR LINEWORK IN PEN AND INK, THEN COLOUR YOUR SUB. USE A WASH FOR THE BODY, THEN BUILD UP A ROUGHER TEXTURE ON TOP WTIH THE SIDE OF A PENCIL. USE A BLUEISH TONE FOR THE WINDOWS, WITH A CONTRASTING COLOUR FOR THE REST OF THE METALWORK. YELLOW MAKES IT LOOK GOLDEN!

Use bands of a slightly darker tone to create the impression that parts of the sub are in shadow.

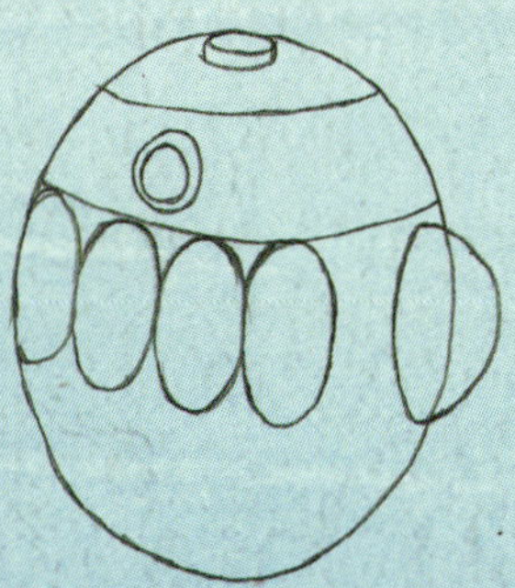

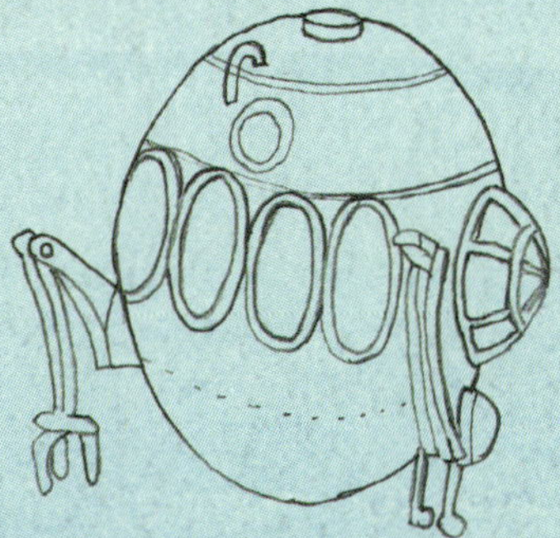

1 USE SIMPLE ELLIPSES AND CURVED LINES TO CREATE THE BASIC SHAPE OF A DIVING BELL.

2 ADD DETAIL BY DOUBLING UP ON THE LINEWORK YOU'VE JUST DRAWN. USE LONG, CURVED SHAPES FOR THE MECHANICAL GRABBERS.

Use a watery blue wash for the sea and add green coral shapes in a variety of different tones.

TROLL

1 USE A PENCIL TO DRAW THE BASIC SHAPE OF THE TROLL. DON'T ADD DETAIL YET – THE AIM IS TO GET THE PROPORTIONS RIGHT FIRST. DRAW THE HEAD LOW ON THE SHOULDERS AND GIVE YOUR TROLL A WIDE BODY AND CLUB.

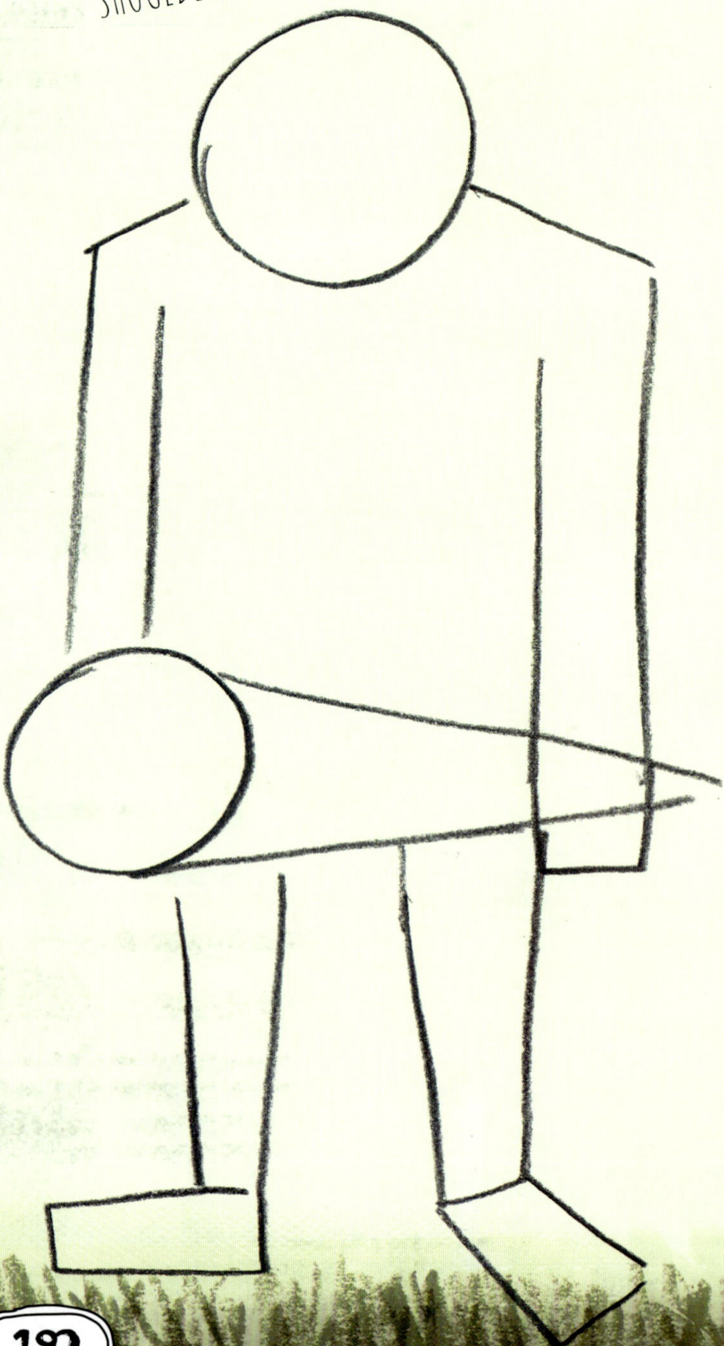

2 ONCE YOU ARE HAPPY WITH THE PROPORTIONS, START ADDING GUIDELINES FOR THE FACE, HAIR AND CLOTHES.

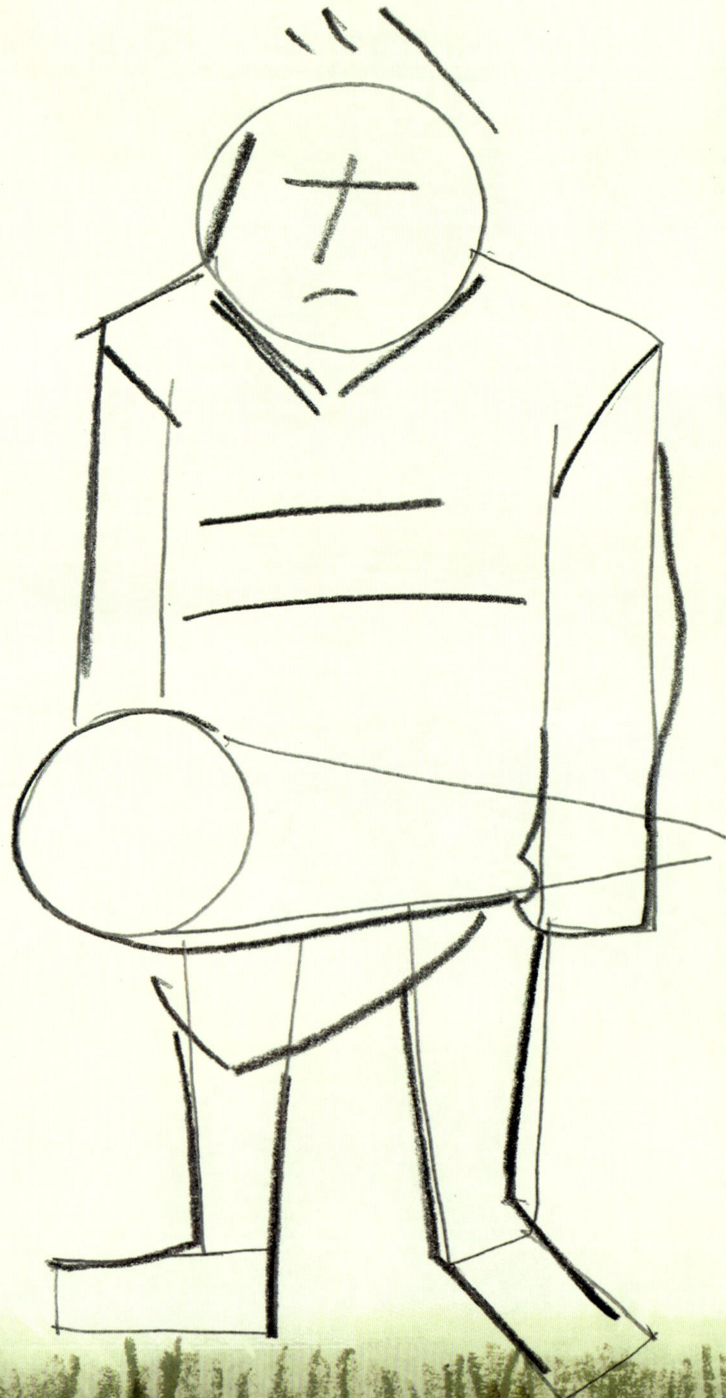

3 NOW BEGIN ADDING DETAIL. DRAW THE HAIRLINE LOW ON THE BROW, HEAVY EYEBROWS, A POINTY NOSE, EARS, A DOWN-TURNED MOUTH. ADD RIPPED EDGES TO THE CLOTHES AND START FLESHING OUT THE BODY AND CLUB.

4 USE SLUDGY GREEN WATERCOLOUR PENCILS AND DRAW YOUR OUTLINE IN BROWN. ADD FINISHING TOUCHES, SUCH AS BITS OF HAIR, WITH PEN AND INK.

ICE-HOCKEY PLAYER

1 LIGHTLY DRAW GUIDELINES FOR THE FIGURE WITH CIRCLES AND LINES. NOTICE HOW THE ARMS ARE MOVING ACROSS THE BODY, MAKING THE FIGURE LOOK DYNAMIC.

2 CHECK THAT THE PROPORTIONS LOOK CORRECT THEN START OUTLINING THE BODY SHAPES. IMAGINE THE MUSCLES AROUND THE SKELETON TO HELP YOU CURVE THE ARMS AND LEGS IN THE RIGHT PLACES.

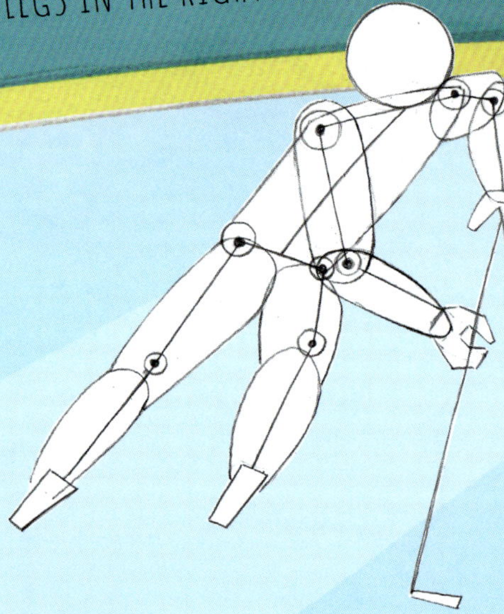

3 NOW START ADDING THE SHAPE OF THE CLOTHING AND KIT AROUND YOUR BASIC SHAPES. THINK ABOUT HOW THE HAIR AND CLOTHES WOULD MOVE WITH THE FIGURE.

4 ONCE YOU ARE HAPPY WITH YOUR SHAPES AND PROPORTIONS, USE A STRONGER PENCIL LINE TO OUTLINE THE FIGURE. THEN ERASE ANY GUIDELINES THAT ARE NOT NEEDED.

Remember to keep your hand relaxed for a more fluid line. This will help your figure look as though she's moving.

6 FINALLY ADD SOME COLOUR! START WITH THE LIGHTER COLOURS AND BUILD UP DARKER COLOURS ON TOP. ADD SCRATCHY SQUIGGLES AT THE BOTTOM FOR A COOL ICE FEEL.

5 ADD DETAILS TO THE FACE AND CLOTHING, SUCH AS FABRIC FOLDS, POCKETS OR TEAM BRANDING. FIND PICTURES IN MAGAZINES FOR INSPIRATION.

GYROCOPTER

A GYROCOPTER LOOKS SIMILAR TO A HELICOPTER AND WAS INVENTED SO PEOPLE COULD FLY THROUGH THE AIR SAFELY AT A SLOW SPEED. DRAW ONE YOURSELF, AS SLOWLY – OR QUICKLY – AS YOU LIKE!

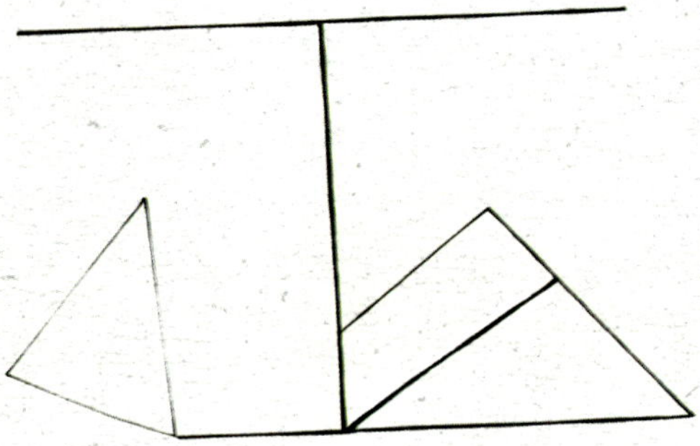

1

SKETCH OUT THE BASIC SHAPES OF THE GYROCOPTER WITH A PENCIL: USE A RULER TO HELP YOU DRAW A T SHAPE AND ADD TWO OTHER TRIANGLE SHAPES AT EITHER SIDE, PLUS AN L SHAPE TO CONNECT ONE OF THE TRIANGLES.

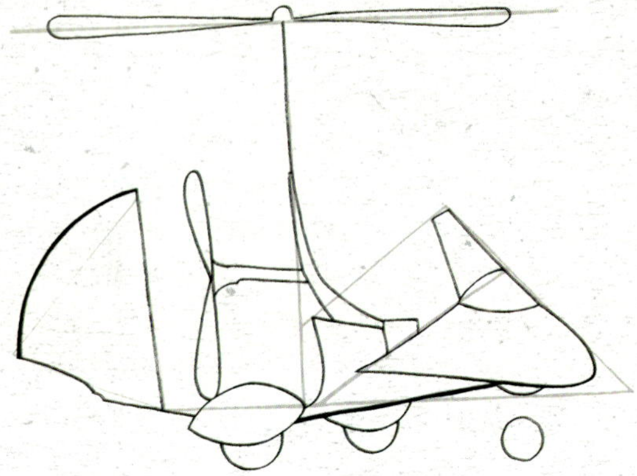

2

DRAW IN THE OTHER DETAILS TO YOUR FLYING MACHINE IN PENCIL. THERE ARE LOTS OF CURVED SHAPES FOR THE WHEELS, WINGS AND BODY. ADD TWO PROPELLERS AT THE TOP OF THE GYROCOPTER, TOO.

5

DRAW IN BLACK DOTS AROUND THE FLYING MACHINE. THIS IS A QUICK AND EASY WAY TO MAKE THE DRAWING LOOK INCREDIBLY DETAILED AND TECHNICAL.

Give the pilot a fun expression and some rosy cheeks!

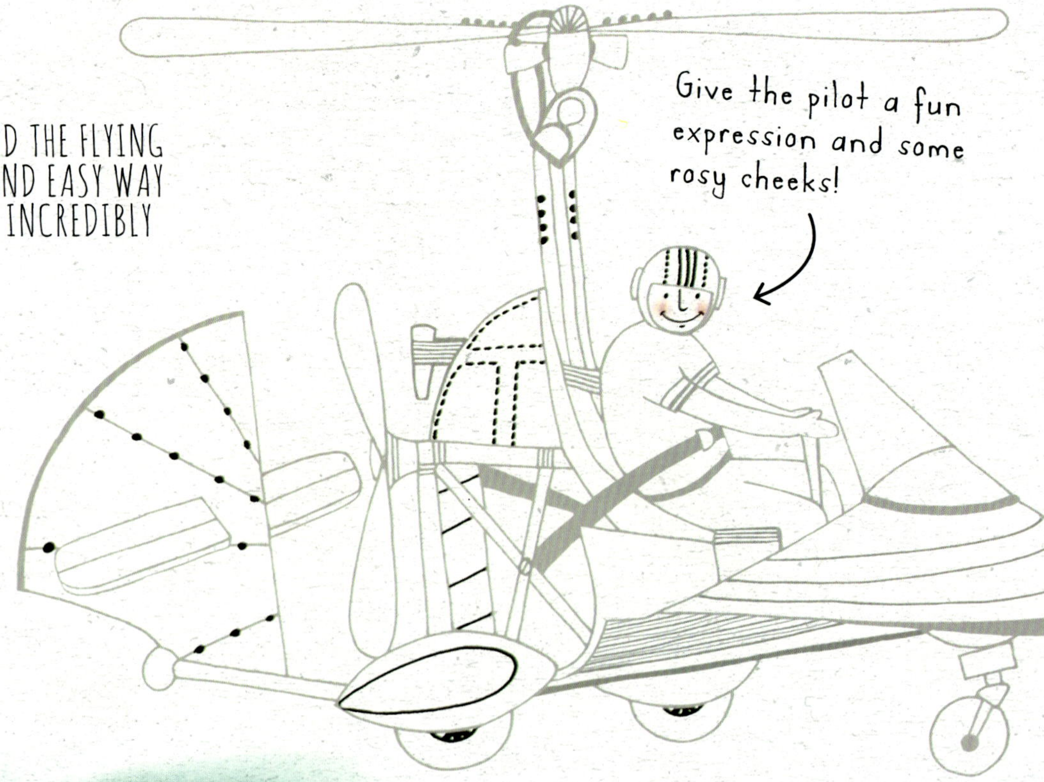

Draw in a background with simple detail to make it look as if the gyrocopter is high up in the sky.

3

ADD DETAIL TO THE GYROCOPTER TO MAKE IT LOOK REAL. DRAW IN THE PILOT, THEN DRAW IN THE SAFETY BELT AND THE MECHANISM THAT RUNS THE TOP PROPELLER.

4

ADD MORE DETAIL IN STAGES. BUILD UP THE FINER TECHNICAL BITS, SUCH AS THE LINES ON THE WINGS AND THE PARTS AROUND THE PROPELLERS.

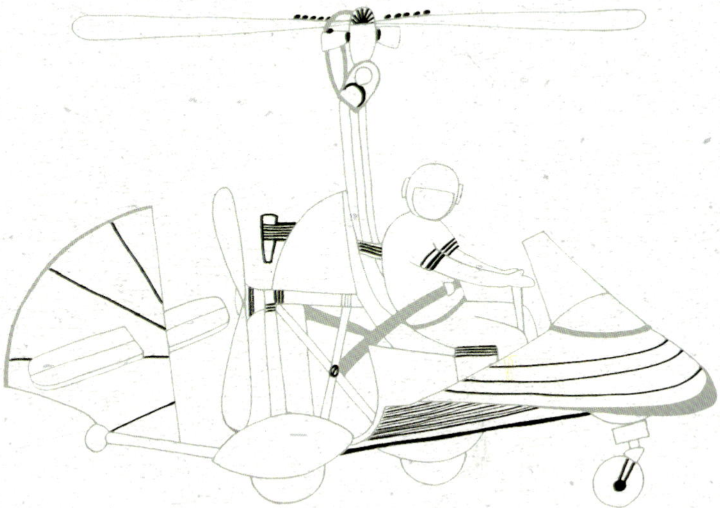

6

USE A FINE-TIP PEN TO COMPLETE THE DRAWING. USING DIFFERENT THICKNESSES OF PEN IS USEFUL TO ADD VARIETY TO THE DRAWING. IF YOU DON'T HAVE DIFFERENT PENS, JUST USE A THIN PEN AND GO OVER SOME LINES A FEW TIMES TO THICKEN THEM UP.

These colours give the machine a metallic feel. The unevenness of the watercolour inks creates a shiny, reflective-looking surface.

DRAGON

Try adding a castle to the background. Build up your design by joining basic shapes together, such as boxes, cones and cylinders.

1 DRAW A DRAGON'S SPINE CURVING FROM THE TIP OF A TAIL TO THE BASE OF THE SKULL. DRAW A ROUGH SHAPE FOR THE HEAD AND EYE, THEN ADD ANOTHER LINE TO CREATE THE BODY. ADD ROUGH STICK LINES FOR THE ARMS, LEGS AND WINGS.

2 FLESH OUT THE DRAGON'S BODY PARTS. REFINE THE HEAD AND DRAW CURVED SHAPES TO CREATE THE ARMS AND LEGS. ADD SOME SPIKES TO THE BACK AND DRAW HORNS ON THE HEAD. USE SLIGHTLY CURVED LINES FOR THE OUTLINE OF THE NEAR WING.

5 YOU CAN ADD EVEN MORE DETAIL TO THE DRAGON'S BODY BY USING LAYERS OF OPAQUE PAINT. START WITH A BASE COLOUR, MAKING THE GAPS BETWEEN THE SCALES EXTRA DARK, THEN PAINT THE HIGHLIGHTS ON TOP. USE IMAGES OF REAL ANIMALS AS REFERERENCE, SUCH AS CROCODILES OR OTHER REPTILES.

The bright flames will light up the dragon's face, so use warmer colours to add highlights to its scales.

Choose muted reds and purples to create an ominous-looking sky. Use thick paint for the clouds and blend the colours and shapes into each other to create texture.

3 RUB OUT YOUR GUIDELINES, INCLUDING THE AREA OF THE BODY BEHIND THE WING. ADD MORE SURFACE DETAIL, SUCH AS BODY SCALES AND WING BONES. ADD DETAIL TO THE HEAD, DRAWING TEETH, NOSTRILS AND A TONGUE.

4 FOCUS ON THE FINER DETAIL. DRAW SMALLER SPINES ON THE TAIL, ADD SCALES TO THE BACK LEGS AND USE SHORT LINES TO GIVE THE SCALES AND HORNS SOME TEXTURE. ADD THE DRAGON'S SHARP TALONS AND USE SWIRLY LINES FOR ITS FIERY BREATH.

CARTOON

LAUGHING

1

USING CIRCLE SHAPES, DRAW EYES AND AN UPTURNED MOUTH.

2

ADD DETAIL TO THE PUPILS AND MOUTH AND LITTLE LAUGH LINES.

PUZZLED

1

DRAW A SLANTED OVAL MOUTH, ONE EYEBROW UP AND ONE DOWN.

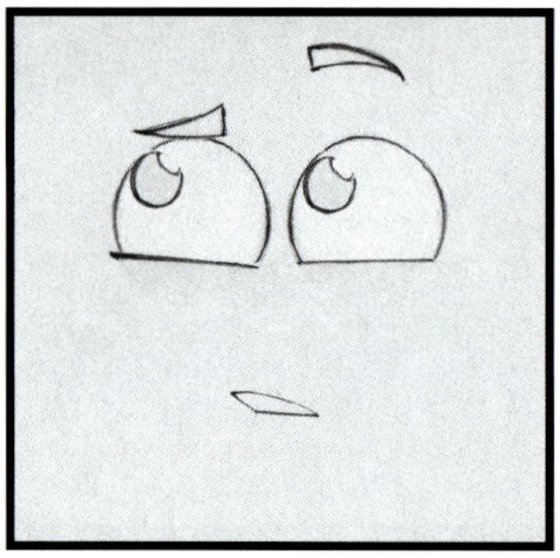

2

FOLLOW THE CURVE OF THE EYEBALL FOR SHADING BELOW THE EYES.

SHOCKED

1

DRAW PUPILS IN THE CENTRE AND A DOWN-TURNED MOUTH.

2

ADD REALLY HIGH EYEBROWS AND DETAIL TO THE EYES AND MOUTH.

Expressions

SMALL CHANGES IN SHAPE CAN MAKE A BIG DIFFERENCE WHEN YOU ARE DRAWING CARTOON EXPRESSIONS. ALL YOU NEED IS CIRCLES, HALF CIRCLES AND LINES.

ANGRY

1

SLANT THE EYEBROWS DOWN AND DRAW A DOWN-TURNED MOUTH.

2

SKETCH IN TEETH THAT LOOK AS THOUGH THEY ARE CLENCHED.

SURPRISED

1

DRAW CIRCLES FOR EYES AND AN UPTURNED MOUTH.

2

REALLY HIGH, SMALL EYEBROWS INCREASE THE LOOK OF SURPRISE.

SLEEPY

1

DRAW DROOPY EYELIDS AND A SLANTED OVAL MOUTH.

2

USE SHADING ABOVE AND BELOW THE EYES TO ADD TO THE EFFECT.

SPACESHIP CONTROLS

CREATE A COMPLICATED-LOOKING, COOL CONTROL COCKPIT BY BUILDING UP BASIC SHAPES.

DIALS

DIALS ARE EASY TO DRAW USING REPEATED CIRCLES. ALWAYS START WTIH TWO LARGE CIRCLES FOR THE OUTSIDE OF THE DIAL AND A SMALL CIRCLE IN THE MIDDLE. THEN ADD DIVISION LINES FOR A GAUGE, NUMBERS, SYMBOLS, HANDS AND/OR EXTRA RINGS DEPENDING ON HOW YOU WANT THE DIAL TO LOOK.

GEAR STICK

START WITH A SMOOTH SQUARE SHAPE AT THE BASE. FROM THERE, DRAW PART OVALS, ONE ON TOP OF THE OTHER, GETTING GRADUALLY SMALLER AS YOU GO UP. FINISH THE STICK WITH A CIRCULAR KNOB AT THE TOP.

SLIDER

TO MAKE UP A PANEL, DRAW TWO RECTANGLES, ONE JUST INSIDE THE OTHER. ADD THREE LONG, VERTICAL RECTANGLES FOR THE SLIDERS. THE SLIDER KNOB IS A CYLINDER SHAPE TURNED ON ITS SIDE. ADD BUTTONS AT THE BOTTOM.

RADIO

USING THE SAME BASIC SHAPES AS THE OTHER COMPONENTS, YOU CAN ADD BUTTONS, LIGHTS, KNOBS AND DIALS TO A RECTANGULAR PANEL TO CREATE ANYTHING, LIKE THIS RADIO! ADD SHADING TO GIVE THE SIMPLE SHAPES SOME DIMENSION.

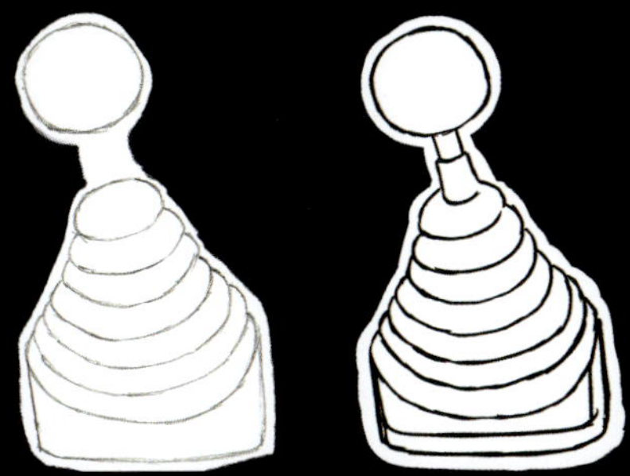

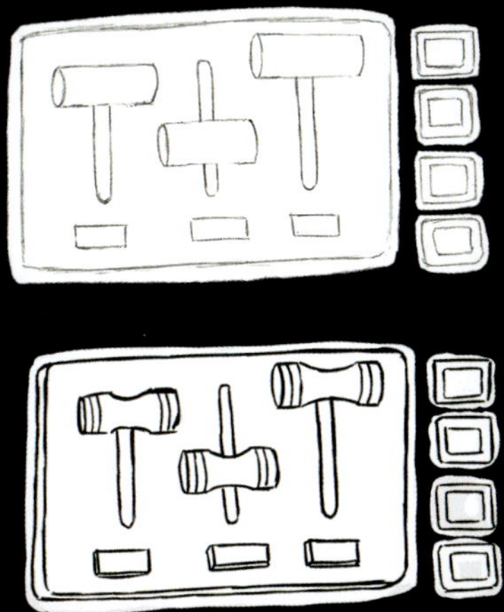

SUPERHEROINE

1

USE A PENCIL TO SKETCH SOME PERSPECTIVE LINES. ANGLE THEM TO MAKE IT LOOK LIKE SHE'S TAKING OFF! AT THE TOP OF YOUR LINES DRAW IN AN OVAL SHAPE FOR THE HEAD.

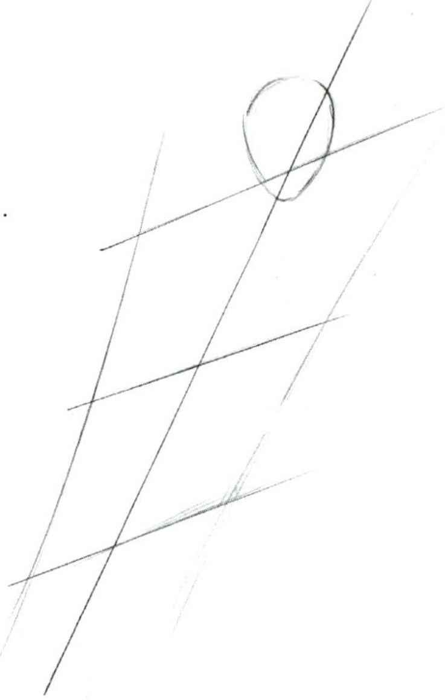

2

DRAW IN THE ANGLED SHAPE OF THE FIGURE.

3

ADD SOME DETAIL FOR THE HANDS AND A LITTLE BIT TO THE FACE AND HAIR. DRAW IN THE CLOTHES AND CAPE SHAPES.

4

WORK IN MORE DETAIL TO THE SKETCH. START WITH THE FACE AND THEN ADD DETAIL TO THE LEGS, HAIR, CLOTHING AND THE ALL-IMPORTANT CAPE.

Remember to relax when you're drawing! This keeps the movement fresh and creates a more realistic illustration.

5

MOVE ONTO A HEAVIER PENCIL AND WORK IN THE DETAIL AND THE SHADOWS. ADD A LIGHT SOURCE IN AT THIS POINT (FROM TOP RIGHT) AND MARK OUT WHERE YOU'D LIKE SHADOWS TO FALL. DON'T BE SCARED TO PUT IN LARGE BLACK AREAS WHERE NEEDED.

6

FINISH YOUR DRAWING WITH CLEAR AND BRIGHT COLOURS. ADD COLOURED MOVEMENT LINES COMING OFF HER BODY AND CAPE TO GIVE THE IMPRESSION OF FAST MOVEMENT SO YOUR SUPERHEROINE CAN GO SAVE THE WORLD!

Here there is a strong shadow under the cape and the skirt as the superheroine zooms up into the sky!

ANIMAL PATTERNS

ANIMAL PATTERNS INSPIRE DESIGNS EVERYWHERE YOU LOOK! THEY'RE USED ON EVERYTHING FROM BOOKS AND BEDDING TO CLOTHING AND ACCESSORIES. USING REFERENCE PHOTOS, LEARN TO DRAW THE BASIC SHAPES FIRST, SUCH AS LEOPARD SPOTS AND ZEBRA STRIPES. EXPERIMENT WITH REALISTIC TONES BUT ALSO PUNCHY FASHION COLOURS. THEN TRY TRANSFERRING YOUR FAVOURITE PATTERNS TO DRAWINGS OF OTHER OBJECTS.

TIGER

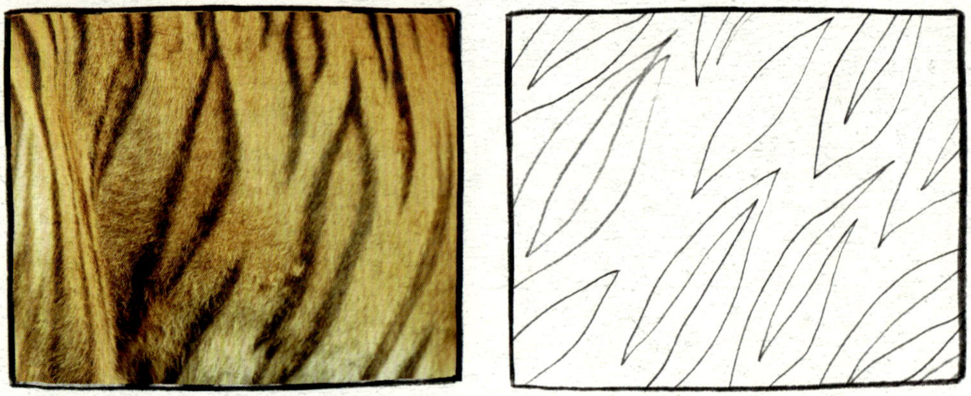

ZEBRA

LEOPARD

GIRAFFE

FISH BOWL

DISTORT YOUR PICTURES USING THIS CLEVER TECHNIQUE.

1

START WITH THE NORMAL PICTURE FIRST. FOR A FISH, DRAW AN EGG SHAPE. ADD A CURVE FOR THE FACE, THEN DRAW AN EYE AND MOUTH.

2

SKETCH THE FINS AND TAIL. USE CURVY LINES FOR THE TAIL TO MAKE IT LOOK AS IF THE FISH IS SWISHING ABOUT IN THE WATER.

3

ADD LINES TO THE FINS AND TAIL, PLUS SOME SHADING TO THE OUTLINE AND EYE AREA. USE SMALL 'C' SHAPES FOR THE SCALES.

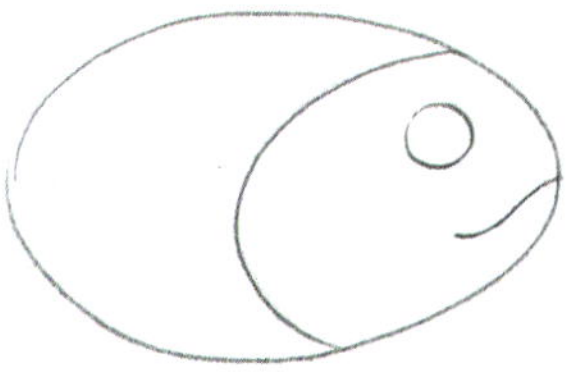

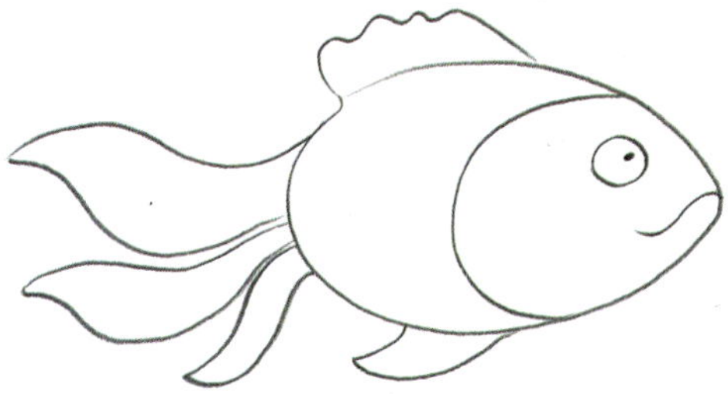

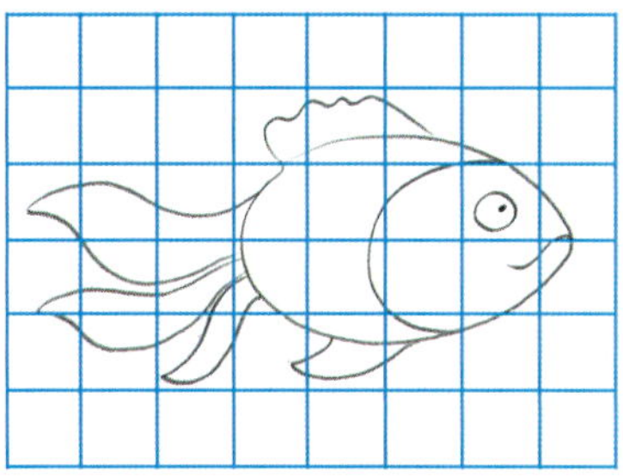

4

USING A RULER, DRAW A RECTANGLE AROUND YOUR FISH. DIVIDE THE SHAPE INTO SMALL SQUARES, MAKING SURE THEY'RE ALL THE SAME SIZE.

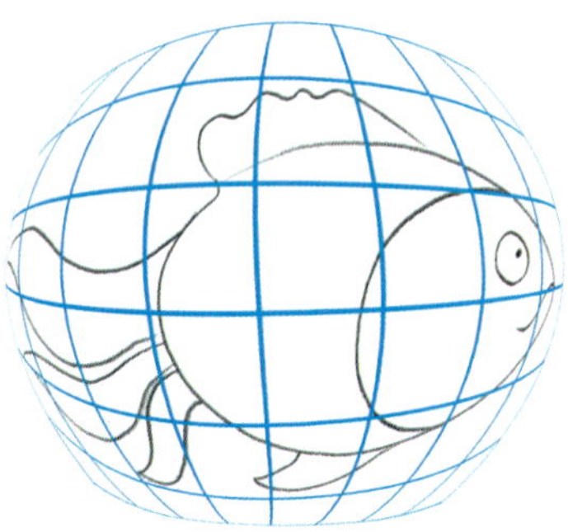

5

SKETCH A CIRCLE. ADD CURVED HORIZONTAL AND VERTICAL LINES TO GIVE YOU THE SAME NUMBER OF BOXES AS THE ORIGINAL GRID. COMPARE AND COPY CORRESPONDING SQUARES TO HELP YOU DRAW A DISTORTED SHAPE OF THE ORIGINAL.

Use different shades of blue to give the impression of movement in the water. Add curved white shapes to create highlights and to make the bowl look 3D!

6

RUB OUT YOUR GUIDELINES AND DRAW A BOWL, SAND AND PLANTS. THEN COLOUR YOUR PICTURE!

CAT LOOKING THROUGH A FISH BOWL!

1

START WITH THE NORMAL PICTURE AGAIN. DRAW AN OVAL FOR THE CAT'S FACE. ADD SIMPLE SHAPES FOR ITS FACE, EARS, PAWS AND TAIL.

2

DRAW STROKES FOR THE CAT'S FUR. SHADE INSIDE THE EARS AND NOSE, AND AROUND THE EYES. DRAW DOTS FOR PUPILS AND LINES FOR WHISKERS.

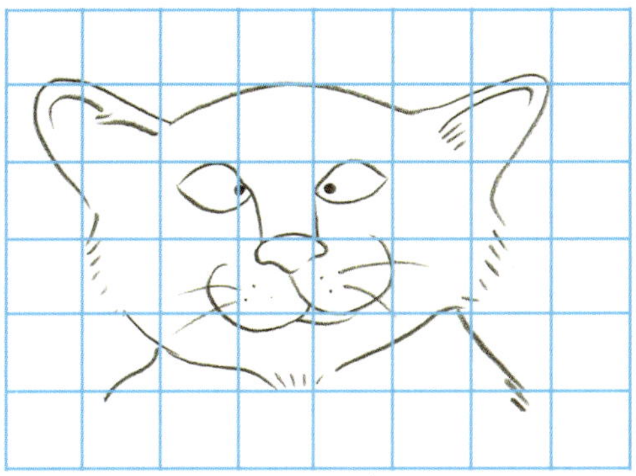

3

DRAW A RECTANGLE AROUND YOUR PICTURE, AS BEFORE. USING A RULER FOR ACCURACY, DIVIDE UP THE SHAPE INTO A GRID OF SMALL SQUARE SHAPES.

4

DRAW A CIRCLE. DIVIDE UP THE AREA WITH CURVED LINES AS BEFORE UNTIL YOU HAVE THE SAME NUMBER OF BOXES AS YOUR RECTANGULAR GRID. COMPARE CORRESPONDING SQUARES AND DRAW IN YOUR DISTORTED CAT SHAPE, BIT BY BIT.

Here is the cat before he is distorted.

Give the distorted cat face a slightly bluish tinge to give the effect of looking through water!

5

DRAW THE FISH BOWL AS BEFORE. USE TRACING OR PARCHMENT PAPER TO COPY THE FACE OF YOUR DISTORTED CAT INTO THE BOWL. THEN, TRACE OR COPY THE ORIGINAL PICTURE TO DRAW HIS EARS ABOVE THE BOWL AND PAWS AND TAIL NEXT TO IT. NOW COLOUR THIS CURIOUS CAT IN!

TOWERING BUILDINGS

1 DRAW SOME SIMPLE RECTANGLES CLOSE TOGETHER. THIS DRAWING USES PERSPECTIVE, SO THE VERTICAL LINES NEED TO COME CLOSER TOGETHER AT THE TOP TO GIVE THE IMPRESSION OF TALL, TOWERING BUILDINGS!

2 TO MAKE THE BUILDINGS LOOK 3D, ADD SOME EXTRA VERTICAL LINES TO THE SIDES OF THE RECTANGLES, BEARING IN MIND THE ANGLE THAT YOU'RE VIEWING THE BUILDINGS FROM.

Find a photo online to give you some inspiration. Look for buildings that have interesting architectural details.

3 ADD ROWS OF SQUARES AND RECTANGLES FOR THE WINDOWS. THESE SHAPES NEED TO BECOME SMALLER AS YOU WORK UP THE BUILDING, GIVING THE IMPRESSION THAT THE UPPER FLOORS ARE FURTHER AWAY.

4 LOOK AT THE TEXTURES AND MATERIALS OF REAL BUILDINGS AND TRY TO IMITATE THE DETAIL USING SIMPLE LINES. ADD SHADING BY DRAWING REPEATED HORIZONTAL, VERTICAL OR CROSSHATCHED LINES.

Paint areas of darker tones to suggest blurry reflections in glass windows.

5 GO OVER YOUR DRAWING WITH PEN-AND-INK LINES. DON'T WORRY IF THE NEW LINES ARE SCRATCHY AND IMPERFECT – THEY WILL HELP GIVE YOUR PICTURE SOME CHARACTER. ADD WATERCOLOUR WASHES TO COLOUR IN YOUR BUILDINGS.

FRENCH CAFÉ

THIS CHIC FRENCH CAFÉ MIGHT LOOK A BIT COMPLICATED TO DRAW, BUT EACH OBJECT IN THE PICTURE IS ACTUALLY MADE UP OF RELATIVELY SIMPLE SHAPES. PRACTISE SKETCHING EACH ELEMENT ON ITS OWN, THEN BRING EVERYTHING TOGETHER TO CREATE A PERFECT PARISIAN SCENE!

For the umbrella, sketch a simple triangle, then draw a curved triangular shape on either side. Add curved lines beneath each segment. Draw a circle on top, then sketch the pole. Add more shapes to make the umbrella look 3D.

Make the café look further away than the people by positioning the building half way up the page. Use a thick pencil outline for the building, picking out certain shapes in pen and ink.

Sketch a big ellipse for the table top, then add a vertical line running through the centre of two much smaller ellipses. Draw swirly supports on one side first before sketching their mirror image on the other.

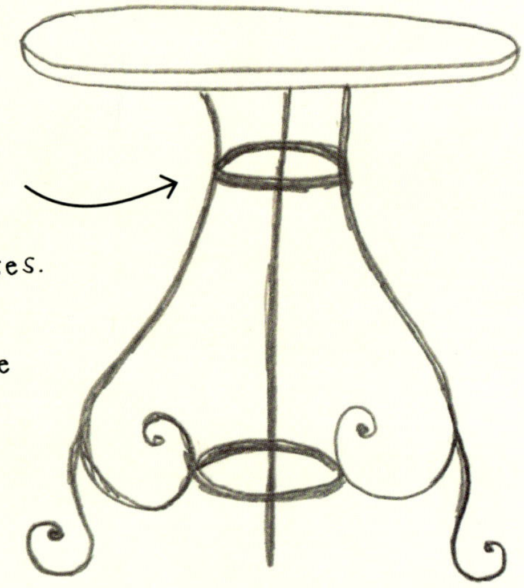

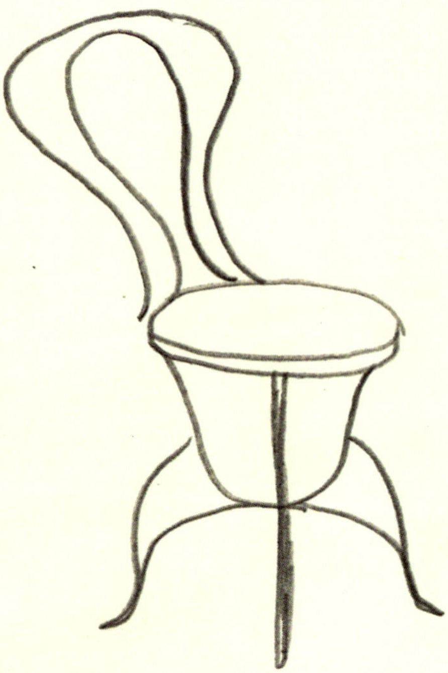

To draw an elegant café chair, sketch an ellipse, adding another line at the bottom to make it look 3D. Draw two curved shapes for the back. Add a big U shape beneath the ellipse, then use more elegant curves for the legs.

Use different-sized ellipses and curved shapes to draw an ornate teapot and cup. Add swirly patterns to the sides to give them some old-fashioned charm!

Use bright colours for key elements in your scene. This yellow-and-white awning works well with the neutral shopfront colours.

Add people and animals to the scene, and make them interact with objects wherever possible.

Using pen and ink, go over the outlines of the objects in the foreground to help them stand out.

OPTICAL ILLUSIONS

OPTICAL ILLUSIONS CAN MAKE PEOPLE SEE THINGS THAT AREN'T THERE. LEARN TO DRAW THEM TO TRICK YOUR FRIENDS AND FAMILY!

CUBES

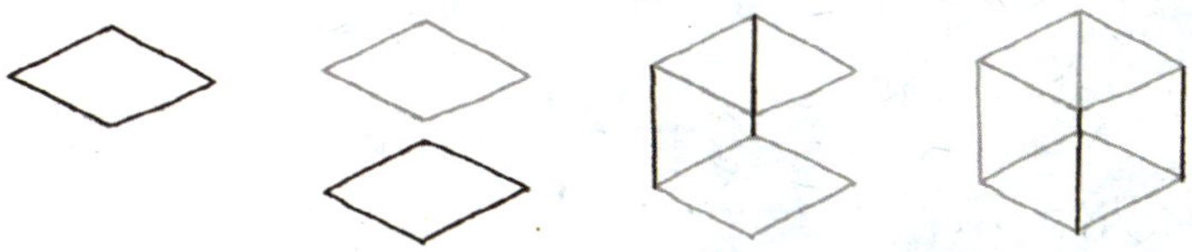

Draw a flattened diamond for the top of the cube, then exactly the same for the base. Draw vertical lines to link the corners together.

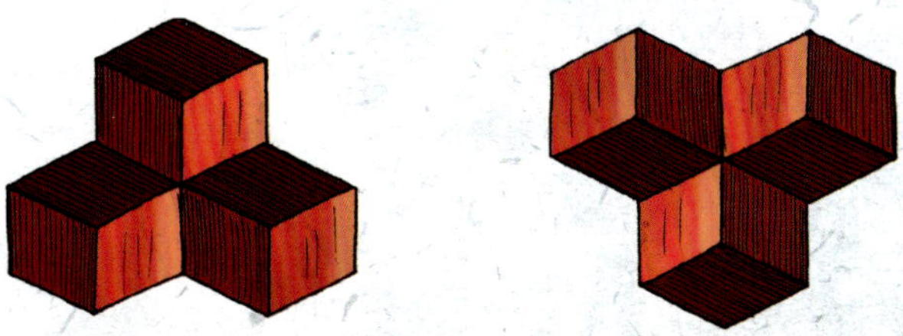

Add shading to some sides of the cube, like this. This helps gives them a 3D look.

Draw a lot of cubes together to get the optical illusion: are the cubes the right way up or upside down? Or maybe you see them flip back and forth!

FACE OR VASE?

Draw a simple outline of a face looking to the right, using only one smooth line.

Then draw or trace the same face again, facing the first.

Darken the gap between the two faces. Some people will see the dark vase, and some people will see the faces!

IMPOSSIBLE TRIANGLE

IF YOU LOOK CLOSELY, THIS TRIANGLE COULDN'T ACTUALLY EXIST. FOLLOW THE STEPS CAREFULLY TO CREATE ANOTHER TRICK OF THE EYES!

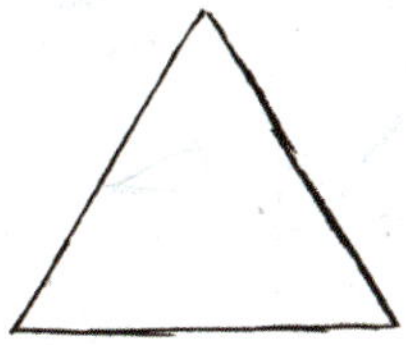

Start with a simple triangle.

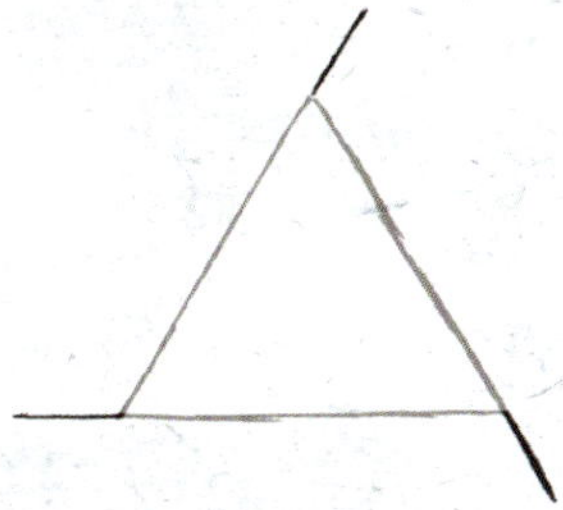

At the three points, extend the lines slightly, like this.

From the end of these new lines, draw parallel lines following the original triangle's sides.

From the end of the last lines draw three more parallel lines. Your impossible triangle should now be taking shape.

To create the illusion, link the last three lines to the rest of the triangle.

Colour up your image. Be careful with the shading, and you'll get the amazing effect!

Draw a simple triangle with the three tips cut off. Then draw four small triangles inside. Extend lines from each point of each triangle. Now draw in the last lines filling in all the gaps. Then add some shading and your impossible triangle is complete and a brilliant illusion!

STREETDANCER

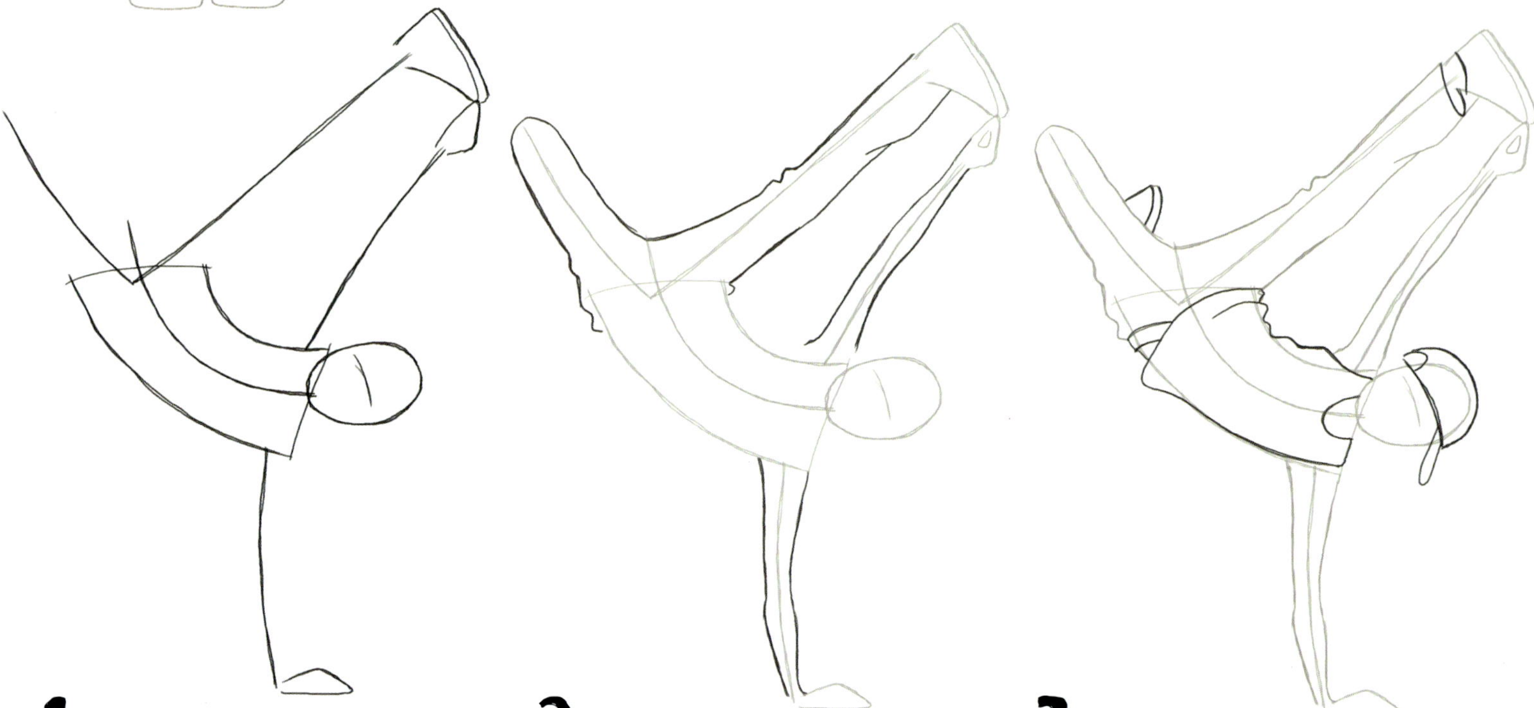

1

USE SIMPLE LINES TO SKETCH THE BASIC POSE. DRAW AN OVAL FOR THE HEAD, WITH CURVED LINES FOR THE TORSO AND ARMS. ADD A BIG V SHAPE FOR THE LEGS, AND A FOOT.

2

DRAW THE DANCER'S JEANS, USING THE GUIDES TO HELP YOU. KEEP THE LINEWORK LOOSE AND ROUND OFF WHERE THE LEFT KNEE IS BENT. DRAW THE SHAPE OF THE ARMS.

3

SKETCH THE SHIRT AND AN ELLIPSE AT THE BOTTOM OF THE TROUSERS. ADD A SEMI-CIRCLE FOR THE CAP WITH AN ELLIPSE FOR THE BRIM. DRAW A FOOT BEHIND THE BENT LEG.

SILHOUETTES

To draw cool silhouettes of streetdancers, find photos of dancers in different poses. Then simply trace over their outlines and colour them in.

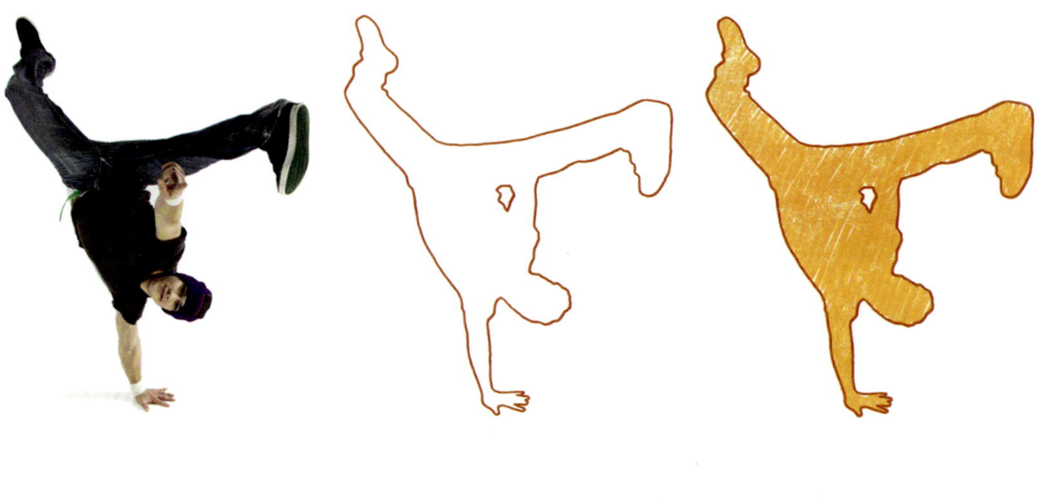

4

REFINE THE OUTLINE OF YOUR FIGURE AND DRAW HIS HAIR AND FACIAL FEATURES. ADD LINES FOR THE CREASES IN HIS CLOTHES. WORK ON THE DETAILS OF HIS BELT AND SHOES. ERASE ANY UNWANTED LINES.

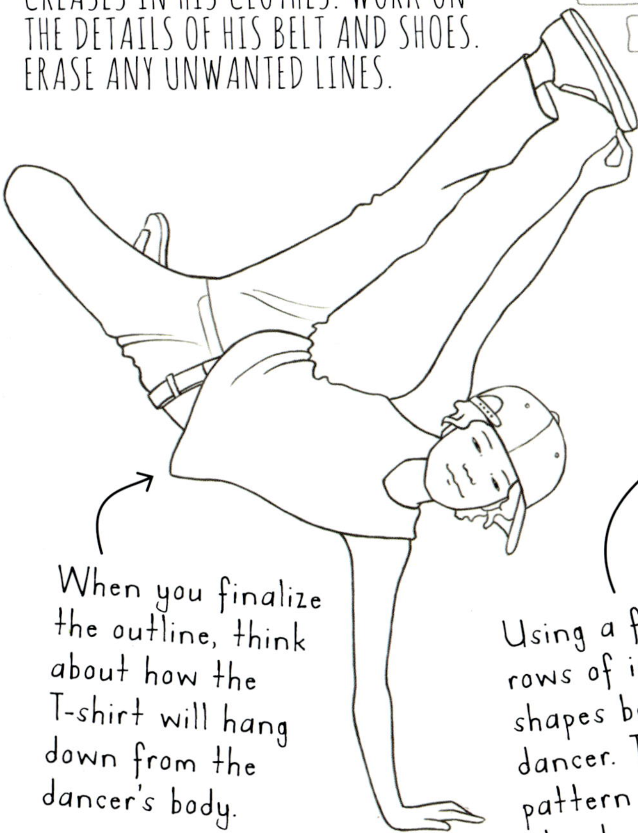

When you finalize the outline, think about how the T-shirt will hang down from the dancer's body.

5

COLOUR YOUR STREETDANCER, USING BRIGHT TONES TO CONTRAST WITH HIS BLACK T-SHIRT AND TRAINERS. DON'T PAINT UP TO THE EDGES ALL THE TIME – THIN STRIPS OF WHITE WILL LOOK LIKE SUBTLE HIGHLIGHTS AND HELP TO ADD DEPTH.

Using a fine line, draw rows of irregular brick shapes behind your dancer. This simple pattern helps the figure stand out from the page.

Keep your colour work loose, allowing streaks of white to show through. These skewed lines help create a feeling of movement.

CREEPY MANSION

1

DRAW A SET OF ROUGH RECTANGLE SHAPES FOR THE MAIN PART OF THE BUILDING. USE TRIANGLES FOR THE ROOF AND TURRETS AND A SEMI-CIRCLE FOR THE DOMED TOWER.

2

ADD SIMPLE LINES TO YOUR SKETCH TO DEFINE THE BUILDING. ADD SMALL TRIANGULAR POINTS TO THE ROOF AND TURRETS TO MAKE THEM LOOK SHARP. DRAW A BASIC DOOR AND BALCONY, TOO.

3 DRAW IN ALL THE DIFFERENT WINDOW SHAPES. THE ROUGHER THE BETTER TO MAKE THE HOUSE LOOK OLD AND CROOKED! ADD ANOTHER BALCONY AND WORK UP THE FRONT DOOR DETAIL. DRAW A CIRCLE FOR THE CLOCK FACE.

Draw lots of bats in solid black ink to make the picture extra creepy!

4 ADD A GHOSTLY FIGURE IN ONE OF THE BIG WINDOWS. THEN DRAW GLASS PANES, SHUTTERS AND BROKEN GLASS. USE LOTS OF RECTANGLE SHAPES FOR THE ROOF TILES, THEN ADD SPIKES AND SPIRES TO THE ROOF AND TURRETS.

5 PAINT WITH DARK PURPLES FOR THE WALLS AND ROOF. USE GREEN IN SOME WINDOWS TO GIVE AN EERIE EFFECT AND MAKE THE SPOOKY FIGURE STAND OUT. CREATE GLOWS AROUND THE LIT WINDOWS WITH LIGHTER COLOURS.

INDEX

A
aeroplane 80-1
aliens 50-1, 60-1
animals 12-13, 18-19, 24-5, 32-3, 52-3, 64-5, 74-5, 82-3, 102-3, 124-5, 154-5, 162-3, 172-3, 180-1, 198-9

B
basketball player 142-3
beards 146-7
belts 94-5
bridge 122-3
buildings 38-9, 118-19, 140-1, 170-1, 218-19, 210-11
bullet train 72-3
burger 130-1

C
café 212-13
cake 166-7
caricatures 152-3
cartoons 7, 105, 188
  animals 124-5, 172-3
  explosions 98-9,
  expressions 200-1
  monsters 62-3
cat 162-3
colour wheel 9
crayons
  chalk 7
  oil 7
  wax 7
crocodile 154-5
crosshatching 8, 34, 104
cyborg 164-5

D
dessert 44-5
dinosaur 112-13
distortion 208-9
diver 70-1
dog 82-3
dragon 198-9
drum kit 58-9

E
editing software 9
Eiffel Tower 76-7
electric guitar 26-7
elephant 102-3
erasers 6
explosions 98-9

F
fashion
  boys 30-1
  girls 16-17
Ferris wheel 160-1
fish bowl 208-9
frames 150-1
Frankenstein 178-9

G
giraffe face 52-3
grizzly bear 18-19
guidelines 8, 10, 14, 16, 20, 24, 30, 31, 38, 39, 40, 47, 50, 52, 68, 71, 72, 73, 74, 75, 76, 82, 84, 92, 95, 101, 106, 120, 128, 141, 152, 160, 174, 180, 181, 188, 194
gyrocopter 196-7

H
hairstyles 78-9
hats 116-17
haunted house 118-19, 218-19
hedgehog 12-13
high street 38-9
highlights 8, 9, 11, 13, 26, 40, 41, 55, 62, 65, 78, 93, 131, 135, 143, 145, 153, 163, 165, 175, 179, 199, 208, 217
horizon line 9, 38
hot-air balloons 14-15

I
ice-hockey player 194-5
inks 6, 7, 14, 15, 18, 21, 34, 39, 43, 51, 56, 57, 68, 69, 77, 81, 91, 98, 99, 103, 104, 105, 108, 123, 144, 151, 157, 169, 181, 183, 184, 185, 191, 193, 197, 211, 212, 213, 219

J
jetpack 126-7

L
light sources 8, 13, 26, 29, 34, 85, 92, 96, 205
line designs 56-7, 59

M
manga
  boy 188-9
  girl 120-1
map 86-7
materials 6-7
meerkats 32-3

monkeys 64-5
monsters 62-3, 158-9, 178-9
motorbike 114-15
mountain bike 182-3
moustaches 48-9

N
ninja 46-7

O
optical illusions 214-15

P
paints
  acrylic 7
  poster 7
  watercolour 6, 7, 15, 39, 53, 61, 77, 85, 97, 117, 139, 141, 151, 175, 211
paper types 6
patterns
  animal 206-7
  circular 132-3
  geometric 110-11, 133
  straight 184-5
peacock 74-5
penguins 24-5
pens 184, 197
  felt-tip 7, 75
  gel 171
  highlighter 7
  marker 7, 49, 85, 189
perspective 9, 38, 60, 69, 72, 73, 88, 90, 96, 109, 160, 176, 190, 192, 199, 204, 208, 210
pirate ship 36-7
pizza 108-9
plant 128-9
pop star 54-5
portraits 10-11, 22-3, 78-9
proportions 8, 9, 14, 32, 46, 92, 96, 116, 142, 164, 188, 192

Q
quad bike 42-3

R
racing car 20-1
robot 168-9
rock star 92-3
rose 28-9

S
shadows 8, 9, 10, 11, 13, 19, 21, 32, 34, 37, 41, 43, 66, 78, 93, 96, 97, 112, 117, 121, 122, 131, 135, 143, 145, 165, 178, 183, 189, 191, 205
shark 138-9
skateboarder 106-7
skateboards 68-9, 106-7
skyline 170-1
skyscrapers 140-1
snowboarder 84-5
space rocket 100-1
  controls 202-3
speech bubbles 66-7
speedboat 148-9
spy car 90-1
Statue of Liberty 40-1
street art 104-5
streetdancer 216-17
stunt rider 114-15
submarine 190-1
sunglasses 176-7
superhero 96-7
superheroine 204-5
surfer 174-5
sweet machine 136-7
symmetry 8, 10, 14, 57, 80, 90, 185

T
T-rex 112-13
T-shirts 34-5
techniques 8-9
tornado 156-7
trainers 88-9
tree 186-7
troll 192-3

U
UFO 60-1

V
vanishing point 9, 38, 72, 90
volcano 144-5

W
watercolour pencils 6, 41, 83, 91, 129, 193
woodland animals 180-1

Z
zombie 134-5

ABOUT THE ARTISTS

TALENTED ARTISTS FROM AROUND THE WORLD HAVE CONTRIBUTED THEIR SKILLS AND ILLUSTRATIONS TO THIS BOOK!

TOM MCGRATH always wanted to be an artist. He likes to use a mixture of pencil, pen and the computer to finish his drawings. Tom now works as a freelance illustrator to support his addiction to ginger snaps.

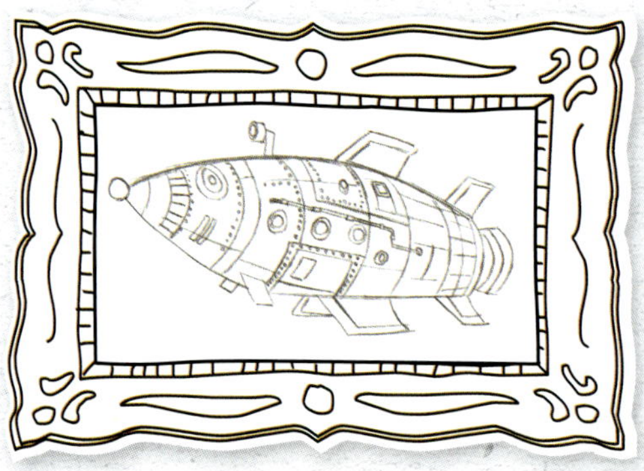

PAULA FRANCO is a children's book illustrator and graphic designer from Argentina. She loves to spend her spare time wandering around libraries.

SI CLARK is an illustrator and animator. He grew up in the countryside but now lives in London. He started drawing at a very early age and has pretty much been drawing every day since then. Si is obsessed with drawing trees and cities, as well as finding strange textures to scan in to his drawings!

YASUKO YASUKO has developed a graphic illustration style, mixing ink work, brush strokes and digital textures. She loves Japanese fashion and sometimes makes her own clothes. Yasuko lives and works in Paris and loves to spend time drawing in the Louvre art museum.

LUCIANO LOCENZO studied an MA in Illustration in Barcelona, Spain, and now lives in that same city. He works as a professional illustrator on books, newspapers and magazines.

STEVE STONE is an illustrator from the North East of England who loves to capture the character of animals. He gets lots of help from his orange cat, Vincent van Mog.

MADDY MCCLELLAN lives in Sussex, England, and works as an illustrator and printmaker. She has illustrated many children's books, including some that she has written herself. She is happiest drawing with a lively, inky line in her studio in the garden, visited by an assortment of animals.

ALEX HEDWORTH works as an illustrator and is currently studying for an MA. Originally from Newcastle, England, he now lives in London. He has been drawing for as long as he can remember - his first drawings were copies of comic books!

JULIE INGHAM is an illustrator and designer who lives and works by the sea in West Sussex, England. Her favourite things to draw are skyscrapers and all things decorative!

STEVE HORROCKS was born in Merseyside, England. He now lives in California with his wife, where he works at a major feature animation studio and continues to pursue his passion for creating art at a personal level too.

DAVID SHEPHARD is a children's book illustrator and designer. He lives in the shadow of a Norman castle in Sussex, England, with his wife, children and several pets. He loves drawing people and faces and works best in his attic, where his family slides his dinners under the door!

Acknowledgements

ILLUSTRATED BY
Si Clark, Paula Franco, Alex Hedworth, Steve Horrocks, Julie Ingham, Luciano Locenzo, Maddy McClellan, Tom McGrath, David Shephard, Steve Stone and Yasuko Yasuko

DESIGNED BY
Belinda Webster at Picnic Design, Clare Phillips and Rachael Fisher

EDITED BY
Laura Baker, Cathy Jones, Moray Laing and Jason Loborik

PRODUCTION BY
Richard Wheeler

PHOTOGRAPHS FROM
Shutterstock, Inc.